# R IN BRADBEER'S PERSONAL COMPUTER BOOK

# Robin Bradbeer's Personal Computer Book

Third Edition

# Gower

© ROBIN BRADBEER, 1980, 1982, 1984

All rights reserved. No part of this publication may be reproduced, stored in a retrieval system, or transmitted in any form or by any means, electronic, mechanical, photocopying, recording, or otherwise, without the permission of Gower Publishing Company Limited.

First published in Great Britain in 1980
by Input Two Nine.

Second edition published in 1982.
Reprinted in 1982.
Third edition 1984.       001.64
Published by Gower Publishing Company Limited,
Gower House, Croft Road,
Aldershot, Hampshire GU11 3HR
Reprinted 1982

Bradbeer, Robin
  Robin Bradbeer's Personal computer book. – 3rd ed
  1. Personal computer systems
  I. Title
  00  1.64'04       QA76.5

ISBN 0-566-03507-3
ISBN 0-566-03506-5 Pbk

884577

Typeset in Great Britain by Graphic Studios (Southern) Ltd.,
Godalming, Surrey, and printed by University Press, Cambridge.

# CONTENTS

| | | |
|---|---|---|
| Foreword | | |
| Chapter 1 | INTRODUCTION | page 1 |
| Chapter 2 | THE COMPUTER — WHAT IS IT AND HOW DOES IT WORK? | page 11 |
| Chapter 3 | HOW DO I TALK TO THE COMPUTER? | page 32 |
| Chapter 4 | WHAT'S IN THE BOXES? | page 52 |
| Chapter 5 | WHAT CAN I BUY? | page 74 |
| Chapter 6 | HOW DO I CHOOSE A SYSTEM? | page 126 |
| Chapter 7 | WHAT CAN I DO WITH IT? | page 133 |
| Appendix A | BINARY ARITHMETIC — OR THINKING IN 1's AND 0's | page 158 |
| Appendix B | INTERFACE STANDARDS | page 163 |
| Appendix C | MANUFACTURERS/DISTRIBUTORS | page 171 |
| Appendix D | CLUBS AND USER GROUPS IN THE UK | page 173 |
| Appendix E | MAGAZINES IN ENGLISH . . . UK/USA/AUSTRALIA | page 204 |
| Appendix F | BIBLIOGRAPHY OF SELECTED MICROCOMPUTER BOOKS | page 227 |
| Appendix G | GLOSSARY | page 251 |
| Appendix H | SOME HINTS ON KIT-BUILT SYSTEMS | page 268 |

# FOREWORD

The response to the first two editions of this book showed the need to explain personal computers in everyday language. There is also need to give advice on how to purchase an initial system. Nobody would claim to have all the answers — and I certainly don't. However, my experience over the past few years, as retailer, customer, teacher, journalist and computer club chairman has helped to crystallize some of the questions that need to be answered.

Most of the material in this, and the previous editions, has been used in a series of talks to novice computer hobbyists at the North London Hobby Computer Club. The positive comments from the listeners have helped me eliminate a lot of material that is not necessary, and also made me include things that I initially didn't consider! Since the first two editions, letters and conversations with readers have shown areas that need reinforcing. These are now fully covered, I hope! Comparison with the first two editions will indicate certain differences. These are basically to make certain sections easier to understand. I am indebted to all those who gave me advice, solicited and unsolicited in this area!

In a book of this sort — where such a wide ranging subject is covered in a few pages — criticisms will always be made about the technical explanations. My apologies in advance to those "experts" who expect a technical discussion to take at least fifty pages! If you have only a page to describe, say a disk drive, then that explanation will obviously be rather superficial. I hope that I have been able to cover the essentials in enough depth to do the machinery justice! At the same time it has been impossible to look at every computer around. In choosing those mentioned, I have looked at machines that are generally available under £1,500. Apologies to those who are offended if their favourite machine is not included. Whenever details are quoted it must be obvious that with specifications increasing and prices decreasing changes occur daily. Please consult the latest edition of a magazine, or chat to your local store, before estimating the cost of a system. Prices and specifications are for guidance only!

In writing this book I have had help from many sources. These include Garry Marshall, Mike O'Reilly, Richard Ross-Langley, G. Winnestein, and Mike Fluskey, and Fred Pipes who did the drawings.

With the BBC and ITV presenting the ideas of personal computing to a massive audience, my hope is that this book will provide more detailed background reading to supplement information coming from those sources.

R.T.B.
June 1983

# CHAPTER 1

## Introduction

Everywhere you look it's computers, computers, computers; on TV, in the press, and on the radio. Words like "home computing", "hobby computer" and "personal computer" are mentioned all the time.

*Computer technology has now grown so cheap that practically anyone can now afford to buy a computer system.*

The home computer is a reality. During the last 3 or 4 years, small, cheap computer systems have begun to appear on the market — many of them as powerful as large computer installations of the 60s. Instead of costing millions of pounds, the price tags now show £50, £100 or perhaps £500.

At the end of 1982 there were around 1,000,000 home computers of various sizes and versions in the UK. The number of people interested is far greater. What has generated this interest?

For the first time in the history of computer technology (which in fact, only goes back about 40 years, counting from the first electronic computer), individuals can now operate and control a computer in their own home.

Previously, large computer systems have been controlled by companies and institutions. Many people have had to co-operate in working with the computer, so it has cost a lot of money to "talk to" the computer. In many cases, this has limited the possibility of using a computer to its fullest ability.

These limitations don't exist any more. We are now in a position to decide **what** we want to do. And **when** we are going to do it.

The words "home computer", can now take on a similar meaning to words like "domestic help", "personal servant" and "private secretary".

### What are computers being used for?

We can play games on the computer or let the computer control various functions in the home. The computer can keep order in our private financial affairs. It can practise vocabulary lists or maths homework with the children — not to mention the value it has for children, allowing them to come into contact with computer technology at an early age (they are going to live in a computer society).

We can keep a check on books, records and other property by storing information in computer files. The computer can help us to write letters, keep a tab on addresses, etc.

It is possible for businessmen to rationalize their work in book-keeping, stock accounting, customer files, the dispatching of advertisements, etc. The personal computer does the job cheaply so that human resources can be freed for more creative occupations.

For those who already have a hobby (model railways, philately, amateur radio, stock investments, rose-gardens or whatever) surprisingly, computer technology can often be integrated with the hobby and enrich the experiences it gives.

Real enthusiasts say, "There is no limit, really, to what you can do with a computer — only your own imagination". What must be remembered is that a computer is just a programmable machine. It's an intelligent idiot! It can do, within reason, whatever you tell it to — and then very quickly and, usually, without mistakes.

This sounds too good to be true. Of course there are limits. One's wallet, for instance! Even though today's computer technology is cheap it **can** run away with the money.

There are technical hurdles to be overcome before the computer can work in the applications one has thought out, but the technology is now developing very quickly. The opportunities are being improved daily by new products, concepts and ideas.

This book offers you guidance in the new computer technology. It points out the possibilities — and warns you of the pitfalls!

**How is it possible?**

What is it, then, that makes this revolutionary development possible?

First and foremost, the answer is semiconductor technology, which has led to the integrated circuit. This new technology makes it possible for a little silicon chip (only 5-6mm square) to contain tens of thousands of transistors.

*Silicon chips can now be made with all of the elements of a computer on them.*

In the early 60s researchers discovered how to miniaturize even further by bringing several transistors together in a single unit during the process of production and the **integrated circuit** was born. Since then, development has proceeded at breakneck speed. Circuits have become even more complex as production methods become more refined. Today, more than 100,000 transistors can be fitted onto a silicon chip measuring 6mm × 6mm.

Manufacturers' predictions suggest that in 1985 there will be one million transistors in the same place. With this technique (Very Large Scale Integration, known as VLSI) manufacturers can build up the exact electronic circuit required.

Manufacturing technology, however, is highly technical. It costs a lot of money to develop each individual configuration of circuits. This is why manufacturers concentrate on integrated circuits that can be sold in large numbers. This makes it possible to reach very low manufacturing costs per integrated circuit. Some simple circuits produced by the million, cost only a penny or two to manufacture. More complex circuits cost more, sometimes as much as a few pounds.

The development that has been of decisive importance in the last few years is the **microprocessor**, which arrived in the early 1970s. In simple terms, the engineers collected all the components of the central parts of a computer and placed them, by means of the VLSI technique, on one small silicon chip. The result was a cheap building component, of universal application, and readily available. Since then, the manufacturers have not been idle and better microprocessors have appeared. Larger memories have also been developed by similar techniques, and more and more functions within the computer have been realized with the VLSI technique.

This has resulted in lower prices, greater reliability, and above all — electronics moving into areas where it had not been practical before.

*The microprocessor has made it possible to place computer power where it is needed.* In cash registers, cars, sewing machines, lathes, industrial automation systems, calculators or vending machines — not to mention the great importance of the microprocessor in building computers, both for professional and home use.

A simple method for looking at these developments is to consider the dimensions of the equipment. Ten years ago, a computer installation filled a fair-sized room. Today the equivalent computer power can be put on a table.

On the consumer side, there have already been advance signs of the approach of the home computer:

The pocket calculator, with its continuous price reduction coupled with ever more advanced technical content.

Anyone who has bought a TV game has in fact taken the first step towards a home computer. TV games are often small computers even though they are made with one purpose in mind, to act as TV games. A real home computer has a more universal range of applications — that is its importance.

Given the direction of present developments, the TV set will become the computer centre of the home — an information centre that provides not only TV programmes but also the possibility of storing, processing and communicating with other similar systems. In a few years, the home computer is likely to be as natural a part of the home as the TV set is today.

### The first hobby computer

The first hobby computer, or personal computer that deserved the name, came onto the American market in January 1975. It was the small New Mexico company MITS that launched a kit for under $500, and gave it the name Altair, which was the name of a star in the TV series "Star Trek".

Altair turned into a real comet. It set fire to the market — and to everyone who discovered how cheaply they could get hold of their own computer.

Altair also attracted a veritable rain of stars! In only a month or so various other manufacturers of hobby computers — and above all of accessories for hobby computers — had appeared by the side of MITS.

The Altair concept became something of a guideline for many of the other manufacturers of personal computers. Several other computers of basically similar design appeared from manufacturers like Imsai, Processor Technology, Polymorphic and many others. Even more firms in the USA established themselves as manufacturers of accessories for these computers. Unfortunately, their pioneering spirit was not backed up by the financial expertise to cope with the massive demand generated, and most of these early companies are now defunct.

The main point about these early companies was their use of **BASIC** as the main programming language, and the development of a common inter-connection system, the S-100 bus. This allowed different manufacturers to have interchangeable components, thus giving the consumer not only a choice of varied supplies, but also a range of accessories that were relatively similar. It was this common bus structure and language that really got personal computing off the ground, and laid the foundation for the present boom.

Quite soon after the first Altair had seen the light of day it was possible in the USA to buy a computer, a keyboard, an interface to change an ordinary TV set into a data screen, and an interface to make a cassette recorder into a computer memory — for a little over $1,000. Then one could work with this system using the programming language, **BASIC**, with the knowledge that most others were doing the same thing.

This meant a properly working computer system at the same price as a good stereo set or colour TV. And an entirely new computer industry sprang up from nowhere. Hundreds of new producers of computer supplies have established themselves in the USA, with many of these and indigenous companies now operating in the UK.

Computer shops began to appear. Today there are something over 10,000 computer shops in the USA. Their numbers are still growing. In the UK we now have around 5,000 — up from 5 in 1978!

There are also vast numbers of clubs for computer enthusiasts throughout the world. They have lively meetings and fast-growing membership.

Dozens of really good magazines have become established in the field of personal computing in the USA, with nearly fifty now in the UK. The leading American one, *Byte Magazine*, a monthly that started in 1976, has a circulation that's going up like a rocket and is now a good bit over 250,000, which makes it the world's largest computer magazine of any type.

Trade fairs, conferences and seminar courses are being organized for thousands of participants. The most popular regularly attract 40,000 or more personal computing enthusiasts.

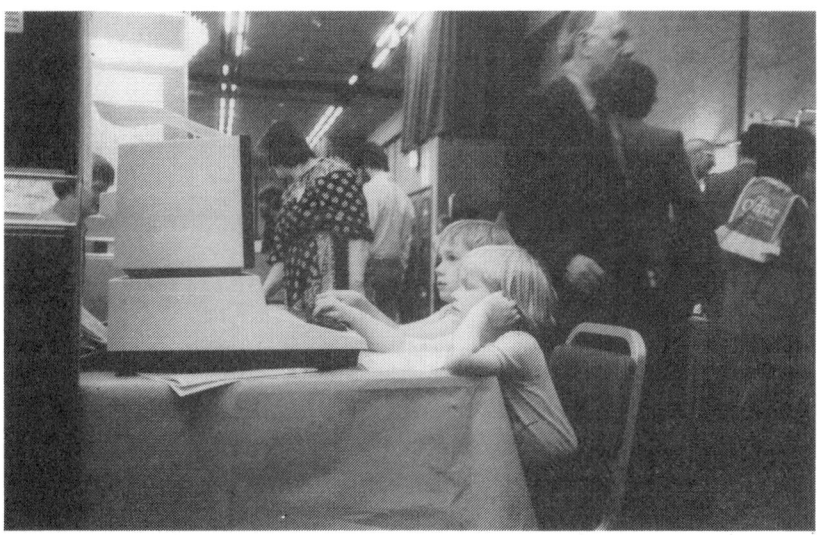

*Computer Fairs attract even the youngest addicts.*

In the UK market predictions indicate that by 1985 around 5 million units a year will be sold, with 1m predicted for 1983 generating a market of around £1,000m. This is larger than the radio/TV/hi-fi market — big business indeed.

**Who buys personal computers?**

What sort of people are prepared to spend £50, £100, £500 — often even more — on building up a computer system of their own at home or in their small firm?

We find that many people with technical know-how are among the converts of personal computing — engineers, programmers, do-it-yourselfers.

Many computer clubs have stands at the popular exhibitions. This is a good way to make contact.

But then there are the Smiths, Joneses and Robinsons of Britain; quite an army of dentists, car mechanics, young people, pensioners, bus-drivers, lawyers, businessmen, teachers, restaurant owners and landlords are buying their own computer systems.

Why do they do it?

It's probably for one of these three reasons:

1 They have one specific application ready for the computer (quite often in connection with their job).
2 They have a general interest in technology and want to learn more about computers.
3 They feel they should know something about this new technology in general.

We can also divide the "personal computer people" into these four categories:

1 The hobby enthusiast pure and simple, who prefers to put his — or her — own computer together. Mainly because it's cheaper that way, but also for the joy of doing the whole job alone.

2 The person with a technological interest who buys a computer kit. The price is not generally the most important question: the most important thing is that the computer can be used for something that's fun and interesting and that the price is more or less reasonable for what may be a life-long friend.

3 The professional person with his eye on the future who wants to use the computer in his work; the writer who wants to build up a text processing system; the architect who wants to rationalize the calculations for his tenders; the businessman who wants a cheap accounting system; or the parent whose children are using computers at school and wants to either learn himself, or provide a similar facility in the home. For this category of people it is of decisive importance that the computer system can do a good job.

4 Schools, institutions and companies with limited budgets have started to discover the personal computer as an answer to their needs that up to now would have been too costly.

**Developments in the next few years**

What is going to happen over the next 3 or 4 years? What applications will be possible then?

Games will be developed further and will become more sophisticated. The educational side of computing will certainly expand. A lot of new software will appear, making it possible to sit at the computer and learn various things; language translation, foreign language pronunciation; or even to run things in the house — home security for example.

Although very many programs are already available, the aim will be more sophisticated applications. Word processing and the control of various functions in the home such as radio/TV, telephone, air conditioning and so forth will gain popularity. In the late 1980s the total domestic information and data processing system, something which we will come to find just as natural as today's electric cooker, washing machine and colour TV, will become a reality. Total systems of this type will provide us with a number of services — all of them in the hope that the quality of life for the people of the 1980s will be enhanced. The system will help us to co-ordinate the functions of all the various items of technical equipment in the home. It will assist us in many errands and serve as a memo pad.

The new developments available through commercial media, such as viewdata, or Prestel, will allow us to communicate outside of the home. We can already order goods using the telephone and television. Our personal computer is the key to communicating with the bank or the grocer.

It will entertain us with an inexhaustible supply of intelligent games. It will give us and our children individualized teaching. It will partly replace the postman by functioning as a telephone-based communication system for information transfer to friends and firms. When we are away we can ring up the system and alter various functions in the home by telephone. The home gains an advanced "secretary" who is really good at text editing.

Today's personal computer is the introduction to all this. The electronics, the hardware, is already there. What remains is to develop the software, to put it all together to form an attractive package — and to convince consumers of the necessity!

# CHAPTER 2
## The computer — what is it and how does it work?

### The computer — confusingly versatile

From the very beginning computers, or computing machines as they used to be called, have had a strange kind of aura, almost as if they possessed supernatural powers.

Well, a computer possesses no such powers.

The computer is just like any other machine, and, just as we are surrounded by masses of different machines we are also surrounded by many different computers. Computers of different capacities, dimensions, appearance — computers with different purposes and names and at different prices. Some are small enough to be held in the palm of the hand, others may need floor space of 100 square metres.

Just like a human being, who in the course of one day can do many entirely different jobs, such as being a filling-station attendant, a parent, an odd-job person, a car driver and a stamp collector, so the computer can change from one specifically distinct job to another.

This makes computers such useful working tools. This very versatility however — together with the fact that computers take so many different forms — probably makes a confusing and obscure impression on anyone starting to approach the computer world. A particular characteristic of a certain computer that you might appreciate and exploit may be quite unknown to another user of the same computer, who may be quite satisfied in his own way.

It is by taking a closer look at the most marked characteristics of computers as a whole that we can gain a sensible overall picture. To use our TV or car, we do not need detailed knowledge of how the channel sector or gearbox works; and neither do we need to scrutinize every little detail of a computer to be able to understand and make use of computer technology.

Take your relationship to a bicycle, for instance: you know what it can be used **for**. You know **how** to use it and you know its limitations.

You can have the same attitude to computers. If you know a little about the general construction of a computer you will also know the range of applications, and how to exploit these possibilities. You will soon learn to see the limitations of the computer and computers do have limitations!

Big computers, or **mainframes**, are found in large firms, institutions, computer centres and government offices, where they are used for a number of different tasks: financial accounts, production planning and follow-up, personnel registers and much else. Since their working tasks are very large and constantly changing, these large computers are characterized by speed, large capacity and flexibility. Often large computers are used in systems where many people need access to information at the same time; this is where the power of a large computer to hold many tasks together really comes into its own.

Somewhat smaller, **minicomputers** are not capable of quite such general use. With a minicomputer it is possible to solve data processing problems more effectively because the system can be built up in a more specialized way.

The user has greater ease of access to his minicomputer installation. Costs do not approach the hundreds of thousands for large computers: one of the more simple minicomputer systems will cost around £5,000 or more. This means that many firms and institutions can afford to invest in minicomputers, which are used for everything from accounting to industrial automation.

Computer power, however, is needed in many different places. The full power of the minicomputer is not always needed. Something cheaper and simpler is often adequate.

So we have the **microcomputer**, the smallest member of the computer family. It is small enough and cheap enough to be built into machines and plant to carry out specific and limited tasks — which are often more complex than one thinks. The heart of a microcomputer is the **microprocessor**. Some special microprocessors today cost no more than £1 to large consumers.

It is possible to extend the microcomputer and equip it with a sufficiently large memory and suitable peripheral equipment. It then approaches the functions and range of applications of a minicomputer. This is true of most of the units sold for personal use. A small system can be extended, and it is therefore possible to have the power of a minicomputer available with a personal microcomputer at its centre.

We all know how to use a washing machine: we put in dirty clothes, the machine washes for a while, and then we take out clean clothes.

It's the same with a computer. We feed in data — figures, symbols or words — the computer processes what has been fed in, and then we are given a result in the form of new figures, symbols or words.

Just as the washing machine has a program to follow during the wash, the computer has instructions on how to treat the data that has been fed in.

Even if the computer can't actually **think** in the same way as man, it may be interesting to make the following comparison with how we function (at least, how we function at times!).

- We receive information at a certain moment (by feeling, hearing, seeing, smelling or tasting).
- We perceive the information, ie. we memorize it.
- We take out other information from another place in our memory.
- By means of logical thinking — in this case by comparing the different information — we arrive at a suitable decision.

We act on the basis of the decision (by using some suitable "output organ" and speaking, walking, using our hands, etc.).

The computer works in a similar manner. It receives its information via an input unit. The computer stores the data it receives in its memory. Thus far, the analogy with the human brain holds good. The computer memory, however, only retains the data it has been programmed to store. Everything else is "forgotten". This saves storage space and it makes it quicker for the computer to search through what it has in store. (On the other hand, the computer lacks the intuition and imagination of the human brain.)

When the computer needs certain data in its work, the data is brought out of store on command.

Processing of data is often similar to our way of thinking logically. One part of this process is to compare two items of information. It is often necessary to compare the item of information being fed in with one that is stored in the computer memory. The item of information already in the memory may itself have come in as "new information" and been stored. Or it may have been given to the computer as part of the working instructions — the program.

The computer may be programmed to compare the new information with information in the memory already so that it can determine whether the information is satisfactory or not, or to divide the information fed into groups and so forth.

The computer could even make a comparison between incoming data and a certain item of information in the memory to see if they are identical — in which case the computer has instructions to proceed in a certain manner; or it may be instructed, when a new item of information is fed in, to search through — and compare with — a number of different data in the memory.

The result — in the form prescribed by the program — is delivered to the output unit of the computer.

**How the computer works, in simple terms**

Two concepts often used when talking about computers are **hardware** and **software**.

Hardware is everything in the computer system that you can in theory pick up and handle — all physically existing items such as electronic connections, wiring, tape recorders, boxes, keyboards and integrated circuits.

Software is the overall term for programs, communication languages, processing procedures, data and stored information.

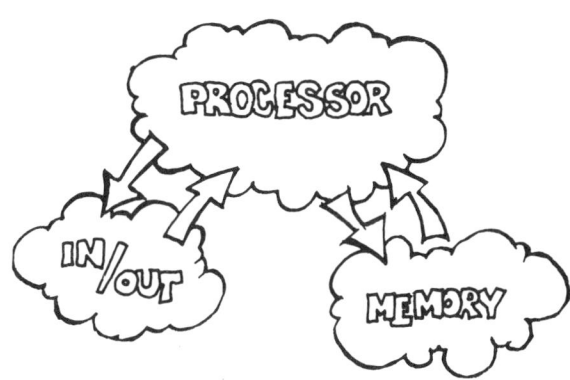

From what has been said so far, it can be seen that the hardware of a computer system consists of three basic parts: **a processing part** (the central unit, CPU, processor, controller — there are many words for the same thing), **an input and output part** (peripheral equipment or I/O equipment), and a **memory** or **store** of some kind.

The software — the program — is a list of **instructions** to the central processing unit or CPU.

Let's look at a highly simplified form of computer — an arrangement consisting of a very simple input unit, an equally simple output unit, and a central processing unit.

This certainly is a very limited "computer": it can only work with a few digits (0-9), and can do nothing more than add two digits together. In fact this kind of machine isn't much use to anybody.

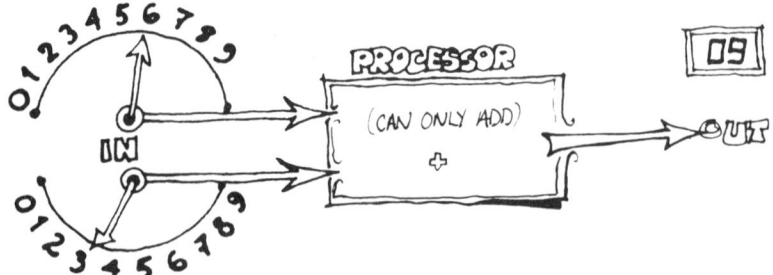

Let's extend the possibilities a little ... we can replace the "adding processor" by an arrangement that can not only add but also subtract, compare and carry out other logical operations. We call this an **Arithmetic Logic Unit** or **ALU**.

Our extended system has now been given a further switch, an instruction switch. We can use this to decide if the ALU is to add, subtract, etc.

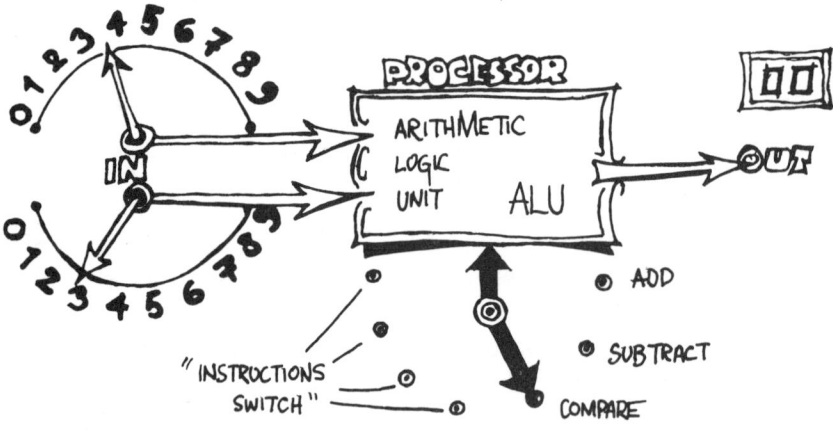

Even though the range of applications in this version is greater, it is not sufficient for the "computer" to have any practical value. Our simple processor can't even work with more than two numbers at once. If we wanted to add several figures together we'd come to a halt.

So we add a unit where the figures can be stored — a memory. This may be a number of switches, a tape recorder, a disk or electronic devices that can store information.

Now we replace the instruction switch by an instruction memory or store. Here we can feed in a number of instructions intended for the processor.

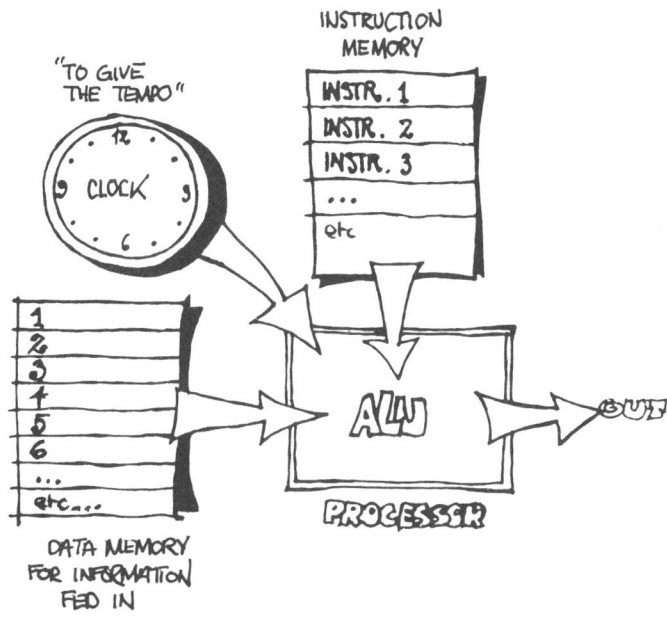

And we add one more thing: we put in a clock (a sort of metronome), which will help the computer through the program step by step and instruction by instruction.

We can now program this system to make the processor carry out the following instructions, for example, one by one:

Instruction 1: Add the first two figures in the store.
Instruction 2: Add the next two figures.
Instruction 3: Compare the two totals.
Instruction 4: Feed out the least total.

There are no essential differences between the basic logical

17

and functional construction of a real computer and this simplified one. In practice, the ALU has the capacity to carry out further operations. There are additional devices to simplify the flow of information and instructions within the computer to facilitate input and output.

The block diagram for a computer looks like this:

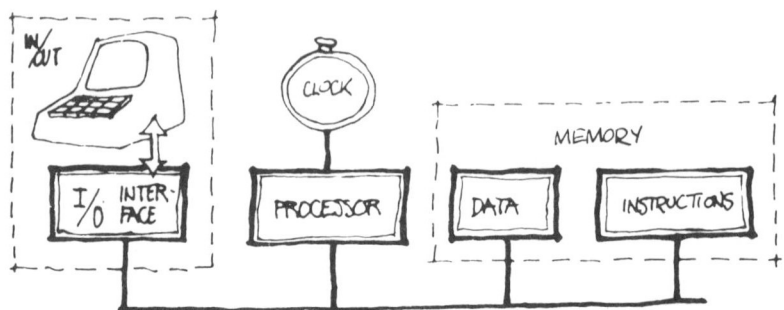

In a microcomputer, each of these blocks could be an integrated circuit. Microprocessors are now beginning to appear with all these blocks enclosed in a single integrated circuit. In minicomputers and larger computers each block is realized in the form of individual circuit boards or modules. Since computers work by electricity there is also a unit for power supply!

A computer is built up of hundreds of thousands of electronic circuits which "think" logically.

Here is an example of a logical electronic circuit — not from a real computer of course — but it will do well enough to explain something on the secret of **how** a computer can calculate, carry out logical operations and so forth.

To drive a car, you need both access to the keys and some petrol in the tank — it won't work with only one of these things. The following illustration is a diagram where all the decisions involved have been broken down into their basic, essential parts.

We can make up a table — a "truth table" — to illustrate the problem and how we can use the above diagram to determine whether it is possible to drive the car.

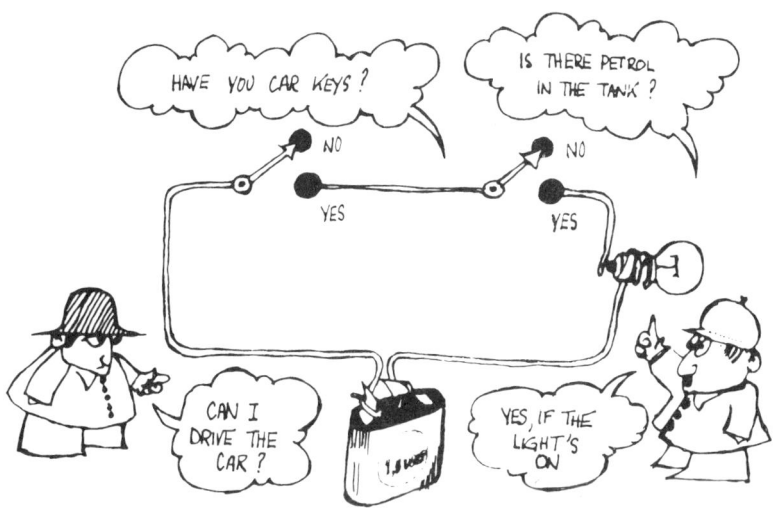

| Keys? | Petrol? | Light? |   | Drive the car |
|-------|---------|--------|---|---------------|
| No    | No      | Off    | = | No            |
| No    | Yes     | Off    | = | No            |
| Yes   | No      | Off    | = | No            |
| Yes   | Yes     | On     | = | Yes           |

The truth table may also look like this:

| A | B | Q |
|---|---|---|
| 0 | 0 | 0 |
| 0 | 1 | 0 |
| 1 | 0 | 0 |
| 1 | 1 | 1 |

A and B stand for data in and Q for the result, or data out. Or in our case A is the condition of the keys and B the condition of the petrol. Q is the condition of the light and indicates whether the car can be driven.

The positions of the switches — "on" or "off" — we have called "yes" or "no", "0" or "1". We can also call them "true/false", "right/wrong", "sun/rain", "high/low" etc. This sort of diagram can be adapted to other purposes.

A computer contains many logical circuits making decisions of this type, in various forms, and this arrangement allows the computer to work in series of logical operations.

### Binary numbers

Let's plump for the alternatives "0" and "1" — these concepts are used very often in computer work. You have probably already heard how computers only count in zeros and ones. We speak of the **binary number system**. It works to the base 2 (only two digits). The **decimal number system** we normally use works to the base 10 (ten digits).

With the binary number system we can simply express the position of the switches in our circuit. "01" means that we have petrol but no keys, "11" that we have both petrol and keys. From the truth table we see that there are four different alternatives: 00, 01, 10, 11.

In each one of these alternatives there are two pieces or bits of information. In information theory — and in computer work — the concept of **bit** is used for the quantity of information needed to answer a question to which there are two possible alternative answers. "Bit" is an abbreviation of **binary digit**.

These bits are very often collected in groups of eight, eg. 00101101.

This group is called a **byte** (pronounced "bite").

Every computer works with a definite number of bits. Most small, personal computers work with data and instructions in eight bit, or byte lengths. Some simpler microprocessors use only four bits or nibbles! Large computers use twelve, sixteen, twenty-four or even thirty-two bits as their working length. The working length for a computer is usually called its word length, and this can vary from machine to machine.

A working knowledge of binary arithmetic is a useful, but not necessary skill in using computers. If you are interested in refreshing your memory, or starting from scratch, then look at Appendix A for some elementary binary arithmetic.

Most of the small computers that we shall be looking at use eight bits, as mentioned earlier. One problem, however, is that although these machines think in eight bit lengths, they actually remember where the information is stored in sixteen bit numbers! It becomes useful to know something about working to base 16 or hexadecimal. This is also described in Appendix A.

### How does the computer handle binary numbers?

It's this kind of information — 00111101 etc. — which is read into the computer memory and thus forms the computer's working material.

How is the memory or store constructed to be able to handle all these zeros and ones?

The store is organized in matrix form somewhat like the pigeon holes used for internal mail: a number of small compartments with room for a certain amount of information. Each compartment has its own address.

Each address in the data usually accommodates a whole byte, ie. eight bits. The memory cell consists of a small space where it is possible to store electronic charges: charge = "1", and no-charge = "0".

In order to make it possible in practice to get a sufficiently large number of store addresses to work with, most computers (microcomputers) are designed for the address to be 16 bits long, eg. 10001111 00011011.

With binary numbers of this length one can express 65,536 different addresses ($2^{16}$).

In the general block diagram for a computer which we drew earlier, there are two types of store, the data store and the instruction store.

As the computer only stores 1's and 0's it is usually possible to mix up the instructions and data, with the instructions taking two bytes and the data, one. It is good practice to "partition" the memory space so that, say, those memory addresses below $0200_{16}$ are used for data, and those above for instructions. In most

21

computers, however, it is useful to have some instructions, or even programs, stored permanently. So if the machine gets switched off it will perform some basic tasks when it is powered up again. The store used in this case must therefore be relatively permanent and, to protect the information stored, fairly difficult if not impossible to erase. This type of storage is called read only memory or ROM. This means that it is only possible to read ie. fetch data or instructions. They are permanently stored and cannot be changed. Another word for this sort of storage is "non-volatile" — meaning that it is not destroyed when power is taken away.

The other type of storage used in computers is called random access memory — or RAM. This means that one can enter any memory address and store or fetch information from it. It is usually volatile ie. it loses all information stored when power is switched off.

Consequently, all the instructions that keep the computer going; telling the clock when to send out certain pulses; when to move data from the memory to ALU or even how to output answers; these instructions are kept in ROM and are usually called the monitor. In most small computer systems the language used to program is also kept in ROM eg. BASIC. Some peripheral hardware also contains ROM — printers and discs for example — so that the information needed to get the electrical pulses in the right format is available all the time.

In the same block diagram there is also something called an **I/O interface**. This is sometimes called a **port**, or an **I/O port**.

The input unit (I) receives data from the peripheral equipment — in this case a keyboard — and adapts this information so that it can be understood and used by the computer. The output unit of the interface (O) takes care of data that the computer wants to read out.

This data is adapted so that the exterior output unit — in the diagram a display — can understand and use the information.

There are basically two different types of I/O — **serial** and **parallel**.

Serial I/O works lengthwise with data, ie. the bits are transmitted back and forth by byte, one by one — rather like a camel caravan.

Parallel I/O works breadthwise, for instance eight bits at once — rather like a platoon of soldiers on the march. Parallel transmission works considerably faster than serial transmission.

A serial interface contains special circuits which determine the speed of transmission, this is called the **baud rate**. This is a measure of the number of bits transmitted per second.

**The processor — the CPU — from the inside**

Though it doesn't look anything special and doesn't cost very much, the processor is the part which determines what the computer is capable of. Generally the processor in a microcomputer is built as a very complex semiconductor circuit. It contains a large number of logic circuits.

The processor has many important functions to perform in the computer. These include the following:

1 Fetching and "understanding" instructions.
2 Transmitting data to and from the store and the I/O units.
3 Performing arithmetic and logic operations.
4 Controlling other parts of the computer.

Basically, the processor can be divided into four functional sections. The first of these — we may call it the **addressing section** — works with the addresses that are needed at any given moment (for fetching or output of data, ie. reading or printing).

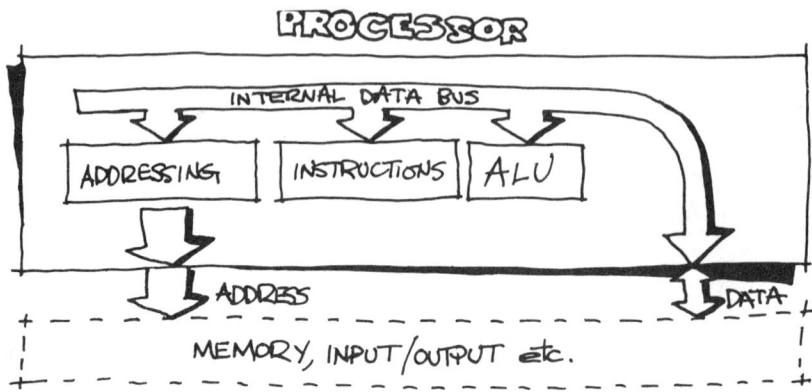

The function of the second section, the **instruction section**, is to translate and "understand" the instructions the computer is to work with.

The third section is an old friend — **ALU**, the arithmetic and logic unit. This is where all the computing and "thinking" goes on.

All these sections in the processor are connected to each other by a complex network called the **internal data bus**, which forms the fourth functional section.

Every one of these sections in the inside of the processor contains one or more **registers**. These are small memory sections used for the temporary storage of instructions, intermittent results and so forth. As a rule these registers are only large enough for one or two bytes (8 or 16 bits).

*How the processor carries out the instructions*

An instruction is the smallest part of a program that has the power to transmit a complete message. These instructions often resemble commands in normal language. The command "Add B to A", for example, may be written "ADD B to A".

For it to be stored in the computer memory, however, and to be handled in other ways by all the electronic circuits in the computer, the instruction must be written in binary digits: the ADD instruction, for instance could be 10000111. This method of communicating is called **machine language**. The processor understands **only** machine code, ie. 1's and 0's.

Each instruction carried out by the processor represents a small step in the computation or process that is programmed into the computer.

There are a number of steps necessary in carrying out each instruction. These are done one by one, not all in one go.

### The instruction cycle

As the program has been stored in the memory, each instruction must first be brought from the memory and placed in one of the registers in the processor. The instruction is translated — ie. the processor finds out the meaning of the binary code — and the operation prescribed by the instruction is carried out.

The total time required for fetching and carrying out an instruction is called the **instruction cycle**. The length varies according to the task performed. For most microprocessors it is in the order of millionths of a second, or a microsecond.

There are thus three steps:

*Fetching the instruction from the memory.*
*Translating the instruction.*
*Performing the prescribed operation.*

### The program counter

To make it possible to fetch an instruction from the memory, the address where the instruction is stored must be known. This is kept in a register in the processor which is called the **program counter**. The space available in the program counter exactly fits the length of the address — 16 bits.

### The instruction register

When the program counter has selected a byte (the instruction or part of it) in the memory, it is sent to the processor and temporarily placed in a register called the **instruction register**.

From this register, the instruction goes to the instruction decoder where its meaning is translated into signals which carry out the operation prescribed.

## The accumulator

The program counter is one of the registers in the addressing section. The instruction register is in the instruction section. In the arithmetic and logic section we find a register called the **accumulator**. This is a register of eight bits which temporarily stores results while the arithmetic and logical instructions are being carried out.

## The interrupt function

One important function in modern microprocessors is called **interrupt**. This function might be described as a "temporary break in the work which the microprocessor is busy on".

An interrupt functions like this: when the processor is working its way through a certain program, an item of peripheral equipment — the keyboard, for instance — may start calling the attention of the processor. The processor makes a note of the point in the program where it is forced to break off, receives data from the keyboard, and then returns to the original task.

### The computer's own road network — the bus

The system of electrical circuitry connecting the processor, the memory or store, the I/O interface and the power supply unit is called the **bus** system.

The bus in the computer is divided into four separate "main roads":

*the power supply to all the blocks of the computer,*
*the control bus along which all control signals flow,*
*the two-way data bus which sends eight bits at a time between the processor and other blocks, and*
*the address bus directed from the processor which handles address signals 16 bits in length.*

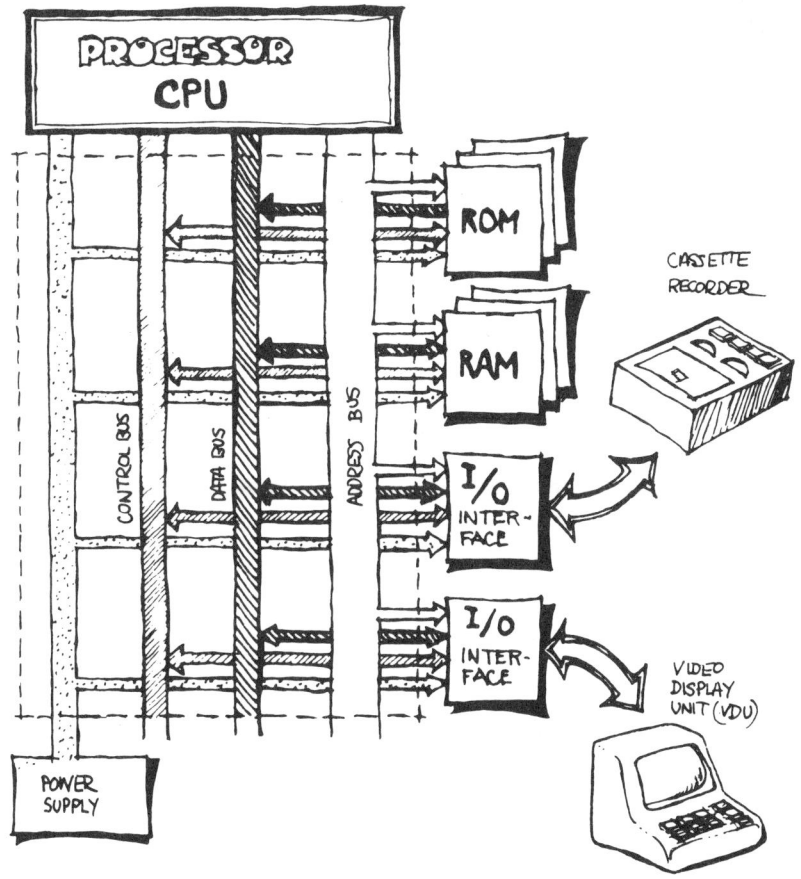

To make a simple, efficient and clear design of the computer possible, the bus is usually constructed in the form of a number of parallel conductors. These are on the printed circuit board on which the computer is constructed.

Sometimes the bus takes the form of a printed circuit "back plane", or "mother board", to which modules containing various parts of the computer can then be attached. The memory, processor, input/output circuitry, can be on separate boards and the user can configure his computer as he wishes.

The most common form of this type of bus is called the S-100 bus, and has the distinction of being not only the first hobby computer bus, but also the first to have its own international standard. The S-100 bus has 100 conductors and details of the pin connections and the international standard are given in Appendix B.

Other buses are the SS-50 (50 lines), SS-44, SS-48 . . . the list is endless. In Chapter 5, where actual real computers available over shop counters are discussed, the bus system used will be mentioned in each case.

Not all boards, or systems, that claim to follow any one bus standard are interchangeable with boards or systems from other manufacturers who claim the same thing! This unfortunate situation has prompted many manufacturers to "invent" their own buses — which is sad but inevitable. The new international standards may overcome this.

**Storage inside the computer**

It is essential that the computer has enough memory to carry out its task of storing programs and data. Memory can be internal, or external. We will consider internal memory here, and external memory in a later chapter.

The internal memory is of a cellular nature and is usually controlled directly by the processor. It should be possible to retrieve discrete items of data from a particular address. With external memory, data is usually retrieved in blocks. The internal memory has a physical limitation in size determined by the size of address that the processor can handle, ie. 64K for an 8 bit processor using 16 bit addressing. The limitations for external memory are determined by the method of storage used.

Internal memory is invariably semiconductor storage. They use the same method of construction as microprocessors and similar large scale integrated circuits, and are thus compatible as far as voltage goes.

The memory in a normal semiconductor memory is arranged in a matrix or grid.

As mentioned previously semiconductor memories come in two types — Random Access Memory, or RAM, and Read Only Memory or ROM. Let's look at RAM first.

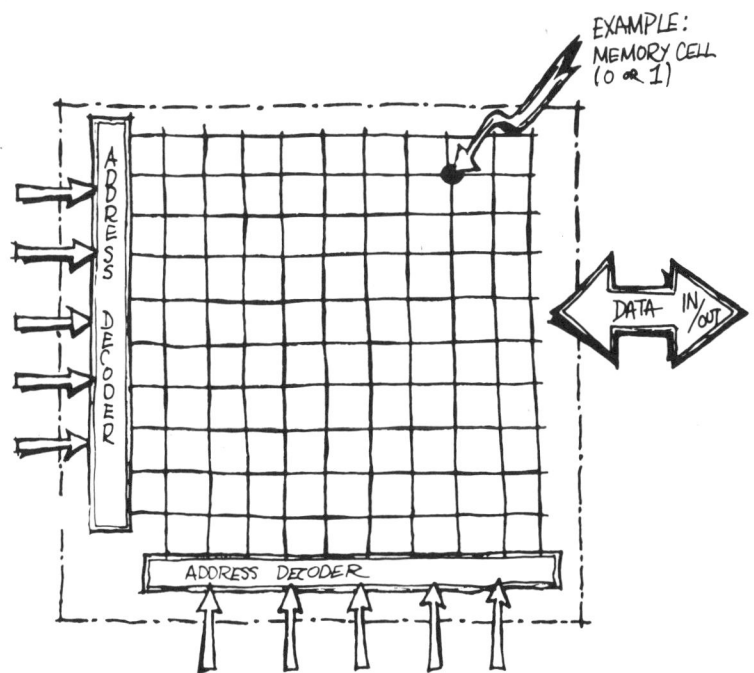

BASIC DIAGRAM OF THE CONTENTS OF A MEMORY CHIP: BY PLACING BINARY SIGNALS AT THE ADDRESS ENTRIES, IT IS POSSIBLE TO SELECT ONE SPECIFIC MEMORY CELL IN THE MATRIX — EITHER FOR INPUT OR OUTPUT OF DATA (ONLY ONE BIT).

Each memory cell can contain a '1' or '0', in the case of semiconductor memory, indicated by a voltage or no voltage at the output of a transistor circuit.

A small memory may contain, say, 32 rows by 32 columns ie. $32 \times 32 = 1024$ or 1K bits. RAM chips come in many sizes but 4K, 16K and 64K are the most common.

As most personal computers have an 8 bit, or byte, word length, a number of chips must be interconnected to form a complete block. If 1K chips are used, eight chips would be needed to store 1 Kbytes. For 4 Kbytes, 32 chips are needed. Some smaller memories, usually used in single-board microcomputers may have their memory organized differently. Instead of 1K × 1 bit, they could be organized as 256 words of 4 bits.

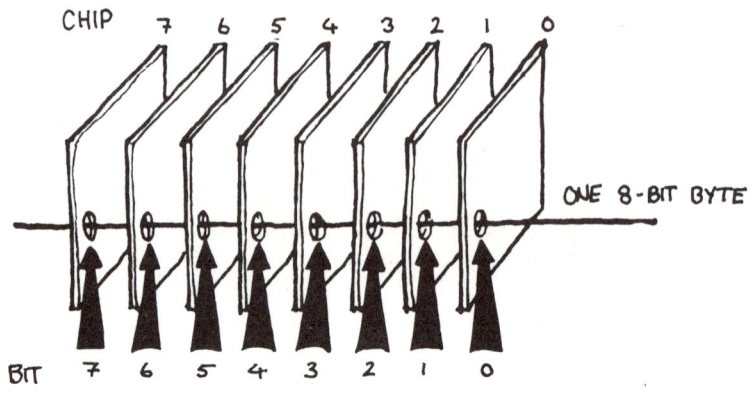

A MEMORY BLOCK IS COMPOSED OF SEVERAL MEMORY CHIPS.

There are two types of RAM — static and dynamic. Static RAM will store information until the power supply ceases or the memory contents are changed. Dynamic RAM will do both the above, but needs extra chips to "refresh" the memory constantly, as the transistor cells cannot hold the information for very long. Static RAM is more expensive than dynamic on a chip for chip basis, but there is little to choose when assembled onto a board, as the support chips for dynamic RAM push up the cost. However static RAM needs more power than dynamic RAM and for large memory systems heat dissipation becomes a problem.

With Read Only Memory the above method of splitting up the memory is also needed. The address lines will only cause a memory cell to output data, as it is impossible to write data into a ROM cell.

It is possible to have ROM's which can be changed if the stored information is incorrect, or needs updating. These are called programmable ROM or PROM and come in many different types. Their principle of operating is similar however. A high voltage or charge of energy, in the form of ultraviolet light, erases the contents. It is then possible to place new information into the ROM with a special PROM programmer.

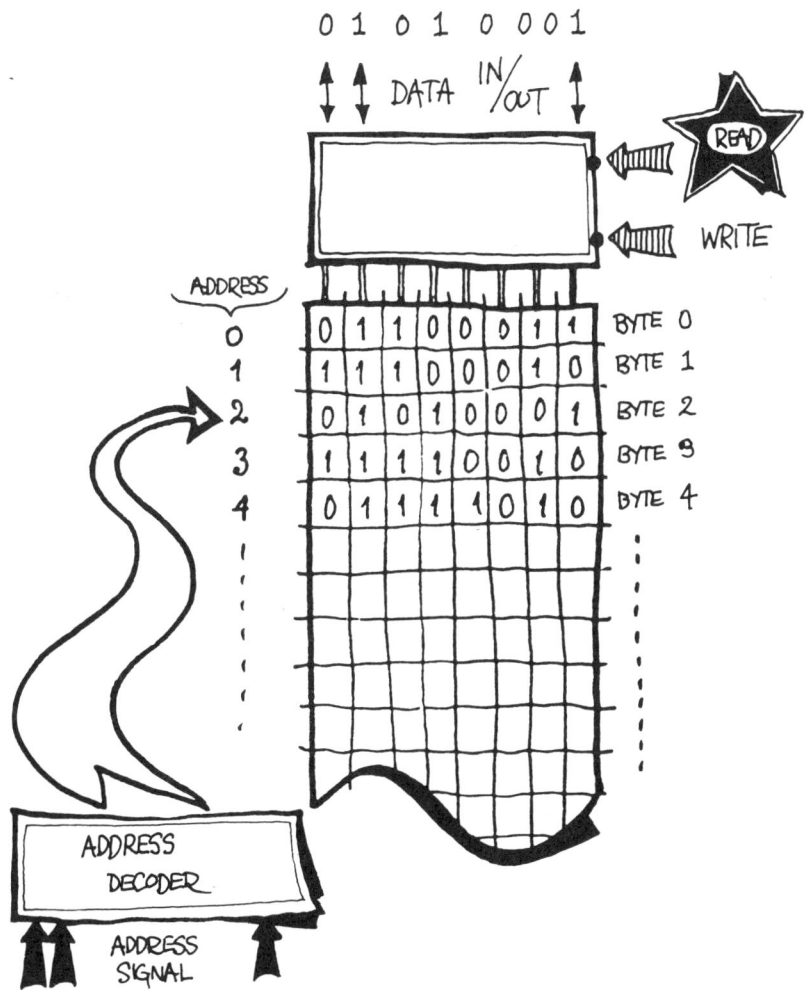

# CHAPTER 3
## How do I talk to the computer?

The actual mechanics of communicating with your computer are detailed in the next chapter. What we are going to look at here is the "language" that is used in talking to a computer.

We have seen in the previous chapter that a computer works in binary code ie. with 1's and 0's. It is clear that if the person operating the computer had to think in 1's and 0's he would soon go mad! Hex is not so difficult, and some people who absorbed computer science with their mother's milk can do it! However, this is not very often the case. Some other method is needed to overcome the problem.

We could just talk to the computer in normal English. Unfortunately, although computers can be designed to understand hundreds of words of the English language, they can't get the meaning of sentences right. The English language is too full of ambiguities. Think how often two people can be talking to each other for, say, half an hour, and both end up with different ideas on what was being discussed.

Our computer needs clear, unambiguous statements if it is to do the job efficiently.

We have seen that the machine language is difficult to use. It's all right for machine to machine communication but not for man-machine communication. It is possible to group the binary coded words together so that each step in the program can be represented by a word, or mnemonic, describing that operation. This is called **mnemonic machine code.**

The next level of programming is to give the variables names, instead of working with their respective addresses. This is called **assembly language programming.**

Finally, there are the so-called **high-level languages** such as BASIC, FORTRAN and ALGOL. These bear a passing resemblance to everyday language, and the computer translates from these to its machine code.

A working knowledge of a high level language is essential for anyone who wants to take personal computing seriously. Consequently, we will look at the most popular language called BASIC. A brief outline of machine code and assembly programming will also be presented so that some idea of what's happening at the higher level can be appreciated.

It is not necessary for the normal user to bother with anything "below" BASIC. Unfortunately, some people in the computing field like to baffle newcomers with jargon. Anything that can deflate a few egos is always worth it!

**Machine language**

Machine language is the most primitive programming language from the human point of view, but it is the only language which the computer can really understand. The manufacturer of a particular processor provides the user with a set of instructions. Each instruction relates to the operation required. The instructions may be quite simple: eg. to add the contents of two registers and place them in a third.

A program of this type may look like this:
```
10101101
01000000
00000000
01101101
01000001
00000000
```

10001101
01000010
00000000

It needs a well-trained eye to see what this program is supposed to do: (a simple addition).

The computer must perform considerably more complex operations than this, which makes it extremely inconvenient to program in machine code. It is *time-consuming* and it is *very easy to make mistakes.*

One way of simplifying the machine language is to equip the computer with a small conversion program to translate the binary figures into hexadecimal code. The program example given above will then read like this: AD, 40, 00, 6D, 41, 00, 8D, 42, 00.

This has immediately become somewhat easier to check, but it is still difficult for the untrained person to state that two numbers are being added here.

The structure of the machine language depends to a great extent on the internal design of the processor, and thus varies according to the type of processor. This example applies to a 6502 processor.

The programmer can make life a bit easier for himself by assigning a mnemonic to each hex byte. For example, the instruction "load the contents of memory address xxxx into the accumulator" could be written as LDA XXXX instead of AD XXXX. This type of machine code programming still needs the programmer to know the address location of the data and instructions.

Our program now becomes:

LDA 0040   ie. load accumulator with contents of 0040
ADC 0041   ie. add contents of address 0041 to number in accumulator
STA 0042   ie. store result in 0042

The programmer has to know that the first number is in address 0040, the second in 0041 and that the answer will be found in 0042. An even simpler method is to give the data variable names and let the computer do the rest.

**Assembly language**

The same mnemonics as previously are used, except the variables are called, for example, NUM 1 and NUM 2.
Our program now looks like this:

LDA NUM 1
ADC NUM 2
STA RESULT

Before it can be run in the computer, this program must be translated into machine language. When the program is as short as in this example, this work can be done by hand. But it is most often done by the computer. The translation is performed by a program called an **assembler,** usually quite a comprehensive program written in machine code, which in its simplest form consists of a large "table" where the computer looks for the meaning of any given mnemonic in binary code. Each instruction is thus translated on a one-for-one basis into machine language.

The assembly language can be considerably improved by what is known as the macro technique. This means that instead of one-for-one translation there is translation of a small number of assembly instructions into a larger number of machine instructions. This increases the efficiency in programming.

**High-level languages**

High-level languages are oriented towards the user and his problems rather than to the machine. A high-level language is comparatively easy to learn and relatively simple to read and write.

There are many different types of high-level languages in use. Some of the most common are **ALGOL** (Algorithmic Language, used for scientific problems), **APL** (A Programming Language, originally an IBM language), **BASIC** (Beginner's All-Purpose Symbolic Instruction Code, simple and popular for solving numerical problems), **COBOL** (Common Business Oriented Language), **FORTRAN** (Formula Translator, a popular all-round language), **LISP** (List Processing), **Pascal** (a further development of Algol), **PL/1** (a general combination of Algol, Cobol and

Fortran. Also available for microcomputers, eg. PL/M). *The most popular high-level language for personal computers is definitely BASIC.*

A simple addition in BASIC, for instance, is written on a single line: LET C = A + B (consider the simplicity compared with machine language and assembly language).

Programming in a high-level language is very efficient as far as programming time is concerned. It is normally reckoned to be at least three to five times as quick as assembler programming.

On the other hand, high-level languages make for less efficient use of the computer's speed and storage capacity. Generally, the processor requires 1½ to 3 times as much time to do its work. The storage requirement increases proportionately.

A program written in a high-level language has to be translated into machine code before the computer can understand it. This work is done by a special, quite complicated system program, normally developed by the computer manufacturer. According to how this program works it is called either a **compiler** or an **interpreter.**

The compiler translates what is called the whole BASIC program once and for all into machine code.

The interpreter, on the other hand, translates one instruction at a time into a number of machine instructions. This takes place continuously at the same time as the program is being executed in the computer — the interpreter and the high-level language program are at work at the same time.

Interpreters are very common on the personal computer scene when BASIC is being used. Compared with a compiler, it is more convenient to use, but the drawback is that it is up to ten times slower.

### At which level do I begin?

Obviously, the skill of the programmer has to be considered when answering this question. Similarly the task to be solved also needs to be considered. A high level language like BASIC is more efficient in programming time, and is generally considered simpler to use. Other programmers can also understand what has been written which aids "portability". Assembly language and machine code, on the other hand, give the programmer the ability to use the computer to its fullest capacity. Programs are shorter and quicker to run.

The following comments are only guidelines:

BASIC: Most suitable for interactive applications, where the operator and computer want to "talk" to each other! Simple calculations, games and other general purpose programs — such as training programs — are easier at this level.

Assembly language: More suitable for control of peripherals and input/output routines, real-time applications and programs within the computer system. It also makes maximum use of the small memory capacity of personal computers.

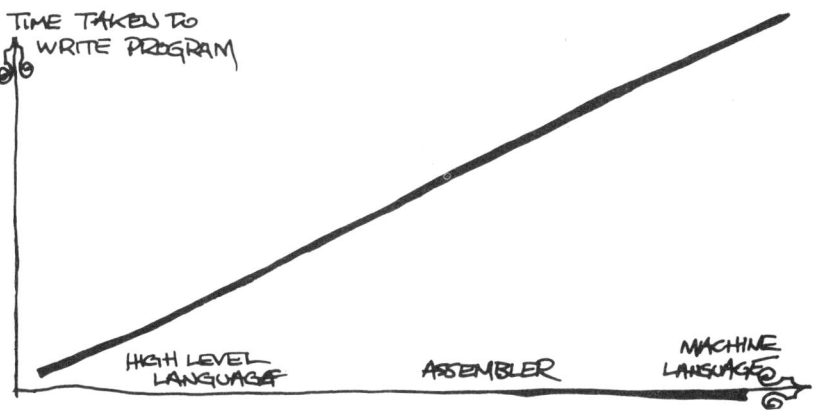

Programming in a high-level language such as BASIC is considerably quicker than in assembly language. Machine coding is very time-consuming.

High-level languages are usually the best method for the majority of personal computer owners. Writing most application programs is a quick and easy business. Troubleshooting (debugging) and testing (a not inessential part of the work!) are also relatively simple. A discussion of the relative merits of BASIC and other languages appears later in this chapter.

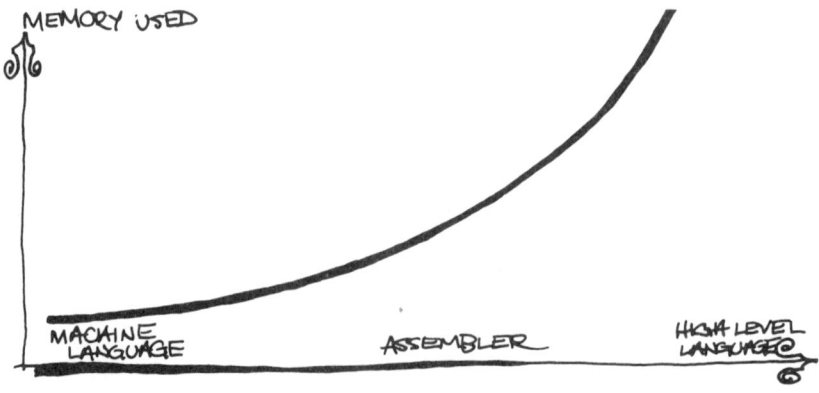

Programs written in high-level language generally require 50% to 300% greater storage capacity than those written in assembly language or machine code.

One must balance out the programming time and the storage costs from case to case.

**BASIC — a convenient language**

BASIC means **B**eginner's **A**ll-purpose **S**ymbolic **I**nstruction **C**ode and was originally developed at an American college in the 1960s. It was mainly intended for people who knew nothing about computers but were keen on using them. Since then BASIC has been further developed and become extremely widespread throughout the world. Hundreds of thousands of different computer programs have been written in BASIC. Many of these are available in books, compendiums, etc.

To make the best possible use of your computer it is advisable to learn at least the fundamentals of BASIC. After a few minutes' study it should be possible to write your own simple programs. For reasons of space, this book cannot give a comprehensive description of BASIC, but an introduction will be given here, and if you want to go further there are several good books recommended in the bibliography at the end.

The art of writing a computer program — in whatever language it may be — can be divided up into four blocks.

The first of these is the most difficult: to define the actual problem. The second step in the program is the actual input of data. The next step is the part of the program which looks after the calculation — the processing — of the problem. The last step is the output of the result.

Like most programs used by computers, the system needs to know the order with which the instructions are to be executed. Hence each statement must be preceded by a line number. It is usual to use line numbers in steps of ten, starting with ten. This allows lines to be inserted in between existing lines if the original program needs amending. On most computers the lines do not need to be typed in their final sequence. Any inserting is done by the computer. If a line number is repeated the original statement will be destroyed and replaced by the new one.

Most computers with an interpreter, and this means most of those available for personal use, can be used without having to write a program. In this interactive mode it is possible to make the computer do something directly from the keyboard.

For example if you typed PRINT "FRED" on the keyboard the screen would respond with FRED when the RETURN or ENTER key was depressed. Similarly PRINT 2 + 4 and the computer would respond with 6 after the RETURN command. This interactive nature of a BASIC interpreter is one of the strengths of using this type of language.

To write a simple program using the above example is quite easy. Say that we wanted to get the computer to display FRED BLOGGS on the screen each time a program was run. First we need to tell the computer where to start so a line number is needed, say 10. Our simple program is then:

```
10   PRINT "FRED"
```

If this is typed in and the RUN command given after RETURN FRED should appear on the screen. If RUN is now typed again FRED will appear again after the RETURN command. One line programs are not very useful so let's look at a two line program:

```
10   PRINT "FRED"
20   PRINT "BLOGGS"
```

If this is entered and RUN the screen will show

FRED
BLOGGS

It is possible to run the two words together, and the symbol ";" after the first line will make the computer print the second line immediately after the first. Similarly "," will space the BLOGGS fifteen spaces in from the edge. The first effect is called concatenation and means that expressions run after one another. The second is a form of tabbing, and usually the semicolon will move a word to the next column defined by the numbers 1, 16, 31, 46, etc., ie. at 15 column intervals. 15 is usual, though some machines use 10 spaces. There is another way of printing words — or strings as they're called — one after another.

This method involves allocating a "variable" or symbol — to the collection of letters being considered. The usual convention calls for a dollar sign, $, to indicate a string of letters. So FRED could be given the symbol A$ and BLOGGS, B$. This can be done in the program eg.

   10    A$ = "FRED"
   20    B$ = "BLOGGS"
   30    PRINT A$ + B$

Notice that line 30 treats the string variables just like the numbers earlier. If this program is entered and RUN the output will show FREDBLOGGS. (Spaces become important, but the rules vary with different implementation of BASIC. Look at the handbook of the computer being used for the convention used.)

So far we have printed out two words, and needed to type RUN each time we needed output. Say we want FRED BLOGGS displayed ten times. It would be possible to repeat line 30 ten times, using line numbers up to 120, but this is tedious. What we need is a form of counter that can keep control of the number of times a process is repeated. This is usually referred to as looping. For example consider a variable I. Let this be given a value 1 to start with and let one be added each time FRED BLOGGS is displayed, then if the computer keeps track of the value of I all we need to do is instruct the computer to stop working when I becomes 10.

   10    A$ = "FRED ",

```
20  B$ = "BLOGGS"
30  FOR I = 1 TO 10 STEP 1
40  PRINT A$ + B$
50  NEXT I
```

Line 30 sets up the initial value of I, the value when to stop and the value to be added each time the NEXT I command is met. This program will now output FRED BLOGGS ten times before stopping. (To be accurate a line 60 should be added with an END command. The example shown is a typical case of "lazy programming"!)

It is also possible to jump around in the program. If we just wanted to display FRED BLOGGS over and over again with no control on the number printed the program could have been

```
10  A$ = "FRED ",
20  B$ = "BLOGGS"
30  PRINT A$ + B$
40  GOTO 30
```

Here the program keeps jumping between 40 and 30 so displaying line after line of FRED BLOGGS! The only way to stop it is to use a BREAK command of some sort — or turn the machine off!

There are many other commands in the BASIC language — but the ones shown are the most common, and less likely to be subject to variation. For further programming examples look in the handbook, or read a good book on BASIC as indicated in the Appendix. This is not a book on programming, and the preceding section is just an example to show how easy it is to program in BASIC!

Some versions of BASIC will only handle whole numbers, and are not capable of working with fractional numbers. These are called **integer** BASICS. Some BASIC dialects, usually called Tiny BASICS, are among these. As most BASIC dialects are based on interpreters, the system throws up errors and indicates the line with the error. Some form of error code will also be shown. If a compiled version of BASIC is used then error checking is more complicated as the whole program has to be 100% correct before a successful compilation is completed.

Most BASIC interpreters used by the more popular computers originate from one company in the United States called Microsoft. Microsoft BASIC is now available for a whole range of processors and there is a certain common thread running through them. These are usually resident in ROM and are available immediately the computer is switched on.

Other BASIC interpreters are available on disk or tape and they have to be loaded into the computer before anything can be done. It is amongst these that the most serious variations occur. It is very important to consider the BASIC interpreter that is going to be used.

### Firmware

When a computer system is switched on a number of things can happen — a) nothing ie. the system sits there waiting for **you** to do something; b) a symbol appears on the output device prompting some action; or c) a message comes up saying that the system is ready for use. The amount of software support available in the monitor ROM — called firmware — determines this response.

The simplest computer firmware puts the appropriate codes into the microprocessor and sets it up ready for operation. The system does nothing more until the necessary program is entered in machine code. Obviously this is ideal for the hobbyist at this level, but does nothing to recommend a computer to the businessman! If the system monitor is more powerful it may have the capability of "booting" the system and allowing a number of alphanumeric characters to be used, eg "M" — to examine memory; "G" — to start a program. If a disk or cassette is used however, a machine code program to translate the information into the correct format, and to send the data to the cassette or data inferface, is needed. On some simple computers this has to be entered from the keyboard. More sophisticated monitors will allow a "D" or "L" (load) command to automatically "boot" the disk or cassette.

Sometimes the monitor ROM can be a very sophisticated development tool. It may contain an assembler, or even editor, that allows quite complex assembly language routines to be written. The most comprehensive firmware, though, is when a high level interpreter is included. This is usually for BASIC.

The Intel$^R$ 2732A 32-kilobit, high-density EPROM.

If BASIC does not reside in ROM it must be first loaded from disk or cassette before any BASIC programming can be done. If BASIC is going to be the main language used then this is a pain in the neck! Systems that have no high level language in firmware — most S-100 bus systems, Sharp MZ80K etc. — can be used for other languages.

There are lots more programs being sold in firmware form than just interpreters or monitors. On some systems plug-in ROM pacs allow quite complicated BASIC or machine code programs to be used. The advantage with firmware is the access time. Whereas a disk or cassette can take between seconds and minutes to load, firmware takes a fraction of a second. Exidy Sorcerer, Texas Instruments TI99/4A and VIC20 are three examples of this approach.

Another form of firmware is available for the Commodore PET or BBC Micro for example. These are in the form of plug-in ROMs that sit inside the machine in sockets that have been left vacant for this purpose. BASIC toolkits, word processors and accounting packages are just three applications of this approach. In the PET, as few ROM sockets are available, a small expansion board can be bought that allows up to sixteen ROMs to be used, all at the same memory address! Each one is "dialled" either by software

43

or a hardware switch, depending on the ROM required.

In fact firmware, in the form of plug-in ROMs, is going to do for the personal computer what the golfball did for the typewriter!

### Software

Most system software does not reside in ROM form, unfortunately. Languages, other than BASIC, are available, and in many circumstances preferable! These would take up too much memory if in ROM format and the only method is on disk or cassette.

The most obvious software that determines a systems capability, especially when using disks, is the operating system. As most cassette operating systems require more hardware than software we will only consider disk operating systems — or DOS — here!

The DOS for any system determines more than anything else its capabilities. It also determines the "portability" of any software developed. Some attempts have been made at standards in this area. On personal computer systems there are four in accepted use.

The standards used by Apple, Tandy and Commodore have become widely accepted, essentially because of the number of machines sold. None has any feature that would recommend itself to outshine the others. Other companies have adopted these standards basically to sell software and/or plug compatible accessories.

The major DOS in use, at the moment, is CP/M developed by Digital Research. It basically lays down a standard for formatting the disk, and encoding the data. In theory it should be portable — and on most Z80 or 8080-based computers using the S-100 bus, it can claim to have some success. Some 6502-based computers like the Apple II or the Commodore PET can accept plug-in units that allow CP/M to be run on them. The most common DOS for 16-bit computers is MS-DOS, developed by the company that wrote the first commercial BASIC.

It is essential when looking at a disk based system to have a very good idea of the software needed. If the programs available can be adapted to your system very easily, and cheaply, then this may determine the hardware requirements!

A brief summary of the pros and cons of different languages and operating systems is given below.

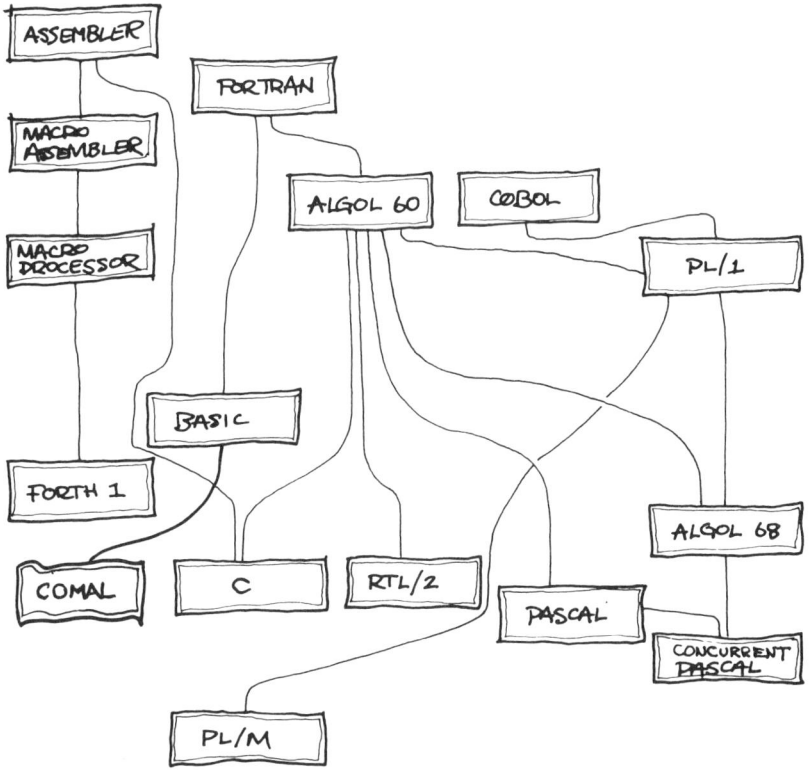

A family tree of some of the common computer languages as used on small computer systems.

## BASIC

BASIC was devised at Dartmouth College in the USA as a high-level language that would be easy to learn and to teach. Its recent rapid increase in popularity has stemmed from the speed with which it can be learnt and from its ready availability on microcomputers. It is the language that is available on the Commodore PET and the Apple. Although there is a standard version of BASIC, so many variations and extensions are currently available, including extensions for text processing or real-time applications, that the standard has little meaning.

Input instructions are interactive, and when executed cause the machine to wait until an input is entered from the keyboard. In BASIC programs, every instruction has a line number. Before executing a program BASIC uses the line numbers to sort the instructions into order.

BASIC provides facilities for handling strings. A variable whose name ends in $ can have a character string assigned to it.

## LISP

LISP is a list processing language. The list is a useful representation in a variety of applications. For example, character strings may be regarded as lists of characters, and text as lists of the obstacles to its movement. It can determine whether a move it proposes to make is obstructed by scanning this list.

LISP is a functional language. Every instruction consists of a function and its arguments, and is executed by evaluating the arguments, applying the function to them and returning the resulting function value.

## PL/1

The facilities possessed by PL/1 include a combination of those of FORTRAN and COBOL. As a general purpose language it is very complicated, and has not achieved its expected popularity. The slowness of its early implementations was a factor contributing to this.

## COBOL

The pre-eminence of COBOL for business data processing stems from the US Government policy that required the provision of a COBOL compiler with any computer bought using their funding. As a commercial language, COBOL emphasizes the handling of alphanumeric data and files, so that tasks such as reading and updating file records and automatic form filling can be accomplished.

## ALGOL

ALGOL 60 is formally defined in a report dated 1960, and although it is a more rational language than FORTRAN, it has never managed to dent the popularity of the latter to any marked degree.

Input/Output is the one language feature not defined in the ALGOL 60 report, so that it varies from implementation to implementation. All variables must be declared before they are used in ALGOL programs. The sub-program in ALGOL is the procedure. Unlike FORTRAN and BASIC, ALGOL supports recursion, that is, sub-programs may call themselves.

## FORTRAN

FORTRAN owes its supremacy over the early high-level scientific programming languages, to its support from IBM. Once established as the language that most scientific programmers knew and in which most scientific software was written, it was naturally difficult to dislodge. Although there are many dialects of FORTRAN, the definitive version is ANSI standard FORTRAN IV.

FORTRAN automatically performs arithmetic operations in the correct order, so that, for instance, multiplications are performed before additions. Brackets can be used to change this order in exactly the same way as in algebraic formulae.

FORTRAN possesses a range of standard functions broadly comparable to that of a scientific calculator.

Input and output are achieved with READ and WRITE instructions. In each READ or WRITE instruction, the key word is followed by a pair of numbers in brackets. The necessity of formats can be aggravating, but it gives the programmer complete control over the layout of his input and output.

Repetition is achieved with a DO loop. This facility gives the automatic repetition of all the instructions between a DO and its matching CONTINUE statement as often as indicated.

FORTRAN supports both functions and subroutines. The function sub-program computes a single value and returns it to the main program. A subroutine can return multiple values besides being executed for its side effects.

The only data structure available in FORTRAN is the array.

The handling of strings and characters in FORTRAN is somewhat limited. However, some dialects permit a solution similar to the one presented in the section on BASIC.

### Pascal

Pascal is descended from the ALGOLs. It was designed as a teaching language to demonstrate programming as a systematic discipline. It was also intended that it should be possible to implement the language compactly and efficiently.

Pascal provides all the control features necessary for structured programming. Arrays and complex data structures are also supported.

### Disk Operating Systems

### CP/M

Originally designed to provide a manufacturer independent operating system for 8080 based computers, it has now evolved to work with most Z80 based systems. Basically CP/M is a collection of routines that sit at the top of the computer's memory, and it takes up around 4K of memory. It allows a whole range of machine code routines, disk utilities and high level compilers/interpreters to be run. For example disk-copy, BASIC, Pilot, word processors, assemblers and Pascal can be obtained. It has now been modified to operate with the 16-bit 8086 processor. This version is called CP/M-86.

There has been some controversy recently as to the actual "portability" of the DOS; and some problems have arisen when using software developed on a different system.

There are now over 1000 suppliers of CP/M software. Unfortunately quite a few systems have DOSs similar to CP/M, but not compatible. For example Cromemco's CDOS has a close resemblance, and needs software "translation" to achieve near compatibility.

In practice at least 24K of RAM must be available to run programs using CP/M. In fact the more RAM the better. Similarly a reasonable amount of disk storage is required, and a dual disk system with at least 250K of memory is useful.

A multi-user version, called MP/M, is also available.

## Flex

Flex is the "CP/M of the 6800" and was developed by SWTPc to do for the SS-50 bus what CP/M did for the S-100. It includes all the file and disk handling routines required for normal running, and has a utility command set eg. copy. Its strength lies in the utilities like dynamic file space allocation, automatic "removal" of defective sectors, space compression and expansion on all text files. Again, a minimum RAM of around 20K is required, and a dual drive system holding around 160K is needed.

## MS-DOS

MS-DOS was developed by Microsoft for the IBM Personal Computer — and has now been adopted by the majority of those manufacturers that use the 8088/8086 processors in their computers.

It is far more "menu-orientated" than CP/M, or CP/M-86, and has been designed for 16-bit processors, unlike CP/M-86 which is just a converted version of CP/M-80. Unfortunately MS-DOS will not support multi-user systems yet, whereas CP/M has a version called MP/M that does this, after a fashion.

There are probably more programs running under MS-DOS for 16-bit machines than at present under CP/M-86.

## UNIX

This DOS has been developed by Bell Labs in the USA. It is written in the high-level language "C" and is probably the most flexible of all the DOSs. It runs on the true 16-bit processors — like the 68000, Z8000 and iAPX 432.

There is not much personal computer software running under UNIX at the moment.

**Which microprocessor is "best"?**

This is a question that will inevitably get asked. It is impossible to answer directly! It all depends on what you want to do with it!

When a microprocessor is chosen for a microcomputer system, a number of things are considered by the designers:

The instruction set: Some micros are better, or more efficient, at performing some instructions than others. Unfortunately, there is no one chip better in all aspects than any other.

Speed: In some uses, especially with BASIC interpreters, some micros are much faster than others.

Programming support: How easy is it to program? A micro which is relatively slow but has a wealth of programs to support it will succeed.

Documentation: The designer doesn't want to spend most of his time working out how it works!

The most popular micros are:

8080 — one of the first microprocessors, and the one on which the S-100 bus was first based. Getting a bit long in the tooth now, and not found in too many machines.

Z80 — a development of the 8080. It is based on the 8080 and runs its instruction set — and a lot more besides. Becoming increasingly popular, as it has a fast speed version — the Z80A — that operates with a clock frequency of 4 MHz. It is ideal for the new IEEE standard S-100 bus.

6800 — again, like the 8080, getting a bit old fashioned. Didn't really catch on as a processor for computational purposes.

6809 – an advanced version of the 6800 — a pseudo 16-bit processor. Its internal registers use 16-bit wide words but communicate with only 8-bits. Not used in many personal computers.

6502 — based on the 6800 but more flexible. Picked up by Apple, Atari and most of the personal computer manufacturers, after Commodore — who designed it — came along with the PET. Incredibly fast when used with the BASIC interpreter from Microsoft Ltd. A 4 MHz version is used in some newer computers — and is **very** fast.

6510 – an upgraded version of the 6502 with more input/output capability and a higher clock speed.

8085 — based on the 8080, but unlike all the preceding chips is not an 8-bit micro. It uses 8-bit addressing and data but has a 16-bit internal architecture — a halfway home to the ...

8088 – a pseudo-16-bit (see 6809) version of the 8080. Used by many of the so-called 16-bit commercial computers. Very much a half-way house to the 8086.

8086 — which is a true 16-bit processor.

9900 — also a 16-bit chip that hasn't really caught on — and used by Texas Instruments in the 99/4 (they designed the 9900!).

SC/MP — used by hobbyists along with the ...

1802 — and ideal for a single board system.

Z8000 — is an upgraded Z80 with 16-bit architecture but is too new to be in many machines at the moment. Coupled with the new S-100 bus, that can take 16-bit processors, it promises to be the system of the future – along with the ...

68000 — a 16-bit processor that is an upgraded 6800.

# CHAPTER 4

## What's in the boxes?

We have seen that a basic computer system consists of an input section, a processing section containing the actual processor and memory, and an output section. This chapter will take a look at the various components of a system, and consider, briefly, how they work.

### Input devices

The simplest input device to a digital computer is an on-off switch! However, programming and entering data using this method is not everybody's cup of tea! The most common means of entering data and information is via an alphanumeric keyboard. Some basic microcomputers that are only programmable in hexadecimal machine code, use a numerical calculator-type keyboard, but most users want a normal typewriter style keyboard so that high level languages can be used.

Although the keyboard is the most common type of input peripheral, other ideas are beginning to emerge. Speech recognition is foremost amongst these. Although outside the scope of this book a brief description is included. Finally it is possible to input information and/or data directly through various devices such as temperature sensors, intruder alarms etc.

**Keyboard-based input**

The simplest typewriter style keyboard consists of a push-button switch. When the key is pressed a contact is made and a pulse is produced, and, if only a few keys are needed, then a wire can come from each key and the computer can be programmed to recognize the input.

However, the usual number of keys on a typewriter is around 50. It is impossible for the computer to decode 50 different inputs efficiently. Hence the keys are linked together in a matrix, with the information being presented as row and column data. Most keyboards are more sophisticated than this and have integrated circuits that take the row and column data and present it to the computer in the parallel eight-bit format that can be handled most efficiently. They also have other circuits that detect only one key at a time, and even ignore keys that are being pressed if the previously keyed information has not been acknowledged by the computer. This stops the system from getting clogged up.

*The PCD MALTRON Ergonomic Keyboard.*

On some systems the keyboard is separate from the main processor, and is just an input unit. On other systems a TV screen is included with the keyboard, and this is called a video display unit, or VDU. The screen not only displays information from the computer, but also shows what is going into the system from the keyboard.

A *visual display unit.*

Sometimes a printer is attached, and this performs the same function as the screen in a VDU. These are called teletypes, which is the name of the company that first invented them. Although a trade name (and a registered trade mark!) the term teletype, or TTY is now used for any printer based system that can be used to enter data from a keyboard.

Most VDUs and TTYs are designed to be machine independent. This means that they can be used on any computer system. However this involves having an interface that is fairly well accepted as a standard. The most common one for these two pieces of equipment is the RS232C interface standard, and this is discussed later in this chapter.

*A Teletype.*

**Speech recognition**

Speech recognition is becoming more widely accepted as its capabilities are being extended with increasingly sophisticated advances in technology. Only one or two personal computer systems can handle speech synthesis at the moment, but with the technique appearing in other consumer orientated electronic goods — such as TVs and calculators — it is only a matter of time before it is generally available.

Basically the computer compares the input information with that stored in its memory. When it recognizes various parts of a phrase or sound it works out what is being said. Most systems can only handle 20 words at the moment, and this requires a lot of memory. The present systems have to be trained to recognize the operator's voice — and then can only respond to that individual. Obviously this has great benefits as far as security goes — but does not recommend the method for general use!

## Direct input

Sometimes it is useful to have input to the computer from various external devices, as well as keyboards. Various interfaces have been designed to deal with these — the most common being the IEEE-488 and RS232C standards. These deal with data in both directions — to and from the computer.

The IEEE-488 interface standard — or GP-IB (General Purpose Interface Bus) is based on a sixteen way parallel transmission of data. It was initially intended as a standard for controlling and interrogating electronic instruments. But Commodore introduced it to the personal computer world and now use it for all their peripherals like disks and printers. A full explanation of the standard as applied to personal computers is given in Appendix B.

Atari$^R$ 830$^{TM}$ Acoustic Modem.

The other standard — RS232C — is much more common — and is used by the vast majority of teletypes, VDUs and modems (devices for sending data over telephone lines). Unlike the IEEE-488 standard the RS232C standard defines the way that data is transmitted and received in serial format, ie. pulses following one another. Consequently only three lines are really needed to get the system working — data receive, data send and earth. (The standard in fact specifies 25 lines, but 15 are usually used as a maximum.) These other 22 lines include facilities for telling the computer to accept the signals. The rate of data send and receive can also be set automatically. Normally this is done by using switches on the input port of the computer and the output port of the peripheral. It is important when using devices that use the RS232C standard that the rate of data transmission is compatible. The usual rates are 110, 300, and 1,200 bits/sec.

When the computer is used to accept or send data to a peripheral, or even another computer, using telephone lines, two methods can be used. An acoustic coupler translates the pulses from the computer into acoustic levels that the normal telephone

This graphics tablet from Ferranti provides a method of translating handwritten data into direct data input.

lines can carry. Alternatively the output can be connected directly to telephone data lines via a box called a modem. Most acoustic couplers have a 25-pin socket that connects directly to the RS232C input/output port of the computer. As prices drop they are becoming more popular and most personal computer manufacturers are offering, or will offer such devices.

**Storage media**

Methods of storing data inside the computer using semiconductor memory, RAM or ROM, were considered in an earlier chapter. The normal 8-bit microprocessor uses 16-bits to address this memory. Thus the maximum amount of memory addressable directly from the processor is $2^{16}$ or 64K bytes. With the monitor and/or interpreter taking up to 20K of this in ROM form, and the video needing up to 8K of RAM to store the screen information, sometimes only 36K is available for user programming space. In fact most small systems are limited to 32K or 48K as a maximum.

Although a single 8-bit microprocessor can only address 64K of memory directly it can be "switched", either by software or hardware, to address a whole series of "banks" of 64K bytes. A number of 8-bit systems, like the Commodore 8096, use this system.

Pseudo-16-bit processors, like the 8088, can also address more than 64K even though they only have an 8-bit data bus. A system called "segmentation", usually software driven, allows the processor to address up to 2 bytes directly. Most systems will only allow up to 1.024 Mbytes as power supply and packaging problems become dominant above that.

It is clear that other forms of storage are needed. Unfortunately none of those generally available come anywhere as close to semiconductor memory in terms of speed and ease of use. Two things are required to overcome these problems. Firstly an interface and/or a program that will transfer the data into a format that can be used by another storage medium, and secondly some method of changing the speed of data transmission from the fairly slow rates required by most peripherals to the faster ones used by the computer. This is usually achieved by using a buffer that accepts an amount of data from the peripheral, storing it and then transmitting it to the processor, or RAM, at the appropriate speed.

**Cassette storage**

The simplest method of storage is to use a domestic cassette recorder. The interface changes the pulses into a format that can be recorded and played back by the cassette recorder electronics. The only problem is that the rate of transmission is very slow — anywhere between 100 and 1000 bits/second. The electronics must be very tolerant of speed variation as the average cassette recorder is not very good at keeping constant speed! The average cassette is also of dubious quality as far as data recording goes. Our ears are far more tolerant of errors than any computer system! When all these problems have been overcome — and the state of technology has reached an adequate level by now — the only major drawback is the speed. For small programs, up to say 4 Kbytes, cassette storage is acceptable. But when it takes up to 10 minutes to load a program, and then still have the possibility of errors, things are nowhere near ideal. Cassette storage is cheap though. Most homes now have a cassette recorder, and if not they only cost a few pounds to buy. Cassettes themselves are also fairly cheap. Hundreds of kilobytes can be stored on an average C60 cassette costing under £1.

The other main problem with cassette storage is the lack of any standard recording format. An early attempt at producing a standard was made in Kansas City. The result is what is now known as the Kansas City standard. This is the only accepted standard for personal computers, and is by far the most common, although used by a small minority. Another one is the KIM standard, and this is used by similar single board computers such as the AIM and SYM and UK101.

Even with cassettes recorded to a single standard, programs may still not be transportable from one computer to another. The BASIC interpreter may be different; certainly the memory map will be and this will affect any part of the program in machine code. There is even the problem of different head alignment on various tape recorders. Even the same tapes may not be played back on a different recorder to that which recorded it.

**Disk storage**

The generally accepted method of overcoming most of the problems of cassette storage is with disk drives. These are not cheap though — and start at around 10 times the price of an average cassette recorder. The disks themselves start around £2 each.

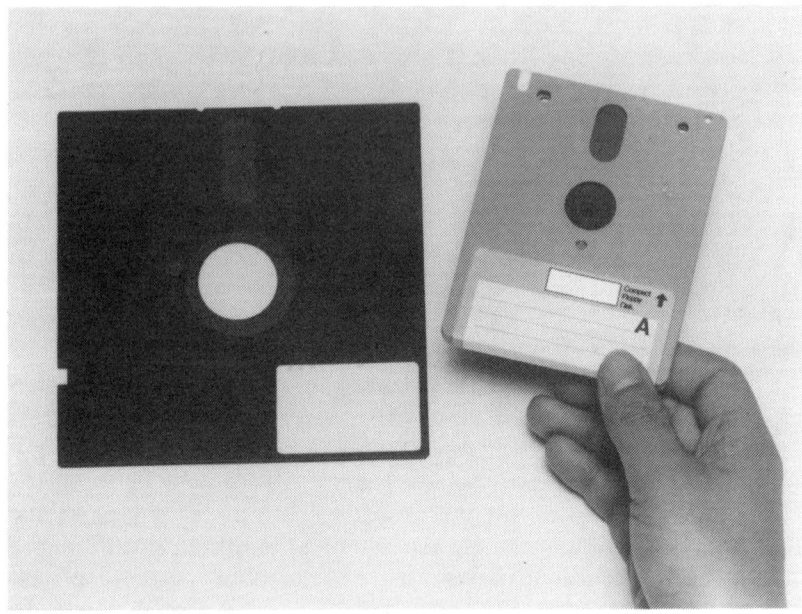

New compact floppy disk (right) shown along-side traditional floppy disk (left).

Unlike records that have information stored in one groove and are accessed serially, magnetic disks are divided into a number of discrete tracks. Each track is then divided into sectors. This can be done by the computer, under software control, or by a separate microprocessor in the disk unit.

There are two basically different ways for the read/write head to find the right place in the different disk sectors — "hard sectoring" and "soft sectoring". A hard-sectored disk has a number of holes punched inside around the centre: each of these holes is a sign for the beginning of a new sector. The soft-sectored disk only has one hole indicating the beginning of each track — the length of each sector is determined by programming (hence the term soft sectoring). These two sectoring methods are not compatible — in other words, a hard sectored disk cannot be used in equipment for soft-sectored disks.

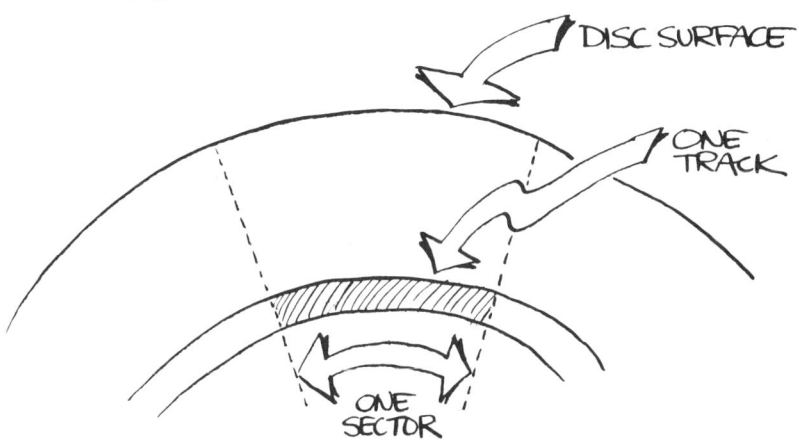

*Diagrammatic representation of a floppy disk, showing sectors, segments and tracks.*

Disks come in various diameters. The most common are 5¼" and 8" diameter floppy disks. The name is indicative of the material used for their construction. It is a flexible plastic with a film of magnetic oxide on each side. Because it is easily damaged the disk is enclosed in a thin card case. A small slit is provided for the record/playback head to come into close proximity to the disk. The exposed sections of the disk must not be touched by greasy fingers, as some of the information stored might get corrupted. Obviously extremes of temperature must be considered, and under no circumstances must any magnetic field come near the disk.

## Disk drive

This is a unit consisting basically of a holder for the disk, a motor driving the disk via a spindle at 300-360 revolutions a minute, and a stepping motor driving a radially movable

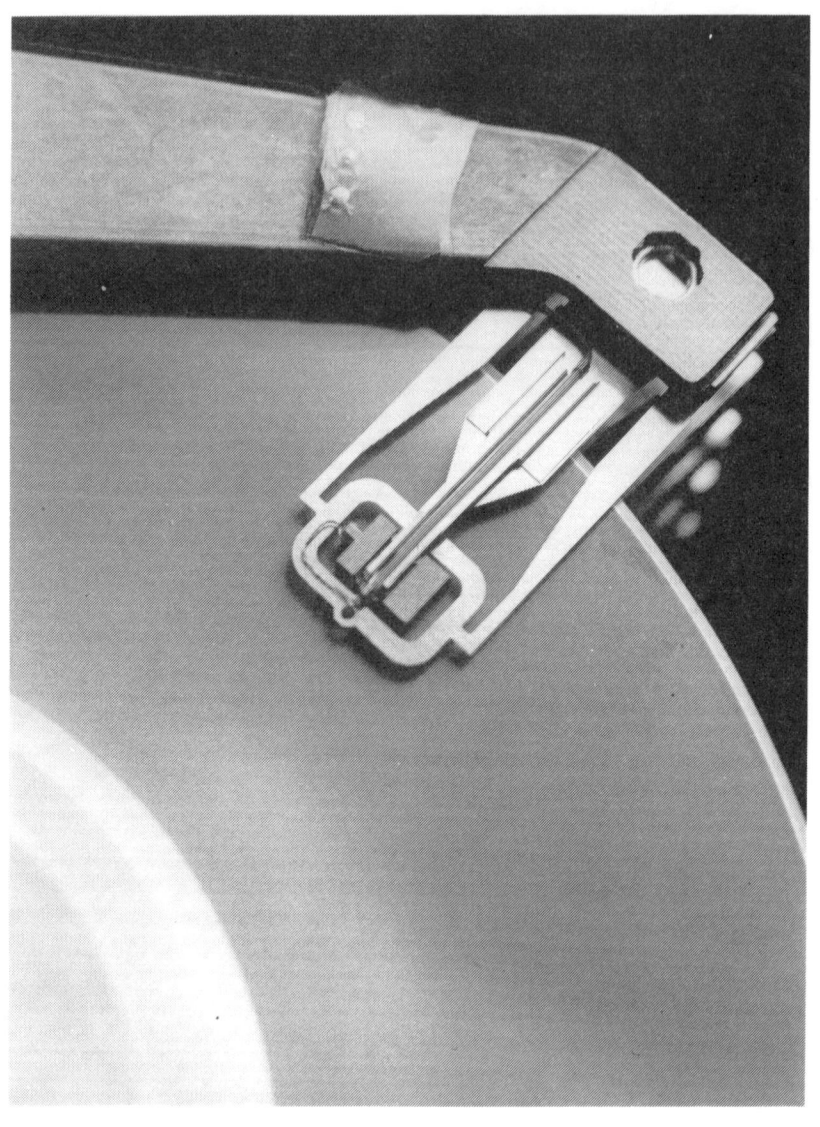

*Read/Write head of Winchester disk drive.*

A 5.25" Winchester, which provides 53.3 Megabytes of storage (unformatted). The drive has a track density of 600 tracks per inch, and bit density of 10,200 bits per inch. Average access time is 50 milliseconds.

mechanism holding the magnetic head for reading and writing. There is also an electronic controller (as a rule in the form of a separate circuit board which is placed in the computer bus). On command, it is the controller which operates the magnetic head of the unit, moving it to the desired track on the disk to read or write the data. The controller can serve several floppy disk units at once.

The normal 5¼" disk has up to 80 tracks with around 16 sectors — although this can vary. According to the method of formatting the information, anything between 75 and 680 Kbytes can be recorded on each side. Some drives have two heads, one for each side, and on these dual-sided drives up to 1300 Kbytes can be stored. It is important to know whether the disk drive is single or double sided, single or double density formatted. The disk manufacturers make different disks for each type. Needless to say it is not possible to exchange a disk between different types of disk drive, however portable it may be between drives of a similar type.

The normal 8" disk has 77 tracks and 26 sections and stores between 256 Kbytes and 1.2 MBytes. 8" disks are usually formatted along similar lines to those used by mainframe computers like IBM and DEC.

One type of disk that is becoming popular for small business applications is the 8" or 5¼" hard disk, or mini-Winnie! The mini-Winnie is a smaller version of an IBM mainframe disk called a Winchester unit and can store up to 26 Mbytes. The main difference between hard and floppy disks is the speed of revolution — around 10× greater for hard disks compared to floppy disks. The record/playback head also sits very close to the disk — somewhere around 1 millionth of a metre away. As this is somewhat smaller than the diameter of human hair, or dust particle, hard disks are enclosed in an air-tight environment usually filled with inert gas under pressure. Speeds of transmission are far greater than floppy disks and approach 2.5 Mbytes/second.

**Other storage media**

There are methods for storing information digitally other than disk or cassette. Small cassette-type packages called cartridges are used by a number of manufacturers like Hewlett-Packard. These can read data very fast and have access times approaching floppy disks.

*The ultra compact Philips Mini-DCR can be easily held in one hand, yet it has a capacity of 128 Kbytes with fast access and a high transfer rate of 6 Kb/s.*

Magnetic bubble memories could become more familiar over the next few years. These are used for storing large amounts of data — in the order of millions of bytes. This method of storage uses similar technology to semiconductor memories, except that small magnetic devices are created into a magnetic medium like transistors are in silicon. The memory is addressed serially, like a cassette, and is thus fairly slow — but takes far less power and space than a cassette. However they are still expensive compared to other types of magnetic storage.

**Output devices**

It is becoming impossible to divorce output devices from input devices as time goes by. It is general practice to have both in one unit — the VDU and teletype are examples. Hence what follows must inevitably contain some information that has gone before.

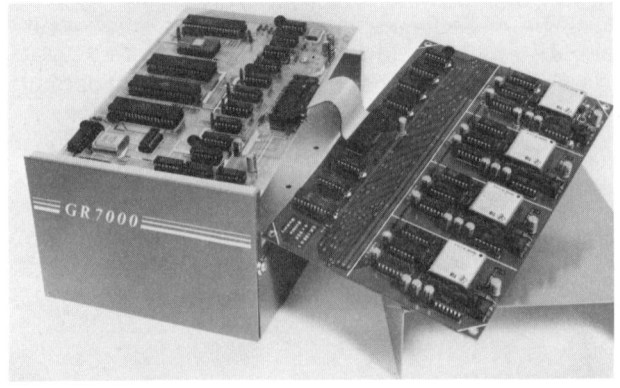

*The GR7000 bubble memory module is a serially interfaced RS232 compatible memory system designed for ensuring data storage in harsh environments.*

## Video output

The VDU is the most common form of video output. The simplest is a domestic television set. Some computer systems, especially those based around a keyboard unit, have a socket for a TV aerial on the back. If this is designed for European sets then all that is required is to tune the set into, say, channel 36 and adjust the brightness and contrast controls. Some of the computer systems that are designed for home use have colour output. In these instances it is absolutely essential that the TV output be the standard for the country of use. It is possible to use systems made for use in, say, the UK and Germany without much difficulty. However, France uses a completely different standard and USA and Japan another system again! Black and white poses less problems, but some instability of picture, and maybe less characters on the screen, could occur with systems designed for the US and Japan when used in Europe.

The most foolproof output is called direct video. Instead of converting the computer's video information to the high frequency used by television transmission, the signal is presented in the form used inside the TV. Nearly all TV sets only have an aerial socket. Some sets, designed for use with video recorders, may also have a video socket. Computers give a voltage of 1 volt peak to peak across their video output, so any TV must be able to take this. With 1v pp video it doesn't matter what transmission standards are used in the country of origin — so as long as you only want black and white, everything's OK. Unfortunately there are still 3 different colour standards around the world — so any system using, say, the American and Japanese NTSC standard, can only be used with an NTSC receiver. Some American colour computer systems have a permanently attached video monitor — Compucolor for example — or sell a specially converted TV set capable of operating on two or more standards — TI for example with the original 99/4.

Whatever form of output is used, nearly every video display uses similar methods of generating the characters. A screen that can display 25 lines of 40 characters requires 1000 memory locations to store the information. In these so called memory mapped systems, each character position on the screen corresponds to a particular memory location in the video memory. All the computer does is transfer the contents of the memory onto the screen. As each memory location can store one byte — of eight bits — this means that $2^8$ or 256 different characters are available. The most common method of encoding characters is the ASCII system. As this only has 7 bits of information, only 128 characters are available. Most personal computer systems add another 128 to make up the number — and they do this by creating graphics characters. There is no standard for these so that PET graphic symbols, for example, have different codes from Spectrum graphics. The codes are interpreted into actual letters and graphic symbols by a ROM called a character generator. It is clear that all this memory detracts from the amount of memory available for use in the system by the user.

Another method of generating video information is to split the screen into a series of discrete points, say $312 \times 210$. This requires a lot more memory. Each point on the screen now corresponds to one **bit** in the memory, hence eight points require one byte of memory. $312 \times 210$ points need 8 Kbytes.

This high density graphics capability is available on a few computers — like the Apple II and BBC. It is a useful facility for educational users — but unless complicated graphical analyses are needed is not really ideal for business use.

Most VDUs in fact take the data in serial format using the RS232C standard. The memory needed to store the information is inside the VDU and does not take up any of the computer memory. As a VDU costs as much as a cheaper computer system however, this method of video output coupled with keyboard input, is really recommended for more expensive bus-structured systems.

## Printed output

There are many different types of printer available for computer users. These range from simple printers for around £40 to word processor output at about £2000.

## Electric typewriter/TTY

The simplest way of generating printed output is to use a converted electric typewriter. There are a number of these around usually based on the IBM Selectric range. The computer uses software, or a hardware board, to convert the signals into the format used by the internal electronics inside the typewriters. Sometimes these will allow the keyboard to be used to enter information as well.

A Teletype is cheap, if you buy it second-hand. There are lots of used machines on the market to be had for anything from £25 to £300 or more. There are three basic model types: RO (receive only), which has no keyboard but is used as a printer; KSR (keyboard, send and receive), which is the one described above; and ASR — a KSR which also has punch and reader for paper tape. Most Teletype machines are made by the American Teletype Corp, but other firms such as Olivetti also make them.

The Selectric machine is an IBM design available in a series of different versions. The spherical type core is common to all of them. This gives very good print quality, it is replaceable, and there are many different type styles.

In its simplest form, the Selectric machine is a normal office electric typewriter. Since the construction is essentially mechanical it must be modified to be able to work with the ASCII signals of the computer. Modification kits are available on the market.

It is somewhat simpler if you can find a second-hand Selectric model 72, 731, 735 or something of the sort. A machine of this type has been used as input/output terminal in various computer systems. The only modification that has to be done is to equip it with an interface for ASCII code.

Several firms have also begun to market Selectric terminals that are reconditioned and modified for ASCII — in other words, completely ready to connect to the computer.

A general word of warning about Selectric machines: the internal mechanics are pretty advanced and may be difficult to repair on one's own. In other words, avoid faulty Selectric machines.

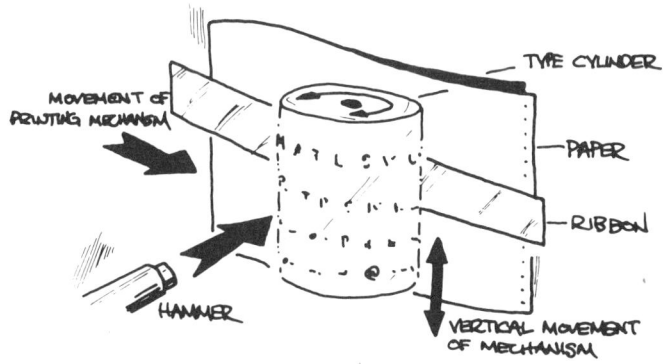

CYLINDRICAL IMPACT PRINTER AS FOUND IN TELETYPE etc.

The Teletype machine is electromechanical in construction with a keyboard for input and an impact printer (a type cylinder) for output on paper which is stored as a roll in the machine. The speed is modest, usually 10 characters a second (110 baud since each character consists of 11 bits — a start bit, eight data bits and two stop bits; in other words series transmission as with the RS232). There are also Teletypes that are faster — 150 or 300 baud. Other disadvantages are that the machine is loud and usually only prints capitals.

**Matrix printers**

Another method of producing characters on a page is by printing dots based on, say, a 5 × 7 matrix. Most characters and graphics symbols can be generated this way. The simplest dot matrix printer cosists of seven needles in a vertical line that are "fired" onto the paper as the head moves from left to right. Five such "firings" are needed to produce each character. A normal typewriter ribbon means that normal paper can be used. The cheapest dot matrix printer is around £40.

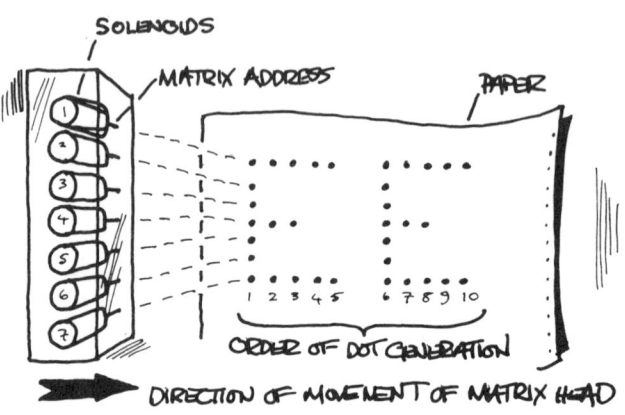

THE WRITING HEAD OF THE MATRIX PRINTER MOVES LEFT TO RIGHT EACH SYMBOL IS BUILT-UP SEQUENTIALLY FROM DOTS, NORMALLY 5-7

It is possible to do quite complicated characters with dot matrix printers as each character can be programmed individually. If the computer system used has a graphics capability a dot matrix printer must be used otherwise these characters will not be printed. And it is here that the non-ASCII standard graphic characters cause problems. Whereas the normal alphabetical and command characters will reproduce on practically any printer with an ASCII interface the graphics do not. A PET computer, for example, **must** have a PET-compatible printer to reproduce its graphics.

It is also important to make sure that the printer can be programmed to reproduce different line widths. The usual 40 characters per line of a small system means a bit of juggling if an 80-line printer is used. Similarly with 64 character systems on a 132 character printer. It is essential that some method of programming the output to take these incompatibilities into account is available.

**Daisy wheel printer**

If good quality output is required then either a converted Selectric typewriter, or specialized printer, is required. The daisy wheel printer is a form of impact printer that has all the characters around the rim of a circular plastic disk. A hammer hits the appropriate character to produce the printed symbol needed. These are rather expensive when compared to other sorts of printers but give good quality at high speed. The print head can be changed to give different type faces. With most daisy wheel printers it is possible to program them, from the computer software, so that right and left justification with proportional spacing is available. They are designed for word processing applications.

*Print heads and ribbon from daisy wheel printer.*

**Other printers**

The printers mentioned above all use impact technology and rely on ink coming from the typewriter ribbon to create the image on paper. They also use normal paper. There are other ways of getting image onto paper and some printers use these methods.

Heat sensitive paper is used by a number of small printers. These usually have about 40 characters per line. A small dot-matrix heating element moves across the paper, and where a hot

*Speech Synthesis Unit.*

spot is created a blue dot appears on the page. They are quick, and because there is no impacting, very quiet. The paper is rather expensive however, and is usually only available in 2" to 3" wide rolls.

There are other forms of heat sensitive paper that has an aluminized finish. This is even more expensive than the previously mentioned paper.

**Speech synthesis**

Like speech recognition, speech synthesis is becoming more important. It is a lot easier to perform than recognition and takes up far less memory space. Around 200 words can be stored in a 128K byte ROM. The quality is very good, and is in fact used a lot by telephone companies to announce engaged lines, for example. Texas Instruments are pioneers in this field, and they sell a board that can be used in a number of computer systems.

One of the most useful applications of speech synthesis is to announce system failures, or even to give directions on how to use the system! It certainly makes using the computer more interesting.

# CHAPTER 5
## What can I buy?

**The computer system**

We've now got to the stage where we know what a computer is, how it works and what's in the boxes. The question now is — how do you actually choose a computer that will serve your needs? This chapter lists the main, generally available, models. Microcomputers can be grouped into four main categories.

First are the single board microcomputers. These originated from the "evaluation" boards that the early microprocessor manufacturers produced to allow engineers the opportunity of familiarizing themselves with the new devices. They have since evolved upwards into self-contained computer systems with keyboards, memory interfacing and even printers. They have also gone down market and can be had for under £30 although at this price they are very basic and are really aimed at the electronics hobbyist who wants to put a simple system together. Also included in this section are a few training computers. These are designed for engineers, scientists and mathematicians who want to learn about machine code programming and interfacing techniques. As these also contain very good self teaching manuals they have been included as some readers may be interested in this area.

Secondly there are the cheaper systems aimed at the home, entertainment or educational use. Like the first category they frequently come as a "naked" circuit board without any casing. This trend has fortunately now ceased and it is even possible to get plastic cases for the early systems that were produced without them. These systems are very versatile and most support cassette drives, disk drives, video display, memory expansion, printers and modems. They can be developed into quite sophisticated systems.

Thirdly, there is the "desktop" category. This term was coined some years ago by Hewlett Packard to describe their self-contained units that were "friendly". What they meant by this was that as soon as the unit is powered up it "talks" to you, and can be programmed straight away. This is because the high level language, usually BASIC, is present in ROM and hence does not need loading with a machine code routine, or "boot" before programming takes place. Commodore were the pioneers of this approach with the PET, and the vast majority of the personal computers around follow this approach. They usually also have an integral cassette unit, although the price of disk drives has been dropping and the size of programs has been getting bigger. Hence they are being replaced by integral disk or optional cassette or disk drives.

The original desktop computers had black and white video output, usually on an integral screen. Apple blew this approach apart when the Apple II with its colour capability came on the market. As most homes have colour TV it is now normal for those computers with colour capability to have an output socket that plugs directly into the aerial socket of a domestic colour TV. There is some problem here for US-made computers as Europe uses a totally incompatible system of TV transmission. Therefore most of these computers have been modified for Europe, or have integral or attached TV screens that do not need altering. These problems also occur with those American machines in the second category, although as they rely on TV output they have usually been modified by their European distributors.

Also included in this category are systems which come in separate "boxes" but can be considered as essentially a unitary system.

Finally we come to the systems that are closest to classical computers. This fourth category has two subsections — those based on a bus system and those that are really glorified desktops. The first sub-section are machines that use the S-100 or SS50 buses. The S-100 bus is undoubtedly the most popular — and in its revamped form as the IEEE 696 standard bus is a very flexible approach. Unfortunately not all components claiming to be S-100 bus based actually implement the standard fully! The SS50 bus only appears with two or three manufacturers and is becoming rather neglected — but it exists. The main advantage of bus structured systems is their flexibility. A system can be configured to particular needs, or expanded easily. However, with plug-in units now available for expanding non-bus structured systems this advantage is not as overwhelming as it was. Most larger, business microcomputers can be grouped in this classification.

Larger desk top systems are capable of supporting large internal memory and large capacity disk units — say 8″ diameter floppy or even hard Winchester-type disks. They are fairly expensive in their basic configuration. The survey does not consider the more expensive examples of this type of computer.

In the brief survey that follows the following points are emphasized:

**Manufacturer:** The actual manufacturer, not the distributor, is given. The country of origin is also given. This is important when thoughts of servicing, repair and software back-up are taken into account. In general European computers are easier to get serviced than American, which are better than Japanese.

**Brief description:** The basic concept of the system is mentioned — with some comment on points of particular interest.

**Peripherals:** The peripherals available are listed whether from the actual manufacturer, or plug compatible manufacturers.

**Keyboard:** Number and type of keys.

**Display:** Number of characters and lines, whether on integral display or on TV output available.

**Interfaces:** Summary of interfaces available on the system, with optional interfaces if plug-in modules used.

**Minimum memory size:** Size of RAM for minimum configuration of the system. This is user available RAM and does not include any RAM that is reserved for memory-mapped displays.

**Maximum memory size:** Maximum user RAM available in largest system.

**ROM:** List of ROM in minimum system. This usually includes size of monitor and, if applicable, size of any interpreter that resides in firmware.

**Power supply:** Indication of voltage needed to get minimum system running.

**Price:** Obviously this will change during the lifetime of this book — if not before it is published! However the prices quoted are approximately those for the minimum available system. An upper limit of around £1500 has been chosen, as most systems above this are for commercial use.

**Software support:** Summary of the main languages available and the general availability of programs is commented on.

# Acorn Atom

The Atom is made by Acorn Computers in Cambridge, England. It is based around the 6502 processor running at 1MHz. The Atom is a keyboard based unit with integral loudspeaker and a 57 key typewriter style keyboard. The minimum RAM available is 2K but this can be expanded to 40K. There are a number of plug-in ROMs, the basic system having an 8K ROM with Integer BASIC and monitor. The ROM capability is expandable up to 126K, including a floating point BASIC. The BASIC uses 32-bit arithmetic, and there is a plug-in ROM to give BBC-BASIC, as used on the BBC Microcomputer (which is also made by Acorn).

The Atom can also be used with Acorn's Econet networking system, allowing up to 255 units to share a central floppy disk.

The video output is both 1Vpp composite, and UHF and gives a display of 32 × 16 characters, or up to 256 × 192 pixels. A colour generator is also available. A cassette interface, and two 8-bit input/output ports supplement a non-standard Acorn bus interface.

The Acorn Atom has a thriving user group, and is well supported by a number of software houses. However, the Atom's demise is threatened by the introduction of the Electron.

Prices:   (2k) £150 (or less)

# Acorn Electron

The Electron is Acorn's answer to criticisms about the cost of the BBC micro. It also gets them out of the BBC's shadow. Essentially the Electron is a cut down version of the BBC Model 'A' (qv) and will run most, but not all, of the BBC software.

The Electron comes with a 6502 microprocessor (2MHz). It has 32K RAM and 32K ROM containing the operating system and a BASIC interpreter. It has uhf tv output and up to 16 colours. The Electron has seven display modes; up to 640 × 256 dots in 2 colours or 80 × 32 characters, or up to 160 × 256 dots in 16 colours or 20 × 32 characters. It does not run BBC Mode 7, which is the teletext mode.

The system has a 56 key typewriter keyboard and uses BBC BASIC. There is no peripheral i/o and an expansion unit is needed for printers, disks etc.

Price:   £199.95

# AIM 65

The AIM is a single-board computer made by Rockwell International in the US. It comes with a 54-key typewriter style keyboard, and uses a 20 character led display. It also has an integral 20 column dot matrix (5 × 7) thermal printer. It uses a 6502 microprocessor running at 1MHz and the minimum system has 1K of RAM and 8K of monitor ROM. It can be expanded to 4K of RAM and supports a 1K ROM-based BASIC (Microsoft) interpreter and also an 8K Assembler. The monitor allows full editing and mnemonic machine code entry.

The AIM-65 has two cassette interfaces — one to KIM standard, the other a faster AIM only standard. It also has two parallel input/output ports.

Disks are available from a number of suppliers, as are cases and memory expansion modules.

Rockwell have just announced an upgraded version, the AIM 65/40 with 64K of RAM on board, and two 6502 processors. It also has a 40 column character display and 40 column printer.

Price:  AIM 65 (1K) £289
            (4K) £307
        BASIC ROM £43
        Assembler £24

# Apple IIe

The Apple II was one of the first personal computers to capture the imagination of the general, and investing, public. This machine dominates its home market in the US, but is behind the Commodore PET in the UK.

The latest version of the Apple II, as marketed in Europe, is designated the IIe.

The system is based around the 6502 processor running at 1MHz. It is a keyboard-based unit with a 53-key typewriter style keyboard. The system can display colour graphics, 256 × 192 pixels, or 24 × 40 characters via a UHF TV interface. The basic system comes with 48K of RAM, expandable to 128K and a 16K ROM containing Microsoft BASIC. There is an integral loudspeaker with sound generator. There are a number of interface slots on the main board that allow RS232C and parallel I/O. Many boards are available giving the system great flexibility. Floppy disk drives (143K), Z80 processor card etc., allow CP/M to be run.

There are many suppliers of both hardware and software in the UK, and, within the limitations of the machine, it is possible to carry out most tasks required of a small computer system.

Prices:  (48K) £776

# Aquarius

Mattel have been in the electronic games and toys market for some years and this is their first attempt at the computer market. Their Intellivision, although successful in America never really caught on over here. The Aquarius is made in Hong Kong by Radofin.

The Aquarius has a Z80A microprocessor and uses a plug-in cartridge memory system. A number of very good games,, and even a home central heating/control program.

The basic unit comes with 8K RAM which is expandable to 52K and MicroSoft BASIC in 8K ROM. The Aquarius has a calculator keyboard (49 keys). There is one sound channel.

The display has 16 colours available and shows 40 × 24 characters or 320 × 192 pixels.

Price:   (8K) £79.95
           4K expansion £19.95
           16K expansion £29.95
           Mini expander (joysticks) £49.95

# Atari 400

The Atari 400 is the "baby brother" of the Atari 800, making two of America's best selling personal computer systems. The Atari 400 has a 57 key touch sensitive keyboard, with four sockets for plug-in ROM packs. The system gives a 40 × 24 character, or up to 320 × 192 pixels, colour display. It uses a 6502B processor at 1.8MHz. There is a built-in loudspeaker with four programmable sound generators. A number of user interfaces give four paddle ports, cassette and UHF TV output and RS232C. The basic unit comes with 16K of RAM, upgradeable to 48K, and 10K monitor in ROM. An 8K BASIC cartridge is available at extra cost, although special offers including the cartridge in the 16K price are common.

A whole range of peripherals are available, including dual floppy disk drives (2 × 88K), cassette recorder and printer. The Atari system has a wide range of software — mostly games, but the ROM-pacs are being used with the disk drives to give some business software. Soon to be replaced by the 600XL.

Prices:  (16K) £129
BASIC cartridge £40
dual disk drive £279
cassette recorder £45

# Atari 600XL

The Atari 600XL is the successor to the rather long in the tooth 400. Although the 400 will be in the shops for sometime it will be replaced by the 600XL. The 600XL is a complete restyling and redesign and is effectively a new machine.

The 600XL comes with 16K RAM as standard with 24K ROM. It has a full typewriter style keyboard with 4 special function keys. It uses the 6502C processor at 1.79MHz.

Like the 400 and 800 the 600XL uses three special chips for graphics, sound and controller ports, and screen functions. It is thus compatible with most 400 and 800 software.

The keyboard unit has a slot for ROM cartridges. The 600XL has 11 graphics modes with up to 256 colours (only 128 at any time). The text display gives 40 by 24 characters or up to 320 by 192 pixels. The sound facility has 4 independent voices with 3.5 octave range.

I/O includes an expansion connector, UHF TV, two joysticks ports and a serial connector.

Price:   £159.95

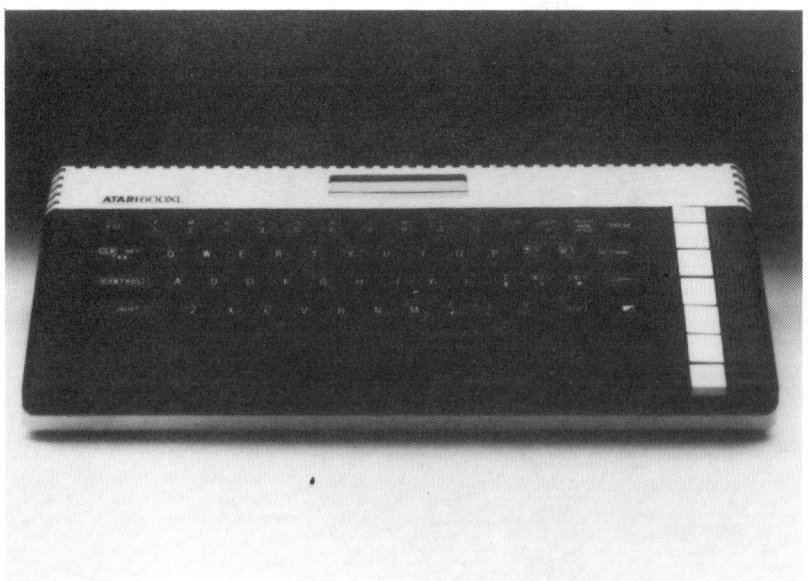

# Atari 800

This system is essentially the same as the Model 400 — except for the keyboard. The Model 800 has a 57 key typewriter style keyboard — instead of a touch sensitive one, with four sockets for plug-in ROM packs. The system gives a 40 × 24 character, or up to 320 × 192 pixels, colour display. It uses a 6502 processor at 1.8MHz. There is a built-in loudspeaker with four programmable sound generators. A number of user interfaces give four paddle ports, cassette and UHF TV output and RS232C. The basic unit comes with 48K of RAM, with 8K BASIC and 10K monitor in ROM.

A whole range of peripherals are available, including dual floppy disk drives (2 × 88K), cassette recorder and printer. The Atari system has a wide range of software — mostly games, but the ROM-pacs are being used with the disk drives to give some business software. Soon to be replaced by the 800XL.

Prices: £199
       dual floppy disk drive £279
       cassette recorder £45

# Atari 800XL

The Atari 800XL is the 600's big brother. Like the 600XL it is compatible with the 400 and 800, it being the replacement of the latter.

The main difference is the 64K RAM as standard and an rgb monitor output as well as UHF TV.

See 600XL for details.

Price:   £249.99

# BBC micro

The BBC micro was designed and built by Acorn for BBC Enterprises as part of the television series "The Computer Programme". The BBC micro has all the hallmarks of being a compromised design. There are also a number of unanswered queries over its reliability.

The BBC model A comes with 16K RAM as basic, expandable to 32K and has 16K ROM. It uses BBC's own version of structured BASIC and also allows Assembly language programs to be entered directly from the keyboard. Both UHF TV and composite video displays are available giving a whole range of display characteristics, up to 40 × 30 characters or 320 × 256 pixels for the Model A. The Model A will be withdrawn soon, due to the introduction of the Electron.

The Model B, which has 32K RAM and 32K ROM has a display of 80 × 30 characters or 640 × 256 pixels.

Both systems have a typewriter style keyboard with ten programmable function keys. Both models use the 6502 processor at 2MHz.

A cassette interface is available on both models with Model B also having one Centronics parallel and five other interfaces, as well as three expansion slots.

The Model A is upgradable to Model B. Both models have three channel sound, a cartridge ROM pack interface and can be modified to use the Econet network, and games paddles. There is also an extension bus for the extension to Prestel and Teletext. A telesoftware interface is also available.

Prices:   Model B (32K RAM, 32K ROM) £399

# Camputers Lynx

The Lynx is based on a Z80A processor at 4MHz and uses BASIC, although other languages are available. It comes with 48K RAM which can be expanded to 192K and 16K ROM. The UHF TV or video outputs give 40 × 24 characters, 248 × 256 pixels, in eight colours.

The Lynx has a typewriter keyboard and cassette storage is at 1200 baud. Other interfaces include one RS232 and a parallel expansion interface. There is no on/off switch, or RESET..

A small internal loudspeaker is provided with single notes available with a BEEP command. A more complex SOUND command allows complete wave forms to be specified.

The Lynx is still too new to have many peripherals but disc drives, printers, light pen etc. are planned.

Price: (48K) £225
      (96K) £299

# CBM 4032

The latest versions of the PET are basically upgrades of the original 2001 system. This can claim to be the world's first mass produced personal computer and it still has a leading position in Europe, although not in the USA. Commodore now manufacture in both the USA and West Germany, most units sold in Europe coming from the latter.

The PET is an integral system with a 12" video screen housed above the keyboard unit. The display has 25 × 40 characters and the unit comes with a 72 typewriter style keyboard with a numeric pad. It uses a 6502 processor at 1MHz and has 8K Microsoft BASIC in ROM. The standard RAM available is 32K. There are five interfaces — IEEE488, 2 × 8 bit parallel, and two cassette I/O ports.

A whole range of Commodore, and compatible, products are available including floppy disk drives, printers, a - d and d - a converters etc. The PET probably has more software and peripherals than any other small computer system.

There are many active user groups, and over 250 retailers around the country. It is now possible to run the CP/M operating system with a special interface unit.

Prices:  4016 (16K) £569
floppy disk drive (2 × 180K) £598
floppy disk drive (2 × 500K) £885
floppy disk drive (2 × 1M) £1029

# CBM 8032/8096

This system is the "big brother" of the ubiquitous PET, and is essentially an 80 column version of the same machine. As such, most of the comments found there are applicable here. The CBM is an integral system with a 12" video screen housed above the keyboard unit. The display has 25 × 80 characters and the unit comes with a 72 key typewriter style keyboard with a numeric key pad. It uses a 6502 processor at 1MHz and has 8K Microsoft BASIC in ROM. The user RAM is 32K. There are five interfaces — IEEE488, 2 × 8 bit parallel, and two cassette I/O ports.

A whole range of Commodore, and compatible, products are available including floppy disk drives, printers, a - d and d - a converters etc.

The 8032 is ideally suited for word processing applications and it is possible to expand the RAM to 96K for modelling and other applications.

The 8096 is similar and has 96K of memory.

Prices:  8032 £776
8096 £914
floppy disks (1 × 170K) £399
dual floppy disks (2 × 500K) £885
dual floppy disks (2 × 1M) £1029

# Colour Genie

The Colour Genie is a development of the Video Genie range made by EACA in Hong Kong. It uses the same processor as the Genie I and II but not the same screen characteristics.

The Colour Genie comes with one RS232, one Centronics and two other interfaces plus one expansion slot. This can be used to expand the system in the same way as the other Genies. It has a cassette interface and comes with 16K RAM as standard expandable to 32K.

The Colour Genie uses a Z80 processor at 2.2MHz and has BASIC in a 16K ROM. Both colour UHF TV and video monitor display can be used giving 40 × 24 characters or up to 320 × 200 pixels. It has 16 colour capability, and a typewriter keyboard with eight programmable function keys. It also has a sophisticated sound generator chip, and light-pen, hifi-audio and cassette i/o.

Price: (32K) £168

# Commodore 64

The Commodore 64 is the first of a new generation of home computers from Commodore, originally designed to replace the Vic 20. Fortunately for Commodore the Vic 20's continuing popularity means that the 64 is now in the middle of Commodore's range instead of being at the bottom.

The Commodore 64 has a standard typewriter keyboard with eight programmable function keys. Both composite video and UHF TV outputs are available giving 40 × 25 characters or 320 × 200 pixels. Sixteen colours are available as well as 62 predefined graphics characters. A new video chip allows the use of high resolution, multi-coloured sprites (moveable object blocks). Up to eight "layers" are available.

A programmable sound chip gives three independent channels with a range of nine octaves. Music envelope, pitch and pulse shape are available to the user.

The Commodore 64 comes with 64K of memory which is split up as the user requires between monitor, language, and user program. Normally 10K of monitor and 16K of BASIC are resident in ROM. LOGO, Pascal, COMAL, and Assembly language are available for the system.

Cassette I/O, one RS232 and three other interfaces are provided. Most of Commodore's peripherals, eg. disc drive, ROM cartridges, printers, joysticks and games paddles can be used on the system.

Prices:  £229
   disc drive (171K) £229
   cassette recorder £39.95

# Commodore 710B/715B

The 710 is the latest development of the original PET computer. It uses all the lessons learnt from the previous models and is, therefore, a far more sophisticated product. Most of the existing Commodore software can be easily adapted to run. The 710 is based around the 6509 processor, which is the latest development of Commodore's original 6502. The processor operates at 2MHz and the system ROM uses Commodore's Kernal operating system. The video display has 80 × 25 characters or 512 × 512 pixels. The keyboard is typewriter style with a numeric pad. The basic system comes with 128K RAM which can be expanded to 896K. The 715 comes with 256K RAM.

There is one RS232 and one IEEE488 interface, plus three expansion slots. There is also an interface for the Commodore cassette recorder. The system has colour capability. Commodore BASIC is resident in ROM but other languages are available. A number of other peripherals, based on the standard Commodore range are available including floppy disks, printers etc. A plug-in Z80 card also allows CP/M to be used.

Prices:  710 £1144
         715 £1374

# DAI PC-1

The PC-1 is made by Data Applications in Belgium. It is based around the 8080 processor, and is a keyboard based unit with colour graphics and fully synthesized sound. It has a 57-key typewriter style keyboard and the UHF TV output gives 60 × 24 characters or up to 335 × 255 pixels, in 16 colours. There are two cassettes and one RS232C interface, as well as a non-standard bus expansion connector, used for industrial control and floppy disk units. There are also three audio outputs and two paddle control ports. The unit is available for PAL, SECAM or NTSC colour systems.

The unit is sold in the UK with 48K of RAM and has a 24K BASIC interpreter, with full colour and sound commands. It also has a very flexible editor and machine language facilities. It is possible to use a hardwired "Maths" chip that speeds maths processing by a factor of ten.

There are many enthusiastic users with a good, Belgian based, user group.

CP/M is available as an operating system.

Prices: (48K) £684
dual floppy disk (2 × 170K) £684

# Dragon 32/64

The Dragon uses BASIC and comes with 32K RAM as standard, expandable to 64K RAM and 16K ROM. The UHF TV or video outputs are available and it displays 32 × 16 characters or 256 × 192 pixels in eight colours. The system uses a 6809E processor at 1MHZ, which is the same processor as the Tandy Color Computer on which the Dragon was based.

Unfortunately the differences between the Dragon and the Tandy Color Computer although sufficient to overcome patent problems are enough to cause software incompatibility.

External storage is by cassette interface, other interfaces being Centronics parallel, joystick, ROM cartridge and system expansion.

Although very popular the Dragon is not a very easy machine to use and seems to be relegated to a glorified games playing system. There are also continuing doubts as to the company's financial future.

Price: (32K) £175
        (64K) £225

# Elan Enterprise

Elan Computers is a new British company based in London with large amounts of money to spend on developing new home computers. The Enterprise is the first of these.

The Enterprise uses a Z80A microprocessor (4MHz). It has 64K RAM expandable to 3,968K and 32K ROM.

Up to 256 colours are available on the screen at any one time. Depending on the amount of RAM available the display can give up to 672 × 512 pixels and up to 84 × 56 characters.

A joystick is built in to the keyboard and a word processor in ROM. The system comes with an RS432 serial interface, two cassette and one Centronics parallel interface. A UHF TV is provided for video. Other i/o ports include RGB monitor, stereo sound (4 voices, 8 octaves), 2 joystick ports and a network interface.

It has a 69 key typewriter keyboard, contoured much like an electronic typewriter. As this is such a new system very little software is available, although other languages like LISP or FORTH are promised.

Prices:  (64K) £199.95
         (128K) £299.95

# Epson HX20

The Epson HX20 is the first truly portable computer system that is totally self-contained. It operates from batteries and has a built-in liquid crystal display showing 20 × 4 characters or 120 × 32 pixels. A 20 character dot matrix printer is also built in to the system.

It comes with 16K RAM expandable to 32K, and 32K ROM. It uses a specialized microprocessor operating at 1MHz. It has a typewriter keyboard with thirteen function keys and numeric pad. Two RS232 interfaces and two expansion slots are provided.

A TV display adaptor and acoustic coupler also available.

Prices: (16K) £472
acoustic coupler (300 baud) £250
UHF TV adaptor n/a

# Genie I/II

The Genie I and II are made by EACA in Hong Kong, and are fully compatible with the Tandy TRS 80/I. The Genie II is a slightly different version of the Genie I, and has a numeric keypad instead of an integral cassette drive, but is essentially the same model.

The Genie I is based around the Z80 processor and the basic system comes with 16K RAM and 12K Microsoft BASIC in ROM. It has an integral 51 key typewriter style keyboard and cassette deck. The video output — both 1Vpp and UHF — displays 64 × 16 characters, or 128 × 48 pixels. There is an interface for a second cassette recorder and an expansion interface. This allows an expansion module to be plugged in giving another 64K of RAM and facilities for discs and printer.

The Genie I and II run the vast software library of the TRS 80/I, and have very active user groups.

Prices:   Genie I (16K) £330 (48K) £365.70
            Genie II (16K) £299 (48K) £341
            Expansion unit (with RS232) £215
            disk (300K) £410
            32K RAM for expansion unit £130

# HP 75C

The HP 75C is a hand held pocket computer that can be expanded to a fairly large system. It comes with 16K of RAM expandable to 24K. It uses a 48K system ROM.

It uses a form of HP BASIC, and the liquid crystal display shows one line of 32 characters. It has a 1.3K integral card reader, and with expansion modules can be plugged into a monitor. The single interface allows connection to the HP-IB, which is a non-standard serial interface bus. There are 4 expansion slots, a cassette facility, and the whole system runs the HP operating system.

Prices: £883
Digital cassette drive £386
Thermal printer £386

# HP 86A

This is really a cut down version of the HP85 and comes without monitor screen or disk/cartridge. It uses a similar custom built processor but has the ability to run the CP/M operating system.

It comes with 64K of RAM expandable to 576K. The system uses HP BASIC in 48K ROM with an additional 80K in ROM pacs. Although it does not come with an integral display, two monitors are available. These give a display of 80 × 24 characters or 544 × 240 pixels. There is a typewriter keyboard and plug-in units which allow 1 RS232 or 1 Centronics interface as well as HP-IL and IEEE488. Other interface modules are also available.

Prices: £1541
        3.5" disk drive (270K) £1052
        3.5" disk drive (2 × 270K) £1553
        5.25" disk drive (270K) £755
        9" monitor £254
        12" monitor £288

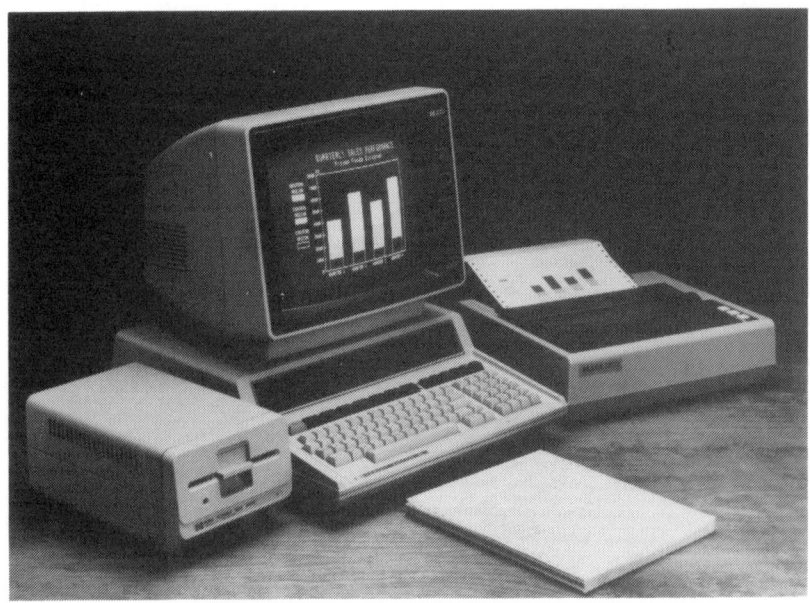

# Micro Decision

This system uses both the BASIC and Pilot languages. It comes with 64K RAM as standard. It uses an external monitor/keyboard which displays 80 × 24 characters. The Micro Decision comes with an integral floppy disk unit (200K) and two RS232 interfaces. It uses a Z80 processor at 4MHz. It uses the CP/M operating system.

Price:   £1144

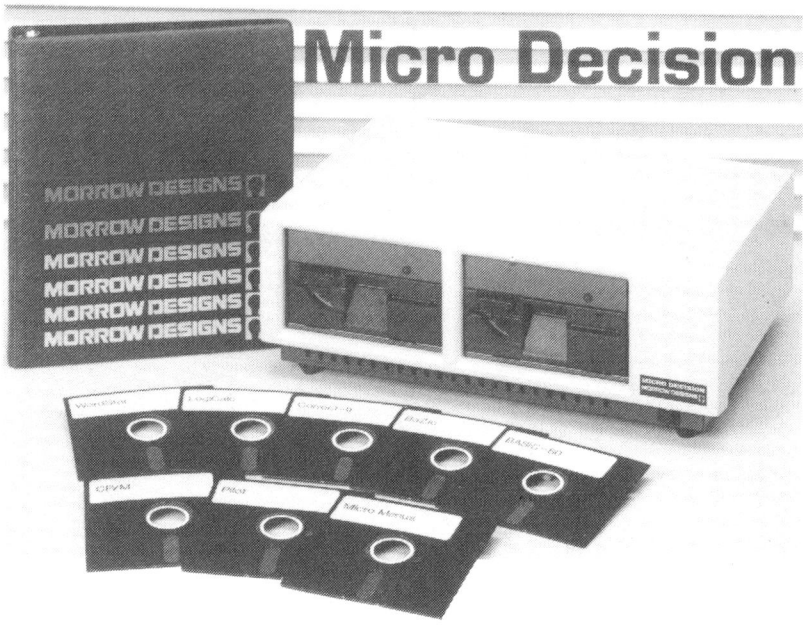

# Multitech MPF II

Multitech is a Taiwanese company which has designed the Micro-Professor MPF II as an Apple compatible system. It is housed in a very low profile casing with a calculator style keyboard.

The MPF II gives UHF TV or video output with 40 × 24 characters or 280 × 192 pixels in up to six colours. It uses BASIC and Assembly language.

The MPF II has 64K RAM as standard and, like the Apple, uses 6502 processor. It has one Centronics parallel interface and one expansion slot. Unfortunately this is not identical to the Apple so that existing expansion cards will not function correctly. The cassette interface uses either a unique MPF II format or standard Apple II.

An extension keyboard with larger typewriter style rubberized keys can be plugged in to the system. Disc drives are promised by the distributors but they will not be standard Apple ones.

Prices:  £269
 joystick £15
 printer £186

# Nascom-2

The Nascom 2 is the big brother of the Nascom 1, Britain's original microcomputer system. It is made by Lucas Logic in the UK. The Nascom 2 is a single board system based around the Z80A at 4MHz. It has a separate 57 key typewriter style keyboard. The basic board comes with 8K of RAM, a 2K monitor ROM and 8K BASIC interpreter. The system can be expanded to 64K of RAM.

There are two eight-bit parallel ports, RS232C and cassette interface. The video output gives 16 × 48 characters. Expansion boards give dual floppy disk capability (2 × 170K). It is possible to purchase a packaged system having dual floppy drives, 16K RAM, case, dot matrix printer and 10" video display.

Like the Nascom 1 this system is well supported by user groups and much software is generally available.

Prices:   (8K) kit £258    built £328
          typical system (16K, 2 × 170K disks, VDU, case, printer) £1500

# Nascom 3

The Nascom 3 is based around the Z80 processor at 4MHz. It has a typewriter style keyboard and uses BASIC and Assembly languages; Pascal is available. It comes with 48K RAM standard and 10K ROM. The UHF TV or composite video gives a display of 16 × 48 characters or 48 × 96 pixels. It has one RS232 interface and four expansion slots, and cassette facility. It uses NAS-SYS operating system.

Disk drives are available for the system using CP/M DOS.

Prices: (48K) £631
 disc drive (2 × 350K) £400

# NEC PC 8000

NEC claim to have at least 45% of their home Japanese market sewn up with the PC 8000. It is a Z80A-based system housed in a keyboard unit in its basic form.

The typewriter style keyboard has a full set of 56 alphanumeric keys with a numeric keypad and ten special function keys. The system comes with 32K of RAM and 24K of ROM containing a Microsoft-like BASIC interpreter. 1Vpp colour video, or UHF TV output is available, with printer, cassette and expansion interfaces.

The colour graphics have eight colours, and display from 30 to 80 characters per line by 20 or 25 lines. High resolution graphics are possible.

A fixed expansion unit allows disks (2 × 163K), an extra 32K of RAM and two RS232C, IEEE488 and one parallel interfaces to be available.

A modular expansion unit gives disk controller and 32K of RAM but also 6 slots for other cards. CP/M can be run with either unit.

Price: typical system (64K, 2 × 163K disks, dual disks, monochrome display, printer) £1454

# Newbrain

The Newbrain has had a chequered history. Originally announced nearly 4 years ago by Newbury Laboratories, it was in limbo until rescued by the new British Technology Group who have now sold the design and manufacture to the Grundy Group. Recently, they have been having financial problems, and the long-term future of the company is in doubt.

The Newbrain is a hand-held unit in three versions. It is based around the Z80A at 4MHz. The main unit has a 62 key calculator style keyboard with a 16-digit alphanumeric display. The outputs include 1Vpp video, UHF TV, and an expansion bus. The video display output gives 24 × 40 or 24 × 80 characters with the possibility of full viewdata/teletext graphics. Screen resolution is 640 × 230 pixels. The minimum memory size is 32K RAM with up to 64K on expansion. An external expansion unit allows up to 2M of user RAM to be accessed. 16K BASIC is available as standard.

The expansion unit can support 4 × 200K floppy disk drives and the RS232C ports a printer and VDU.

Prices:  Model A (no built in display) £219
           Model AD (built in 16 character display) £249

# Oric

The Oric uses BASIC language with 16K ROM and comes in two versions. One has 16K RAM the other 48K. Both UHF TV and video outputs can be used, giving 40 × 28 characters or 240 × 200 pixels. It has a calculator keyboard and uses external cassette storage at two speeds, one fast one slow. There are eight colours available and it has one Centronics and one expansion interface.

The Prestel characters are available and a communications modem can be attached giving simple access to any Prestel based system.

The Oric comes with a very flexible sound generator with some more common sound functions, such as ZAP, PING and EXPLODE being available directly through BASIC. It is possible to put the audio output through a hi-fi amplifier.

Prices: (16K) £79.95
       (48K) £149

# Osborne 1

The Osborne 1 was essentially a new concept in computers, and has been designed by the guru of the personal computing world, and ex-patriate Briton, Adam Osborne. The Osborne 1 is based around the Z80 processor and comes housed as an integral disk and screen unit with attached keyboard. The whole unit weighs around 20 pounds and has a carrying handle to make it portable.

The screen is a small 5" monochrome display and gives a window of 24 by 50 characters or a longer display of up to 128 characters. The user RAM supplied as standard is 64K and there is another 2 × 100K available on the dual 5¼" disk drives. Two interfaces are provided ; one RS232C and one IEEE488. A modem with acoustic coupler plugs into a special jack socket. The keyboard is a standard typewriter style unit with numeric keypad. It is attached to the main unit by a 9" cable. The system comes supplied with the CP/M operating system and BASIC, Word Star and a version of Visicalc.

Osborne has recently been having trouble with manufacturing in the States, and this could affect the future viability of the company.

Price:   1 £1091

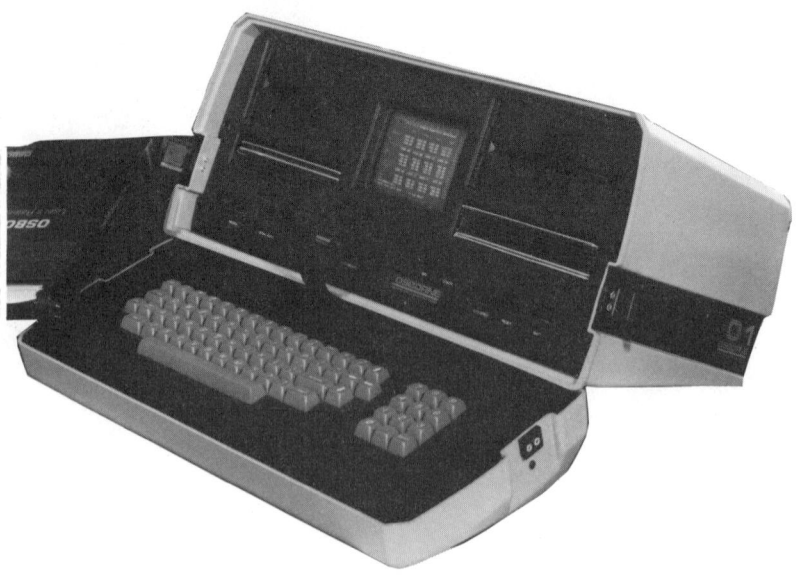

# Positron 900

Positron are a long established microcomputer company whose systems are designed mainly for industrial/commercial use. The 900 is the most basic system in the Positron range, the more expensive ones having exceptional colour capabilities.

The Positron 900 uses the 6809 processor at 1MHz. Consequently it uses the O/S9 operating system, which is a development of FLEX the 6800 based DOS.

BASIC comes as standard and an external VDU uses one of the four RS232 interfaces. Other interfaces include one IEEE488 and three expansion slots inside the housing.

Price: (64K) £1259

# Powertran Cortex

The Powertran Cortex comes in two versions, as a self assembling kit or ready built. The system uses a TMS 9995 16 bit microprocessor. It is therefore very accurate, having 11 digit accuracy on most maths functions. The TV or monitor display has 40 × 24 characters or 256 × 192 pixels. 16 colours are available with fast line drawing and point plotting available from BASIC. High speed colour shape manipulation is also available as standard.

The system comes with 64K RAM expandable to 1Mb. BASIC resides in a 24K ROM. An Assembler and Disk Assembler are standard with up to 16 I/O devices possible of support.

Other languages like Pascal, Forth, SPL, etc. are available.

An RS232 interface kit and floppy disk interface allow up to four disk drives to be used. The system uses a typewriter keyboard with 12 function keys and a numeric keypad.

Prices: (kit) £340
(built) £455
RS232 interface £9.20
floppy disk interface £100
disk drives (2 × 250K) £400

# Research Machines Link 480Z

The 480Z is the baby brother of the 380Z. It runs as a cassette-based, Z80A system and has a minimum 32K of RAM on 8K of ROM-based monitor. The system is keyboard-based and has 65 typewriter-style keys with four cursor-control and four user-definable keys. There are two display modes, 80 by 24 using 1Vpp video, and 40 × 24 using UHF TV output.

Two graphics modes are available, 160 × 72 single-tone or 80 × 72 two-tone. Two cassette interface standards are available and the unit has an integral loudspeaker. One eight bit parallel and one RS32C ports are standard, with a joystick or pushbutton and analogue inputs and output. The ROM can be upgraded to 16K, allowing 16K BASIC in ROM to be used.

Expansion options allow 640 × 192 monochrome, 320 × 192 — four colour — and 160 × 95 — eight colour-graphics. The RAM can be expanded to 64K and an IEEE488 interface is being developed. Research Machines is also working on a memory expansion module allowing 256K of RAM and a network capability. The 480Z is upwards compatible with the 380Z.

Prices: (32K) £564
(64K and network i/f) £685

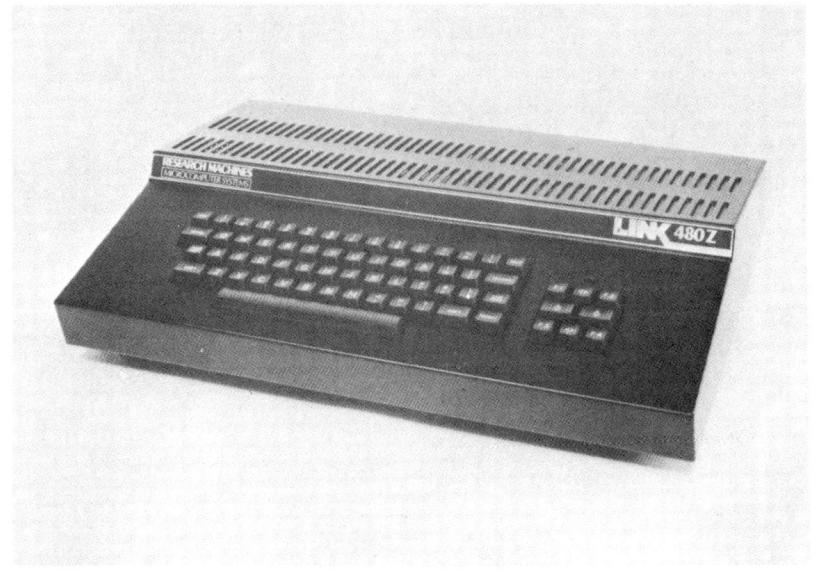

# Sanyo MBC 1000

The MBC 1000 comes with 64K RAM and uses a Z80 processor at 4MHz. It uses BASIC language, although other languages are available. The monitor display gives 80 × 25 characters.

There is an integral floppy disk drive (320K) and one RS232 and one Centronics interface. It uses the CP/M operating system and has a typewriter keyboard with seventeen function keys and a numeric pad.

Price:   (64K) £1195

# Sharp MZ 80A

The MZ 80A is the development of the very successful MZ80K. It has a similar specification to its predecessor.

The MZ 80A has 48K RAM as standard with 4K monitor ROM. BASIC and other languages like Forth are loaded from the integral cassette recorder. The system is based on a Z80 running at 2MHz.

It has a full sized typewriter keyboard with numeric keypad. A large range of graphics characters are available directly from the keyboard. The integral monitor displays 40 × 25 characters or 80 × 50 pixels.

An expansion interface allows up to five peripherals to be attached eg. floppy disks, printer, RS232 etc.

There are many programs now available for MZ80 series and it has a good dealer network and many user groups. CP/M operating system can be run with the aid of the expansion unit.

Price: (48K) £399

# Sharp MZ-80B

Made in Japan by Sharp, the MZ-80B is an upgrade of the very successful MZ-80K.

The MZ-80B has integral 9″ video display and cassette recorder. The calculator style keyboard of the MZ-80K has been replaced by a 78 key typewriter style keyboard, with ten user definable keys.

The 9″ display has either 40 or 80 × 25 characters, or 320 × 200 pixels. There is a partial rolling display. The system uses a Z80A processor and the basic unit has 64K RAM and 2K monitor ROM. Like the MZ80K language programs are loaded from a cassette, or disk. The unit needs an expansion unit to drive floppy disks (2 × 280K), printers and other peripheral devices.

Price: £799

# Sharp MZ700 Series

The MZ700 series from Sharp has a novel approach to displaying information. Although it doesn't have a screen, you can plug in modules containing a printer and cassette recorder.

It is based around the Z80A chip and comes with 6K of ROM and 64K RAM. Video RAM takes another 4K. The UHF TV output display 40 × 25 characters or 320 × 200 pixels. Up to 8 foreground and background colours are possible.

Optional cassette recorder and four colour printer/plotter can be added to the keyboard module.

Prices: 64K Model 711 £249.95
Cassette recorder £39.95
Printer/plotter £129.95

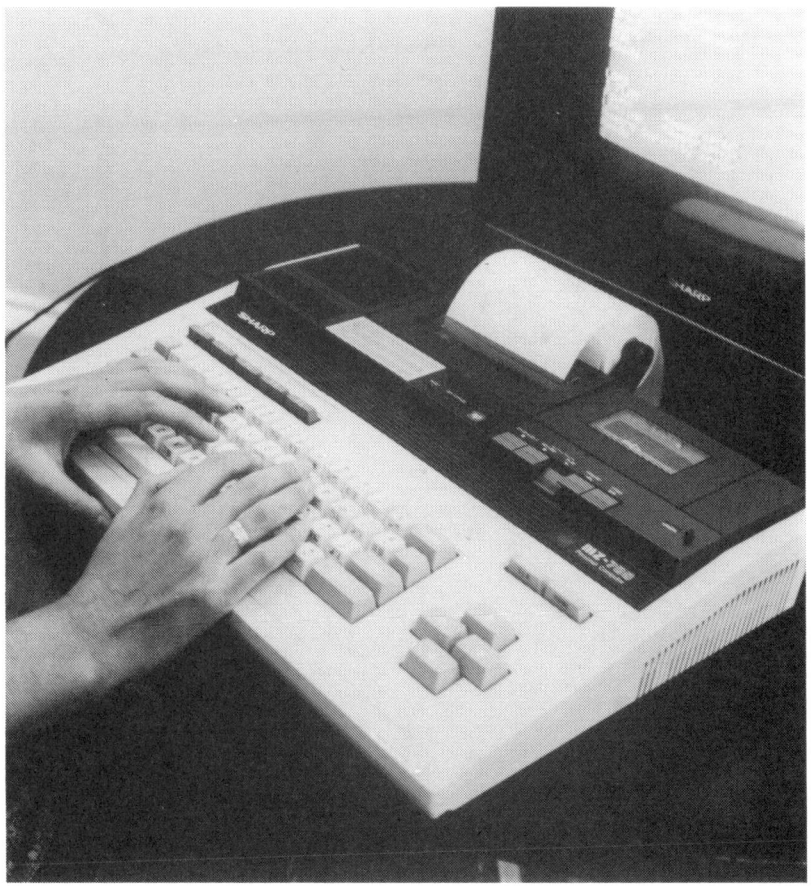

# Signet 10025

Shelton Instruments were the people behind the original design of the Nascom 1. Sig-Net is a totally new concept, whereby a series of boards — processor, interface, memory etc. — are interconnected by flexible wires. Each board has its own power supply, and many variations of computer can be evolved from the basic system components. Shelton Instruments are based in London.

The Signet 10025 uses a Z80B processor at 6MHz and CP/M and Macnos operating systems. It comes with 64K RAM and uses 2 × 200K 5.25″ floppy disks. It has a monitor output, colour capability and an expansion slot. The display gives 80 × 24 characters or 512 × 512 pixels. There is a keyboard typewriter and numeric pad. It has two RS232 and one Centronics interface.

Price: £1599

This photo shows the unique interconnections used in the Sig-Net system.

# Sinclair ZX-81

Manufactured by Sinclair Research in Cambridge, England, the ZX-81, successor to the ZX80, can claim to be Europe's largest selling computer.

The ZX-81 is a small, keyboard based unit with 40 touch sensitive keys. UHF TV output, as well as cassette and power supply sockets, are available. There is one expansion interface that allows a 16K RAM expansion pack to be used. The system comes ready built, or in kit form. The basic unit has 1K RAM and 8K BASIC/monitor ROM. The video gives 24 × 32 characters or 64 × 44 pixels.

The BASIC interpreter carries out dynamic syntax checking on key entry.

A small 40 column electrostatic printer is also available. The system is supported by many user groups who generate most of the available software.

Prices: (1K) £39.95
16K RAM £29.95
printer £39.95

# Sinclair ZX Spectrum

The Spectrum is the most popular micro in the UK. It is based upon the best selling ZX series of microcomputers and uses Sinclair BASIC as its main programming language in a 16K ROM. Other languages, such as FORTH and LOGO are also available.

The ZX Spectrum has eight colours and gives a UHF TV display of $32 \times 24$ characters or $256 \times 192$ pixels.

The system comes in two versions, one with 16K RAM the other with 48K. It uses a Z80A processor at 3.5 MHz and has a rubberized, calculator type keyboard. The system has a small internal speaker giving limited single channel sound.

The Z80 bus is available on an expansion port and a whole range of peripherals are available. Sinclair plan a micro floppy disk drive and RS232 and networking interfaces.

Prices:   (16K) £99.95
           (48K) £129.95
           ZX printer (32 columns) £39.95
           Expansion interface £59.95
           ZX Microdrive (140K) £49.95

# Sord M5

Sord are the fastest growing Japanese microcomputer company. The M5 is the first Japanese attempt to break the domination of the British companies in the UK market.

The M5 is based around the Z80A processor at 4MHz. It also uses a very flexible video controller chip and sound generator chip. It uses BASIC in an 8K ROM and comes with 20K of RAM of which 16K are used for video and only 4K for the user. It can be expanded to 16K of user RAM. It has a rubberized calculator-type keyboard with good graphics functions on the keys. 32 sprites are available for animation and the display, with 16 colours available gives 40 × 24 characters of 256 × 196 pixels.

Both UHF TV and composite video outputs are available, with external storage on video cassette. Other interfaces include sound output, Centronics parallel and ROM/interface cartridge.

Two joysticks can be used and the system includes a real time integral timer.

Price: (4K RAM) £149

# Tandy Color

Unlike other models in the Tandy range, which are based around the Z80 processor the Tandy Color computer uses a 6809E processor operating at 1MHz. UHF TV display gives 32 × 16 characters or 256 × 192 pixels. Eight colours are available.

The system comes with 16K of RAM expandable to 32K with BASIC residing in a 16K monitor ROM. One RS232 interface is provided as well as a cassette I/O. The system uses a standard typewriter keyboard. A plug-in ROM cartridge gives extra memory and firmware based games etc.

The Dragon 32 computer was based on the Tandy Color design so a number of programs written for the former can be easily modified to run on the latter.

Prices: (16K) £240
        disc drive (175K) £449

# Tandy TRS-80 Model 3

The TRS 80 Model 3 is the successor to the TRS 80 Model 2, which was one of the original microcomputers.

The Model 3 has 14K ROM and 16K RAM which can be expanded to 48K. It has a parallel printer interface and a cassette interface with provision for adding disk drives and RS232C.

The Model 3 has a built in 12" black and white screen can display 64 or 32 characters by 16 lines. A whole host of applications software is available. The disc drives can be fitted into the front of the casing. The 65 key keyboard is not detachable.

Prices:  16K RAM £599
48K 2 × 184K disc drives £1299

# Tandy TRS-80 Model 4

This system uses a Z80A processor (4MHz) and the TRSDOS operating system. It comes with 64K RAM upgradeable to 128K, and 14K ROM. The basic system comes with cassette based storage although it is possible to upgrade with either one or two built-in, double density 184K 5.25 inch disk drives.

It has a 70 key typewriter keyboard with numeric pad. The basic system comes with a Centronics parallel interface, with RS232C as an optional extra.

The built in 12" screen displays 80 × 24 characters, or 64 or 32 by 16. A sound function, duration and tone, is available on an internal speaker.

Prices:  Cassette version £749
  (1 × 184K disk) £1499
  (2 × 184K disk) £1299

# Tandy TRS-80 Model 100

This is a portable computer weighing just under 4lbs. It operates at 2.4 MHz and comes with 32K ROM and 8K or 24K RAM expandable to 32K. It has a liquid crystal display with 8 × 40 characters or 240 × 64 dots. The Model 100 has a full size typewriter keyboard (56 keys) with 8 programmable function keys.

It has a word processing program built in as well as a schedule and address book program. The unit comes with one RS232C, cassette and parallel printer interfaces. It is battery driven and these should last up to 100 hours.

Prices: (8K) £499
(24K) £649

# TI CC-40

The Compact Computer 40 from TI is a battery driven portable machine with a built in single line liquid crystal display with 31 characters. Batteries should last up to 200 hours.

The CC-40 comes with 34K ROM and 6K RAM which can be expanded to 18K. It uses BASIC and TMS700 Assembler languages. The computer uses the BASIC operating system and has a full size typewriter keyboard with numeric key pad.

A cartridge slot on the CC-40 takes a whole range of programs which can use up to 128K bytes of memory. The CC-40 has a sophisticated peripheral connector bus – the Hex bus – which allows a whole range of other units to be added on. These include a bar code reader, xy plotter, RS232/parallel interface and many others.

Price:   £179

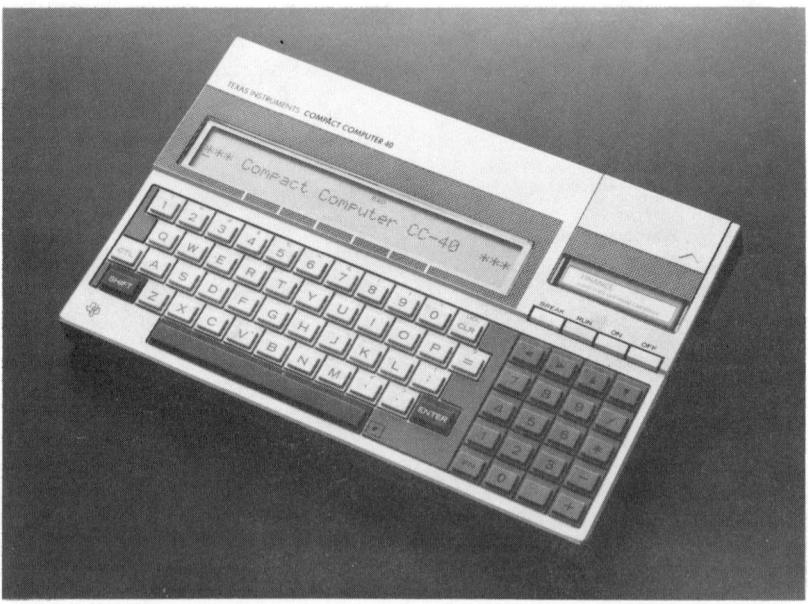

# VIC 20

The VIC-20 computer is Commodore's first product in the computer field that represents a challenge to the market below the PET. The VIC-20 is based on the 6502 processor, and can run most of the PET software. The main difference is the 22 × 23 character screen. VIC-20 has 16 screen colours, four internal sound generators using TV loudspeaker, and uses plug-in ROM pacs that can be up to 27K.

The basic unit comes with 5K of RAM, expandable externally to 32K. Standard PET Microsoft BASIC is in an 8K ROM. The system is a keyboard based unit with 66 typewriter style keys, including four user definable keys.

A range of accessories are available including printer, floppy disk (120K), IEEE488 cartridge, joysticks, light pens, etc. Most peripherals should interface with the VIC. "Starter packs" now include a free cassette recorder.

Price: (5K) £139.95
      cassette recorder £39.95
      disk drive (1 × 170K) £229

# CHAPTER 6

## How do I choose a system?

We now have a fairly good idea of the systems on the market — their capabilities and how they interconnect with various peripheral devices. As there are as many ideal systems as there are applications ie. a near infinite number, no system will be ideal. It is worth stressing that it is very unlikely that any computer system will do **all** that you want it to do — some compromise must be sought. Mainly this is in the area of cost. It is possible that the more expensive the system the more likely it approaches your ideal. The trade-off between price and performance, or when you stop looking for something too complex, is up to the individual. Guidelines are possible, and an attempt to have a comprehensive list follows.

The first thing to do is to find out why you want a computer in the first place! Here we come across a circular argument — how do you choose the right system when you've never had a computer before and are not sure what they can do? How do you define your application if you haven't chosen the system? This is where this book, and your local computer retailer comes in. Chat to the retailer, join a club — read the magazines; in fact everything that was mentioned in the earlier chapters.

Once you have got a good idea of the type of system, and amount of money to spend, things become slightly easier.

The obvious starting point is the power of the system. If you just want to learn how a microprocessor system works, and are interested in programming at the machine level — and even controlling electronic apparatus — then the single board computer is your baby. Unfortunately, the accompanying literature is pretty sparse. As the system is really for learning about a specific microprocessor your choice is limited to three or four systems per processor.

With the cheaper, personal computers the questions are fairly obvious, and simply answered. These can be summarized as follows:

a. Is the computer built around a popular processor? This really means the 8080, Z80, 8085, 6800 or 6502. If you choose one of the others, how good is the software support?
b. Is there a good operating system built in to the ROM on the computer board? You must of course be able to work through the program one instruction at a time, and the editing functions are important. Reading in the program from magnetic tape (is there an interface?) must be possible without difficulty. Is there facility for expanding to disks without difficulty?
c. Is it a simple matter to connect peripheral equipment via serial or parallel interface?
d. Can you actually afford the storage capacity? Where is the ceiling? Is it in fact simple to expand the computer to a complete system?
e. Does it plug into the mains, or is another power source needed — at additional cost?
f. Can the computer be interfaced to an acceptable bus? What does the additional equipment cost?
g. Are there provisions for using high-level language? Most computers have this in their basic form. Don't count on being able to use another language other than BASIC for instance.

Things get a bit more difficult when more complicated systems are required. The basic question usually is — do I need a system that can grow with my needs and inventiveness, or am I getting a system to learn on and then buy a more sophisticated one? Only the user can answer this. If the answer is yes to the first part — expandability — then a system based on an accepted bus standard, or with plenty of peripheral support is required. If the answer is yes to the second part — a simple system to learn on — then a small desk top system may be all that is required.

Expandability and software/hardware support usually determine the choice of system. It is not possible to say that one system is better than another with any objectivity. It all depends on where you live, what your local supplier is like, and whether you have, or want, any software expertise.

The first thing to do is to get to know the supplier. Is he a retailer who has recently come into computers having spent many years selling electrical or consumer electronic goods? If he has a reputation to consider he may not be too hot on software but the servicing backup and help in this area may compensate.

Is he a computer specialist? If so, why does he only stock three or four machines? Why does he consider one better than his competitor up the road, or in the next town? Has he access to software expertise, someone who can help you when you get into a fix?

The main point is — does he know what he's talking about, and is he financially secure? There have been a number of cases recently of computer stores going out of business. Their technical competence was never in question — but the overall management structure was very weak. The last thing wanted is for your supplier, who you will depend on a great deal to start off with, to go bust just when you need him!

This is true for smaller systems that are advertised at discount rates in the magazines. Reading these journals is one way of finding out what is going on. But cheap prices usually means lack of after sales support. It really does pay to shop around in person — go to the exhibitions — and stick with somebody once you've built up trust. If there is a computer club in your locality, a few visits will soon tell you who has a good reputation.

In fact talking to existing users is the best way of getting to know a system. Try and find somebody locally that has solved, or is trying to solve, a similar problem. Their experience can save a lot of time and money.

If I'm sounding a bit vague, then it's because there are as many answers to the question as questioners. A process of elimination will identify a group of three or four machines. This elimination contest will consider the following:

> Cost; physical size; memory size; ease of use; software support; servicing support; reputation of manufacturer; local support.

When these have been considered try out the systems selected, and make your choice. In some ways it's a bit like buying a car, washing machine or hi-fi system — don't think that different considerations apply. They don't!

## Ten hints to help you on your way

1 *Become computer conscious.*

Look around you, in your firm or at school — how and where are computers used today? Think about the developments taking place at this moment: the very highly centralized computer centres of the 50s and 60s, with the computers in their ivory towers, are turning at breakneck speed into computers in almost every home. Consider the possibilities this development opens for society and for yourself.

Before you know where you are, your fingers will be itching to play with your own computer...

2 *Learn more about computers.*

If you are a novice in the computer field it may be wise to read a good introduction to the subject. Keep on reading this book — read several books; look in the bibliography in the appendix. You'll also find there quite a number of useful magazines.

Read product brochures, discuss matters with sales staff and — above all — with other people who are interested in personal computers. Go to some of the computer exhibitions that are becoming quite frequent. The magazines usually advertise these.

3 *Get yourself some computer friends.*

A group of like-minded people is the place to bring up "stupid questions". The place to find crazy ideas and the place to give and find help with tricky problems.

During the last few years, hundreds of computer clubs have been formed in the UK. If you can't find a club in the place where you live, then start one! You're bound to find more interested people at work or school.

4   *Which type are you?*

Are you the type who mainly prefers to **build** a computer system or to **use** it?

It's important to know . . . from the start.

There are a number of computer kits available. Most of them are comparatively simple to assemble for a handy person with some sort of experience. But they may be rather time consuming. Sooner or later you get involved in purely electronic questions: trouble shooting, interfacing of different units, or quite simply new design.

If you want to concentrate your interest on programming and using the computer, then you should buy a complete system in full working order.

If possible try out several different computer systems before deciding.

5   *Make up your mind what you want.*

The main question is: how are you going to get hold of some form of computer power? Here are some of the possibilities:

Buy a second-hand computer.

Borrow computer time at work, at school, or from an acquaintance.

Invest in a personal computer of your own.

Evaluate these alternatives and compare them. They all have their pros and cons.

6   *Check your wallet.*

Go through your budget, and cut your cloth according to your purse. When you see all the good things coming on to the personal computer market it's all too easy to lose your head.

Make up a financing plan **before** you start buying your computer stuff. Try to see what you will need to invest a year or so ahead. Finances **are** important. You will soon find yourself with the same kind of costs as a yachtsman, a motor-boat owner, a motorcycle enthusiast or a hi-fi convert.

### 7 Look ahead.

At the present rate of development, today's ideas will be out of date in a year or even a month and prices are falling. You are getting more and more for your money. But that's no reason for waiting. Try instead to get an idea of how developments are going. That way you'll stand a good chance of avoiding expenditure on things that have no future.

The fastest development is taking place on the electronics side, in highly integrated semiconductor technology. There are new and better processors, but above all larger and faster semiconductor memories.

On the peripheral side things are moving slower. Keyboards still cost the same as last year; so too do tape recorders and cassettes. However, prices are beginning to drop on printers, and mass storage, such as floppy disks, are getting cheaper all the time.

### 8 Try to find a partner.

Sooner or later you will need help — in finding a fault, in learning some operating trick or other, or in developing some specific application.

Maybe you will need some programs.

At such times, two's good company! Especially if you find a good friend who has the same system and ways of looking at things. This will save you both a lot of trouble. And you will both make faster progress. (Some people even club together to buy a system. If you are on really good terms then this is quite a good way of sharing the capital costs.)

### 9 When the system is up and running — start using it.

Once your new computer system is set up and everything

seems to be working properly, you may perhaps ask, "What do I do now?"

The answer is "Use it, of course!"

All too often, it seems, many personal computers are used to run test programs or various types of demonstration program. This is rather like looking at the test picture on the TV or scraping, painting and equipping the boat without ever sailing it! For many people, the reason for this kind of hesitation may be the lack of suitable program material.

Take it easy! Now you've come this far you have started to look at life differently. You've got a working computer system at your fingertips. Applications which those without a computer cannot even imagine will occur to you. Not everybody wants to learn how to program. If you do, then have a look at what other people are doing. Most colleges, polytechnics, computer clubs etc. run courses on BASIC programming.

Call them and see what's going on. When you do start programming, remember that often the best way to program is plagiarism!

10  *Get other people interested in computer technology.*

Look at your own changing interest in computers. Once it was only lukewarm — maybe even unconscious; now you are an active computer user, full of enthusiasm at all the possibilities this technology places at your disposal. Nobody's a better advertisement for personal computers than yourself.

Demonstrate your own system to friends and acquaintances. Get hold of a suitable set of demonstration programs. Tell people about them and answer their questions. In return, you may get some new ideas for applications for your own system.

# CHAPTER 7
## What can I do with it?

There are many fascinating applications for cheap microcomputers. It is practically impossible to make a complete list — new ideas are flooding in all the time. Each application of personal computers places individual demands on equipment and programs. A personal computer system for book-keeping etc. has quite a different design from the computer you buy to control the central heating at home.

### Games

It is quite fashionable among so-called computer experts to run down the playing of games on a computer. This is rubbish! One of the easiest and most pleasant ways of learning how to program is to get hooked on a game, and then want to learn how it works. Among the reasons given by many computer professionals for joining Computer Clubs is that it is not possible to play games on the computer at work! Certainly programming for graphics, or presenting information in a way that anybody can understand it, is a very important part of computer development. The greatest boost to speech synthesis, and integral sound capabilities, was the need to amuse the operator!

Games do provide light relief though, and the value of this must not be underestimated. Many a sceptical, or concerned, user has been converted to the computer by such means. If the computer you have chosen is to be used in the home, it most certainly must have a games capability. That will mean ability to have games joysticks attached, and possibly sound output. A colour graphics video output is also desirable.

Computer games can also be "mind stretching". Most desktop systems can now play a passable game of chess, backgammon or bridge. In the latter case it's just a matter of turning the machine on and loading the program. You don't even have to hunt around for three other people!

*Even the smallest children can play with computer based games.*

Many magazines devote a large proportion of their editorial space to games programs, and this is usually a way to keep your library up to date with the latest developments. Program libraries available commercially on cassette or disk are usually fairly expensive.

The great thing for both educational and fun use is the interactive nature of the computer. In computer aided instruction (CAI) it will not make you go faster than your learning capability.

In games you are playing with "somebody" who will usually prove a worthy opponent — at whatever level of difficulty you agree on!

**Education**

One of the major areas of interest, and one place where children are being introduced to aspects of computing, is in education. Unlike the Americans most Europeans put educational use of the personal computer above most others. With systems like the Sinclair ZX81, costing under £50 and many others under £200, schools and colleges are able to enter computing for a modest amount. Even where budgets are being slashed, the need for a computer is high on most schools' equipment requirements. Most schools in the UK now have at least one computer.

The use of computers in schools though is limited by the knowledge of the teacher. Cheap computers can be bought by students and used in the home and this is where a lot of adults will use them for the first time. It's the calculator effect all over again — and with computers now available for the price of a calculator five years ago (in real terms) they will probably have a similar effect.

The Sinclair ZX Spectrum personal computer being used at a Primary School in Cambridgeshire, to teach Geography.

Programs for use in a school environment can be divided into five categories. Drill and practice; simulation/modelling; games; tutorials; and a combination of these four.

Drill and practice programs are used to develop and master skills associated with specific objects. Maths, spelling, syntax etc., are typical examples. The sudent is expected to continue with the program until the program has been mastered. Unfortunately students soon get tired or frustrated with this type of program.

*Colourful, animated alphabets are a beneficial learning aid to children between two and eight years of age.*

With simulation/modelling programs, which are more difficult to write, real world events are simulated or modelled. It is not necessary for the students to physically encounter the actual problem. Data collected from real events is often entered into the programs, decision making skills are developed and group discussion evolves.

Games programs are fun — as previously mentioned. If educational games programs are well designed they assist students in developing their thinking skills.

Tutorial programs are probably the most difficult to write. Students are expected to acquire specific knowledge through well designed frame sequences. They are usually designed for a specific student.

There are thousands of these programs around. Most, unfortunately, are rubbish as software development has not kept up with hardware. There are many suppliers with long lists of computer aided instruction — CAI — software but little has reached into our schools. The software that is available is fairly poor at the moment, although there are some good programs available in the maths and science area. This is to be expected, of course, but it is only a matter of time before programs for language learning, for example, get better.

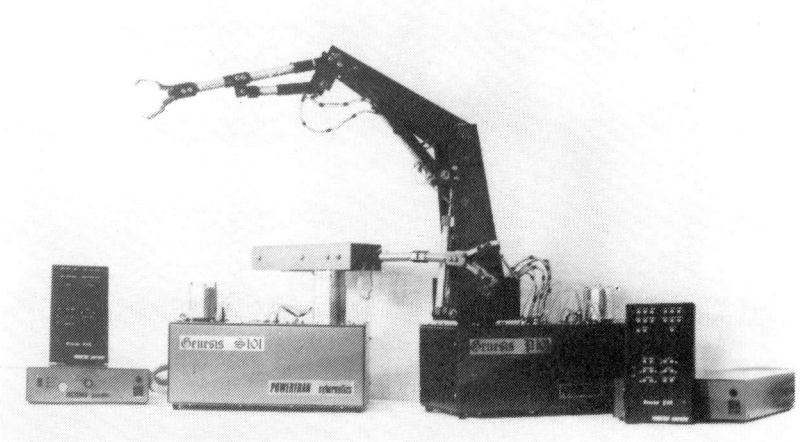

*For educational purposes small robot arms can be attached to educational personal computers.*

### Business use

When we come to consider business use, the ways of using a computer are virtually infinite. Many domestic finance programs exist for keeping a check on your bank balance; calculating

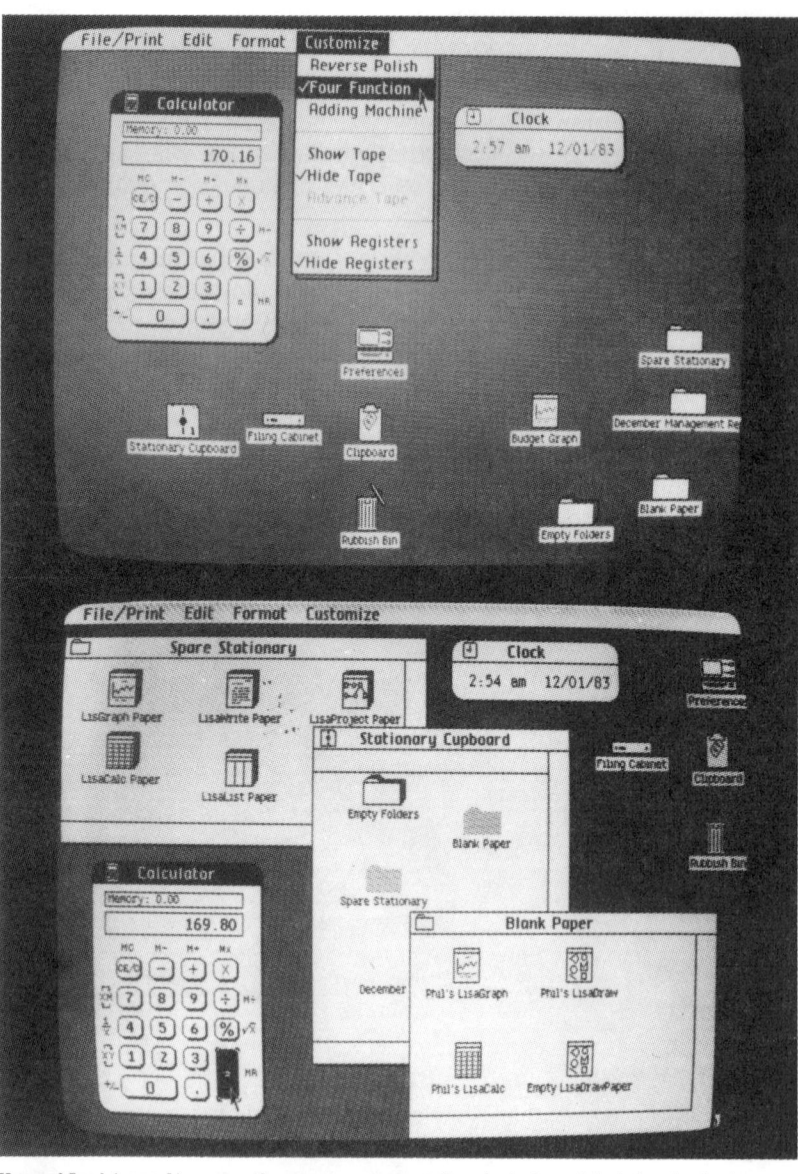

Users of Apple's new Lisa see on the screen a representation of a desk top. It includes simple pictures of things they commonly work with, such as folders and documents.

income tax returns; acting as an address and telephone file; simple diary-keeping; and even cataloguing books and records!

In a commercial environment the investment of a few thousand pounds will usually pay for itself within one year.

Book-keeping — in all its forms — is an obvious job for computers. You only have to look at the development in the business world: large and medium-sized companies make use of computer technology. Inexpensive personal computers now make it possible for even small companies (including one-man businesses) to rationalize their book-keeping, order processing, current-account ledgers, invoicing, salaries, stock accounting, budget, etc. Many of the people who have embraced personal computers are small businessmen: doctors, consultants, shop-keepers, stockbrokers, garage proprietors and others.

One thing is clear, however: relatively simple personal computer systems will not get you far. This is because, for the system to work in a rational and convenient manner, it needs a lot of storage. The handling of data files separately from the application program itself is also necessary. Many personal computer BASIC interpreters can't manage this. Above all, well written — and easily modifiable — software is needed.

The minimum system for a small company should contain the following:

A fast CPU based around a common microprocessor;

At least 64K but preferably 256K of user RAM;

A reasonable printer. If letters, invoices or other "official" stationery are going to be printed, a daisy-wheel type printer is essential;

A video display unit with at least 80 characters/line;

Dual floppy disks with a capacity of more than 1 Mbyte;

A good disk operating system that is "portable", or at least popular and well-supported, eg. CP/M; Flex; PET; Apple etc.

A decent, flexible BASIC interpreter;

And plenty of applications software, carefully tested and with good documentation.

*The Apple Stock Quote Reporter receives a current display of stock prices and allows the operator to place a corresponding bid. The Reporter also ascertains the closing price, the high and low price for the day, and the current volume of the stock. Stock portfolios can be easily changed to suit the individual operator.*

When choosing software it is very important to consider the following; ease of tailoring and accounting system used. In the first case most programs will need tailoring for your particular use. If a £100 program is going to cost £500 to get going for your particular application, it is going to be cheaper to buy a £400 program and pay £100 for tailoring. In general if a program needs modifying by more than 10% forget it.

It is sometimes worthwhile paying for a program to be written especially for you. In most cases this will cost as much as the machine. But if you can justify it in terms of eventual saving then it is probably the best thing to do. Do not think that a £15 invoicing package will be capable of reproducing a £15,000 mainframe package. It won't!

The second point, accounting system used, is very important. Many American packages conform to American accounting procedures and will not be any use in Europe. This is specially true with packages for calculating tax. In fact for VAT calculations many programs sold in Europe do not meet the Inland Revenue standards. If you want to use your computer for tax calculations find out where it is acceptable to the tax man first.

**Word processing**

Next to business accounting, word processing is the fastest growing area of use. Information handling is being revolutionized by the personal computer.

It may be simple enough to write a letter by typing but an attractive and faultless text is considerably more difficult for most of us.

A word processing system built around a cheap personal computer makes the whole procedure much simpler and reduces frustration.

The concept of word processing means that you type the text in the normal way on an electric typewriter or VDU connected to the computer. With the assistance of the computer you then correct and edit the text until it is exactly as you want it. After this the computer supplies a perfect printout, with as many copies as needed, and the text can be stored for later use.

Professional word processing systems usually cost anything up to £10,000 or even more. For personal use you can get a long way for considerably less.

**This is what's needed...**

Let's see what is needed to turn the personal computer into a word processing system in micro form.

First of all: *suitable terminal equipment* for handling input editing and printout of text. There are several possible arrangements for such terminal equipment. One example: an electric typewriter of the IBM Selectric type modified for use with a computer system plus a video printer. A VDU with a decent printer will also be acceptable.

Text input takes place at the keyboard, editing on the screen and the output comes on the printer.

The printer is really the bit that costs money in word processing systems, especially if you want attractive copy.

And then you need a suitable program — a *text editor*. This makes it possible to produce the text body on the screen on command, to correct spelling errors, erase, add, exchange sentences or paragraphs and get a printout made. There are many different types of text editors, both simple and more complex ones.

One word processing program very popular, especially on CP/M machines, is Wordstar.

"Complete Business System" from Micropower.

Wordstar has on-screen visual text composition and dynamic justification and re-margination. There is no need to hit "return" at the end of a line, for example, as Wordstar moves you to the next line. The preceding line is re-displayed justified to the left and right margins. You can centre in a line with one keystroke and set boldface or underline even in mid paragraph. The text can be rejustified to new margins when necessary. Dynamic pagination shows the printer page breaks during text entry, correction or review. Page headings, page numbers etc. can be easily entered. Selected pages, pauses between pages and headings can be inserted during printing. This system costs around £200 and is available in most disk formats.

One example of how you can have practical use of your own word processing system: letters. For a letter, you write your rough copy, edit it on the VDU until you are satisfied, and then get a fair copy printed out. When it is a question of a large number of letters that are basically the same, you also input an address list of the persons who are to be sent the letters. It is also possible to input particulars for each individual case. In this way each letter will be a personal one despite the fact that the printout has been done with the aid of the computer. Very time-saving.

In the mass memory of the system you can store a number of standard phrases which can be called up when needed and put together, for example for a contract. A newspaper article or a memorandum can be composed and edited without the heap of unsuccessful attempts filling the waste paper basket. The paper only comes into the picture in the final phase.

A lot of letters we get have been addressed by a computer. The personal computer can be used for the same purpose: for storing, updating and printing out names and addresses. It may be a list of members or customers — or perhaps even a list of Christmas cards to be sent.

The word processing system — described above — can with advantage also be used for mailing registers. For the sake of mailing registers alone, though the software does not need to be all that advanced. A good mailing-register program should of course contain search routines so as to make it possible to find a certain person in the register, or to print out all those with a certain code designation or postal code, or to sort in alphabetical order (good for lists of members) and so on.

Another very popular word processor is Word-Pro. This is available for Commodore computers. Although initially designed as a "home" computer — and unfairly dismissed by its competition as a toy! — the PET, and its successors, make a good starting point for a small system. Word-Pro does most of the things that Wordstar does — and a few more. Unfortunately it is only designed for Commodore computers, and is therefore not portable. This is the decision that has to be made when choosing a system for business use — portability and expandability — or off-the-shelf. It is similar to buying a hi-fi system — the choice is between separate units, with all the problems of matching impedances and leads hanging around, or a music centre with everything in one box.

**Information handling**

This is going to be the growth industry of the 80s — and the personal computer is at the heart of the exercise. The Post Office and broadcasting authorities are spending millions on giving us an information retrieval system that will revolutionize our lives. Prestel, Viewdata, Ceefax, Oracle, Antiope, Captain or ... — call it what you will they are all basically similar in concept. Many personal computers will soon have the capability to retrieve and display the information stored by the central computer. Apple have a teletext/viewdata card that plugs into one of the I/O ports. Some personal computers designed in Europe have been designed from the start to plug into the national and international networks. One problem in Britain is the need to get PO approval before any device can be plugged into the telephone system.

Most personal computers can now be plugged directly into the Prestel network. A small adaptor — either modem or acoustic coupler-casting under £100 can be plugged into any I/O port of the computer. Software then allows Prestel graphics to be "translated" into the computer's graphics.

A number of organizations have been formed to allow computer users to access Prestel — the largest being Micronet 800.

You can choose from hundreds of free games for all the family from Micronet's "Aladdin's Cave". They're changed quite frequently so it is possible to choose from over 100 that are compatible with most computers. You can download the game to your own machine, and use it whenever you like. It's just about as easy — and as cheap — as a local phone call.

To download games and other free telesoftware, you follow a simple routine explained in the instructions you receive when you join Micronet.

Kenny Everett filling his bytes with Micronet 800.

There's plenty of scope for education at home too. Micronet offers schools and colleges an inexpensive way to expand their range of software and gain computing experience.

Schools can use Micronet at a special low day-time rate for call charges, and link in with other schools and educational users around the country to swap ideas, techniques and programs written by students and teachers — using the system's educational exchange library.

It's fertile ground for sharing new ideas, it cuts down the huge costs and problems of normal distribution, and you can link into news, information and a diary of events.

Business users will also plug into the communications possibilities of the system — like telex and electronic mail.

There's also access to all the current business information instantly available on Prestel.

Even more important — business users can operate "closed areas" of Micronet for company communications. It means they can send information like new prices, special promotions, memos and so on to all retail outlets, branches, or perhaps the field force of salesmen or engineers.

"User groups" for the major micro manufacturers maintain news and reference information on Micronet. And users can send messages to their group, or any other Micronet or Prestel users — straight from the keyboard.

Messages are held on Prestel's "mailbox" service — but can only be accessed with a personal subscriber number. You can send Prestel messages even if you're away from home. Call Prestel by phone and they'll send messages to the Prestel user for you.

Another communications bonus means telexes you send through Prestel are picked up by a carrier and despatched

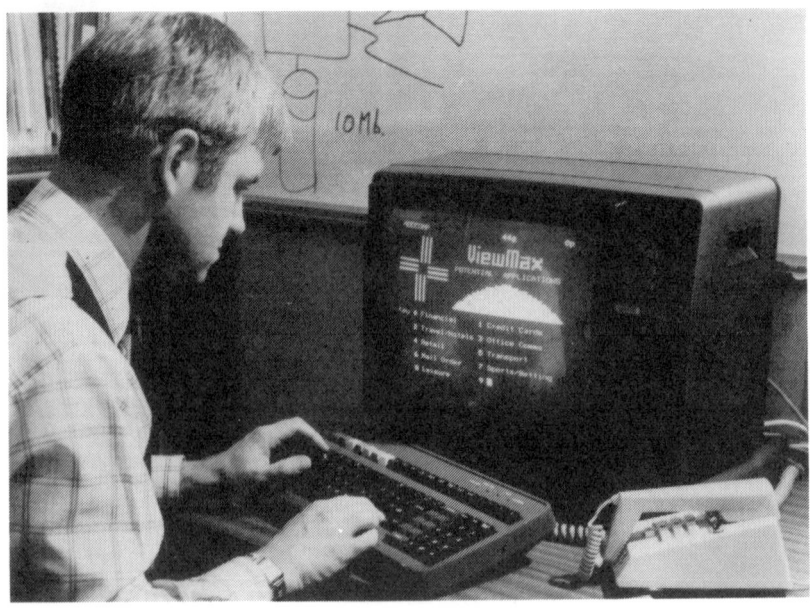

Viewdata can now be accessed from a personal computer.

through the normal telex system. You get charged for telexes on the quarterly bill.

As the service grows it will become even more interactive — directing the user to additional information on a subject. Suddenly with Prestel your own small computer takes you into a lively national network, whenever you like, at a fraction of the cost of other communications methods.

Once you've got a computer that can handle these information retrieval systems, it is useful? It must be possible to integrate the information into the applications required. Expenditure of a couple of hundred pounds on a teletext decoder would be better spent on having it inside a domestic TV. If the TV is used as the display unit, however, then it is better to have the decoder inside the computer. Most people will use viewdata/teletext as a simple data base. It is possible to use it in a quasi-interactive mode — really interrogating the data base to selectively get information. In fact many large firms are getting their own viewdata systems to hold their company information.

## Multi-user systems

A multi-user system allows a number of different users running different applications to use the computer at the same time.

There are a number of methods to set up a multi-user system for business use. The simplest is to connect a number of microcomputers together using various networking devices.

There are two basic types of network:

A "ring" network is a loop of wires which connects all the computers on the loop. Data for transmission is put into the ring at one point — the source — and taken off at another — the destination. That means that each point — or node — on the ring needs to have some form of identification — or specific address.

Each node has to recognize information destined for it and also generate information in such a way that the desired destination recognizes it. It is usual to allow any two or more points on the ring to converse with each other. The destination therefore needs to know who is sending the information and there can be two successive transmissions to one destination.

The other form of network connects the computers in the system in a pattern rather like the spokes in a wheel. Thus a central controller is needed through which each computer must communicate.

*A typical 6-node Acorn Econet at Long Road Sixth Form College, with a 400 kilobyte file station.*

Interfacing computers in the network via disk drives is one of the most popular methods for personal computers.

Typical are systems based on the Corvus Winchester disk. The simplest is called the Miracle and is constructed around the Corvus Constellation network. In addition to his own dedicated computer and associated memory, each user has access to a central hard disk memory, without interference from other users.

Miracle also makes it possible for similar computers to communicate with each other in the network and for peripherals to be shared.

The Miracle system can connect a wide range of micros in any combination. These include the Apple, Alpha, Altos, Superbrain, TRS-80 Models I and II, Digital Equipment LSI-11 and all S-100 bus computers.

**Sharing**

Peripherals — such as printers, VDUs, devices for speech output and voice recognition, colour graphics, light pens and digitizers — can also be linked. A single-level Miracle network can have up to eight computers and a two-level network allows up to 64 computers to share the disk memory.

A device called the Constellation shared data multiplexer is used to connect the computers in the system to 10 or 18 megabytes of Corvus hard disk memory. Using four disk drives, the total capacity of a Miracle system can be extended to 72 megabytes. Corvus will work with existing software and give a disk accessing speed which is normally 20 times faster than floppies.

Miracle makes use of a range of computer languages, from BASIC, COBOL and FORTRAN to Pascal, ALGOL and APL.

The latest local networking facility from Corvus is called Omninet. It can link up to 64 different or identical microcomputers or varied peripherals.

According to Corvus, Omninet is 100% compatible with the Constellation. Corvus anticipates that many users of its large installed base of Constellation units will opt to combine that system with Omninet.

A similar system, from Zynar — called Cluster/One Model A or Nestar — is also designed for the Apple. Information can be transmitted from machine to machine directly, without going through disk files and without the need for modems.

## Shared access

All stations share access either to private data or to a common read-only library of programs and data, and they can update databases simultaneously.

All information can be shared among users or, using the protection mechanism of the system, can be password-protected so that only one designated individual or group has access to special data. As an example, a number of people may have permission to read specific data but may not have the ability to modify that data.

In the Nestar Model A network, a standard Apple with 48 kilobytes of processor memory can function as the dedicated central controller/mass storage manager, with connections to the Nestar storage subsystems and to other Apples which serve as user stations. Each station is connected to the ClusterBus which can be up to 300 metres of 16-wire ribbon cable or standard round cable.

Programs written in languages supported by Apple — Applesoft, BASIC, Integer BASIC, machine language, Pascal — will function without change in the Model A. Any hardware in the Apple universe obeying Apple standard conventions can be used. Most applications in automation, accounting, legal or small business use can be put to work immediately without reprogramming.

The Model A has utility programs for initializing new floppy disks, making back-up copies and copying certain data selectively for off-line retention. Program files, data files, binary files, picture files and random access on sequential text files may all be saved on the disk.

Nestar supports multiple printer stations. An application program can run in a user station and can search for files prepared for printing. It can then print those files with any Apple-compatible printer. The system can be upgraded in the field by adding more individual stations, up to 65 units, at any time.

Nestar consists of a compact metal box with two double-sized 8" floppy disks with formatted available storage of 1.26 million bytes; the necessary electronics which plug into the central controller Apple; the ClusterBus communication card; the communication cards required for each Apple station; and all necessary software. Also available as an option is the Nestar hard disk drive with either 16.5 or 33 million bytes of formatted available storage in a single unit.

The user station communication cards contain 2 kilobytes of ROM, 1 kilobyte of RAM and all necessary bus electronics. They are compatible with standard Apple interface cards, including those for mini-disks, serial and parallel printers, modems, sound and graphics tablets.

The ClusterBus communications card plugs into any of the

peripheral connectors inside the Apple and is perceived by the Apple to be an Apple mini-disk controller card and thus will be initialized automatically when the Apple is turned on.

The Apple is not the only microcomputer with at least two network options. The PET has the Mu-PET and the KC Netkit. Both use a hardware approach, with the Netkit having some software in ROM — firmware.

Essentially the KC Netkit is a hardware/firmware package which allows a relatively inexperienced programmer, assisted by 10 new BASIC commands, to achieve configurations without recourse to tedious machine-code routines. The PET can act as a smart or dumb terminal, which can accommodate virtually any protocol and character conversion the user may require.

Additionally, by allowing the serial port to equate with the keyboard, the PET can exchange data and program files freely and can also be controlled remotely, opening a wide range of high-speed networking and also, more important, be grouped with others to achieve greater real-time number-crunching.

The firmware includes re-location routines which avoid clashes with other devices demanding access to memory. The expansion bus, on which the Netkit unit is placed, is duplicated, and the only way one can recognize that an apparently standard PET has been modified is a small connector clipped unobtrusively into the expansion port.

Mu-PET allows up to eight PETs to share one or more Commodore disc drives and any compatible printer. The hardware runs via the standard PET-IEEE bus and each PET accesses the disk as if it were the only user.

Tandy has a fairly primitive system which allows a teacher in a classroom to switch each computer into a master disk unit. That is obviously not so sophisticated as other manufacturers' products and should not be considered as a true network.

There are many other developments which will allow multi-user access to information. Systems using the disk operating system CP/M 2.2 should be converted easily to its multi-user equivalent MP/M. As that is a slightly different concept from a dedicated system based around a specific microcomputer, it will not be considered here.

More expensive microcomputer systems — costing around £7,000 or more — usually have the multi-user system built in.

**Controlling things**

Most of the systems considered in this book have at least one programmable input/output port. This allows information to be sent to and from the computer in the ones and zeros needed by the CPU, and thus lets all sorts of things to be connected up to the computer.

Simple things like switches need little interfacing as they are essentially binary devices. Thus burglar alarm systems lend themselves easily to computer control. In the other direction things can be switched on and off fairly simply by pulses — suitably amplified — coming from the computer. Those systems with internal timers or clocks obviously help there.

*PERSONAL COMPUTING FOR PROFESSIONALS* — The HP-85 computer from Hewlett-Packard, is designed for personal use in business and industry by professionals such as in engineers, scientists, accountants, and investment analysts.

If other signals are required special interfaces called analogue-digital converters are needed. These convert varying voltages into equivalent digital signals as required by the computer. Thus it is possible for the computer, for example, both to simulate sound and also to manipulate and process it.

Computers with control buses — like the IEEE488 — can be used to control, and get information to and from various instruments. Thus they become intelligent controllers in a laboratory.

One area where personal computers can be fun is in robotics. A number of companies sell small robots that can be operated from small systems. Intelligent machines are obviously going to become more important in the future and, again, a small computer system is ideal as an entry into this area.

## Making money

One factor in choosing a system, or even buying one in the first place, is the possibility of earning some money with it! There is still a lack of good programs at the moment. This is the first area to look at. If you're good at programming then the purchase of a well-known and popular system could be the key to a prosperous future! Many people are now making a living writing software for the major software distributors. These companies work on a straight royalty basis. 10% on a £10 program works out a reasonable amount even if only 10 a week are sold!

Many local retailers do not have the resident software expertise they need. If you are good at tailoring — or are an accountant, for example, with programming ability — then your local retailer will probably welcome you with open arms.

Advertise! Most of the computer monthlies have special advertising slots for the one-man band. These cost about £20 and usually pay for themselves quickly. Contact your local computer clubs. If they have a relatively "high profile" in your locality then those with software problems will contact them at sometime for help. If the secretary or chairman knows your name and area of expertise then he will pass it on.

If you have hardware experience then helping people get their kits working is one area of need. Or selling the "boxes" that are needed to interface various systems together. A number of companies are doing very well selling interfaces that convert, say IEEE488 signals into RS232C, and vice versa. Small control systems are also worth investigating — as well as voice recognition and speech synthesis. Most of the early work in this area was done by one or two engineers in their spare bedroom or garage. It certainly isn't worth trying to design a computer system from scratch now — not unless you have a few hundred thousand pounds to invest anyway. There are just too many successful companies around.

### Examples of personal computers in use

Some examples of the uses to which personal computers have been put will illustrate how versatile a system can be. It is clear that the number of uses is only limited by the human imagination.

i) A college in London has adapted a Nascom 1 computer so that severely handicapped people can communicate effectively. Two foot operated switches move a cursor around a matrix of letters and characters. These can then be assembled on the video display showing the message required.

ii) The PET computer has been programmed to carry out many of the functions in hotel reservations and billings. The software allows the PET to keep a record of room availability — with immediate viewing and blocking for up to 12 blocks of rooms, 400 days ahead with up to 99 rooms per block. Entering a date gives screen display of availability of all blocks for that date and following 6 days. Guest billing is also available and caters for up to 200 rooms. Final accounts include service charge and VAT. A printer can be used as an integral part of the system.

iii) The best example of financial modelling is Visicalc, a forecasting program that was a worldwide best seller.

Virtually any problem that can be entered in tabular form can be solved using Visicalc. A recalculation feature allows the user to change only one figure for the program to adjust all the others automatically. This enables one to ask a series of "What if?" questions such as "What if interest charges increase by 3%?" or "What if sales fall by 12½%?"

Visicalc is essentially a general purpose utility and it is widely used for budgeting and financial planning as well as engineering and scientific applications. It has been described as software which allows you to program without having to learn a programming language. (More sophisticated utilities are under development, including a number of program generators which, given precise instructions, will automatically write programs to suit your purposes. But contrary to some claims, these program generators do require some knowledge of systems analysis in order to prepare the correct instructions.)

iv) Solicitors are using a number of packages to carry out the following applications: time recording and costing; financial accounting; debt collection and word processing. Other areas being considered are information retrieval, conveyancing support and probate support. The time recording and costing relies on each fee-earner maintaining a daily or weekly time-sheet. The information on the time sheets is fed into the computer and stored in a client/matter sequence. A fee-earner can then, subsequently, enquire on any individual matter to see how much time has been spent — and how much it costs! Solicitors have found their income has been underestimated by up to 50% on non-computerized systems. The legal accounting system involves a vast number of different types of transactions and these are governed by very strict rules. The computer can make this process easier — and more accurate. Debt collection is a natural spin-off from accountancy and the uses of word processing, especially when dealing with repetitious documents, are obvious.

v) A public relations consultancy had a package written for

them to handle most of their daily routines. This includes an activity planner, mailing system and accounting tasks. The activity planner gives a daily check-up, client by client, with matters pending according to client, date and type of activity. Clients are sent end of month summaries as activity reports. The mailing system allows up to 300 names and addresses to be categorized in up to 100 ways. Hence selective mailings are possible. The accounting tasks include clients' costing accounts. Output is available on a dot-matrix or daisy-wheel printer, and can be used in conjunction with a word processor package.

vi) Estate agents have been offered a package on the Apple II. There are routines to handle the entry of new property details, amend and update these details, enter potential purchaser details and a sales checklist. The program also gives a home sale negotiation analysis, and allows routine letters and transfer of records to archives. It is claimed to handle an unlimited number of records.

vii) Telesoft has been developed by the IBA for use with adapted TV sets receiving Oracle teletext transmissions. This allows schools and colleges access to programs held by the IBA's central computer and broadcast with as-normal teletext characters. When the TV set receives the software it puts it into RAM and this becomes available for use on any computer plugged in to it. It is designed mainly for educational use at the moment.

viii) A kitchen outfitters are using an Apple II to help design layouts for kitchen designs. It replaces the traditional drawing board. The computer gives both speed and accuracy and also appeals to customers. The Apple's high resolution graphics are used, with sub-assembly plans held on disc. This allows customers to move units around and seen them displayed on a screen immediately. Five programs are available: plan and design the kitchen; price and design a kitchen for any range of any manufacturer; draw and calculate tile requirements; draw the plan of the kitchen on to a graph plotter or daisy-wheel printer; or design the worktops. To draw an average square or

L-shaped room takes two minutes and around 15 minutes to design the plan.

ix) A pharmacist in Hertfordshire is using a PET computer to keep track of his prescriptions. Not only does it do stock control, but also prints labels — in a way that customers can read easily! There are plans to link the dosage with a data bank so that over-prescription is avoided. Most of the information is held in code, so that the operator can produce a complete label with only a few key strokes. The pharmacist is also investigating the possibility of using the computer to check for drug incompatibilities.

x) A group of independent lorry drivers in the States have got together to use a computer based information system to help them to be more efficient. A central office uses the computer to link the various truck stops — and the drivers who frequent them — with customers having loads for carrying. The system interfaces directly with the telephone network. A customer calls the computer and uses the telephone keys to communicate their latest load information — both for new jobs and updates on old jobs. The computers, located at key truck stops display the information on a monitor. The drivers then scan the monitor, identify jobs they may be interested in hauling and person to contact. There's even an up-to-date information listing where and when fuel is available on the road ahead. The truck driver is saving time and money and has immediate access to available work, wherever he may be. And the customers are getting maximum exposure to the independent lorry drivers.

Well, these are just a few of the uses for personal computers. You'll agree that they are very varied — and the surface has only just been scratched!

Now that you've been fired with enthusiasm, go out, get yourself a system and contribute to the fund of knowledge available!

# APPENDIX A

**Binary arithmetic — or thinking in 1's and 0's**

Almost as soon as we get to school, we have to learn the decimal number system with digits, 0-9. This means that we know how much 27 is, or 56, or whatever number.

The computer is designed to calculate with the binary number system which has two digits, 0 and 1. Despite this, the computer has no difficulty in expressing numbers like 27 or 56.

This is how it works:
$27_{10} = 11011_2$ Marvellous isn't it? (The little 2 or 10 denotes the number system used.)

How can it be 11011? Let's first take a look at how the number 27 is built up in the *decimal number system* ...

27 in decimal actually means $2 \times 10^1 + 7 \times 10^0$, where $10^1$ is 10 and $10^0$ is 1. Similarly, $10^2$ is 100 and $10^3$ is 1000. (The little number indicates the number of zeros after the one.) This is sometimes called the multiplier. We can therefore make a simple table:

| Multiplier | $10^1$ (10) | $10^0$ (1) |
|---|---|---|
| Digit | 2 | 7 |
| Product | 20 | 7 |

which, added together, give 27.

Similarly, the number $1234_{10}$ really means:
$1 \times 10^3 + 2 \times 10^2 + 3 \times 10^1 + 4 \times 10^0.$

Exactly the same method is used with the binary system, except that the 10 is replaced by a 2. Therefore $11011_2$ really means:
$1 \times 2^4 + 1 \times 2^3 + 0 \times 2^2 + 1 \times 2^1 + 1 \times 2^0$ or
$1 \times 16_{10} + 1 \times 8_{10} \phantom{+ 0 \times 2^2} + 1 \times 2_{10} + 1 \times 1_{10}$
which should give $27_{10}$.

A practical method of converting 27 to a binary number is as follows:

$27/2 = 13$ remainder 1
$13/2 = 6$ remainder 1
$6/2 = 3$ remainder 0
$3/2 = 1$ remainder 1         READ UP
$1/2 = 0$ remainder 1
$\phantom{1/2 = 0 remainder}$ 1  1  0  1  1

Then what does the decimal number 56 become in binary code? The same method gives a quick answer: 111000.

**Adding binary numbers**

There are four extremely simple rules for addition: $0 + 0 = 0$, $0 + 1 = 1, 1 + 0 = 1$, and $1 + 1 = 10$. We express the last rule like this "one plus one is one zero".

This table illustrates the addition of binary and decimal numbers:

| Binary | Decimal |
|---|---|
| 0 + 0 = 0 | 0 + 0 = 0 |
| 0 + 1 = 0 | 0 + 1 = 1 |
| 1 + 1 = 10 | 1 + 1 = 2 |
| 10 + 1 = 11 | 2 + 1 = 3 |
| 11 + 1 = 100 | 3 + 1 = 4 |
| 100 + 1 = 101 | 4 + 1 = 5 |
| 101 + 1 = 110 | 5 + 1 = 6 |
| 110 + 1 = 111 | 6 + 1 = 7 |
| 111 + 1 = 1000 | 7 + 1 = 8 |
| 1000 + 1 = 1001 | 8 + 1 = 9 |
| 1001 + 1 = 1010 | 9 + 1 = 10 |

## Octal, Hexadecimal — or how do you pronounce 1001000111110010?

Even if the computer thrives on such an expression, it's very inconvenient for human beings to deal with!

It's much simplier if you make the binary number a number with the base 16 or 8, i.e. sixteen or eight symbols instead of the 2 for the binary system or the 10 for the decimal system.

A system with the base 8 is called *the octal number system* and has eight symbols: 0 1 2 3 4 5 6 7.

The base 16 gives what is called the *hexadecimal system*. This has sixteen symbols: 0 1 2 3 4 5 6 7 8 9 A B C D E F.

This is how these number systems correspond to the binary system:

| Binary | Octal | Binary | Hexadecimal |
|--------|-------|--------|-------------|
| 000    | 0     | 0000   | 0           |
| 001    | 1     | 0001   | 1           |
| 010    | 2     | 0010   | 2           |
| 011    | 3     | 0011   | 3           |
| 100    | 4     | 0100   | 4           |
| 101    | 5     | 0101   | 5           |
| 110    | 6     | 0110   | 6           |
| 111    | 7     | 0111   | 7           |
|        |       | 1000   | 8           |
|        |       | 1001   | 9           |
|        |       | 1010   | A           |
|        |       | 1011   | B           |
|        |       | 1100   | C           |
|        |       | 1101   | D           |
|        |       | 1110   | E           |
|        |       | 1111   | F           |

It is simple to convert a long binary number, say 11101011, to octal form:

11 101 011

3   5   3 = $353_8$

We just group the binary number in threes, and express each group of three as its equivalent octal number.

Converted into hexadecimal form:

| 1110 | 1011 | Here we group the binary number in fours and then express each group of four as its equivalent hexadecimal. |
|------|------|---|
| E | B = EB$_{16}$ | |

How about the long binary number in the section heading?

Well it's certainly easier to remember $91F2_{16}$ than $1001\ 0001\ 1111\ 0010_2$!

Generally it's wisest to learn to use the hexadecimal number system, or hex as it's usually called. The octal form is less common. This is because each symbol in hex expresses four binary bits. Since most computers are constructed to handle data in groups of eight bits (i.e. one byte), one byte can be simply and exactly expressed by two hex symbols; $00_{16}$ is a byte with nothing but zeros, $FF_{16}$ is a byte with nothing but ones.

The address consisting of sixteen bits can conveniently be expressed by four hex symbols, e.g. FA01.

## The ASCII Code (a practical use of binary)

ASCII, the American Standard Code for Information Interchange, is the standardised code normally used for communication between the computer and the peripheral units. While human speech is relatively sophisticated a computer only understands machine language, i.e. zeros and ones. ASCII serves as a translation between man and machine (and vice versa).

If we strike the A key on the keyboard, the internal circuitry of the keyboard effects a transformation, according to the ASCII rules, into machine language: 1000001. Striking the M key gives binary 1001101.

And in the other direction, if the terminal printer is to print for example the digit 8, the computer has to feed it with the binary code 0111000.

The letter combinations in the table are machine instructions which are not printed out.

**TABLE A-1.** ASCII Code

| $b_7$ $b_6$ $b_5$ → | | | | | 0 0 0 | 0 0 1 | 0 1 0 | 0 1 1 | 1 0 0 | 1 0 1 | 1 1 0 | 1 1 1 |
|---|---|---|---|---|---|---|---|---|---|---|---|---|
| bits | $b_4$ ↓ | $b_3$ ↓ | $b_2$ ↓ | $b_1$ ↓ | column → row ↓ | 0 | 1 | 2 | 3 | 4 | 5 | 6 | 7 |
| | 0 | 0 | 0 | 0 | 0 | NUL | DLE | SP | 0 | @ | P | ` | p |
| | 0 | 0 | 0 | 1 | 1 | SOH | DC1 | ! | 1 | A | Q | a | q |
| | 0 | 0 | 1 | 0 | 2 | STX | DC2 | " | 2 | B | R | b | r |
| | 0 | 0 | 1 | 1 | 3 | ETX | DC3 | # | 3 | C | S | c | s |
| | 0 | 1 | 0 | 0 | 4 | EOT | DC4 | $ | 4 | D | T | d | t |
| | 0 | 1 | 0 | 1 | 5 | ENQ | NAK | % | 5 | E | U | e | u |
| | 0 | 1 | 1 | 0 | 6 | ACK | SYN | & | 6 | F | V | f | v |
| | 0 | 1 | 1 | 1 | 7 | BEL | ETB | ' | 7 | G | W | g | w |
| | 1 | 0 | 0 | 0 | 8 | BS | CAN | ( | 8 | H | X | h | x |
| | 1 | 0 | 0 | 1 | 9 | HT | EM | ) | 9 | I | Y | i | y |
| | 1 | 0 | 1 | 0 | 10 | LF | SUB | ★ | : | J | Z | j | z |
| | 1 | 0 | 1 | 1 | 11 | VT | ESC | + | ; | K | [ | k | { |
| | 1 | 1 | 0 | 0 | 12 | FF | FS | , | < | L | \ | l | \| |
| | 1 | 1 | 0 | 1 | 13 | CR | GS | — | = | M | ] | m | } |
| | 1 | 1 | 1 | 0 | 14 | SO | RS | . | > | N | ∧ | n | ~ |
| | 1 | 1 | 1 | 1 | 15 | SI | US | / | ? | O | — | o | DEL |

most significant bits (top); least significant bits (left)

NUL  Null
SOH  Start of Heading (CC)
STX  Start of Text (CC)
ETX  End of Text (CC)
EOT  End of Transmission (CC)
ENQ  Enquiry (CC)
ACK  Acknowledge (CC)
BEL  Bell (audible or attention signal)
BS   Backspace (FE)
HT   Horizontal Tabulation (punched card skip) (FE)
LF   Line Feed (FE)
VT   Vertical Tabulation (FE)
FF   Form Feed (FE)
CR   Carriage Return (FE)
SO   Shift Out
SI   Shift In

DLE  Data Link Escape (CC)
DC1  Device Control 1
DC2  Device Control 2
DC3  Device Control 3
DC4  Device Control 4 (Stop)
NAK  Negative Acknowledge (CC)
SYN  Synchronous Idle (CC)
ETB  End of Transmission Block (CC)
CAN  Cancel
EM   End of Medium
SUB  Substitute
ESC  Escape
FS   File Separator (IS)
GS   Group Separator (IS)
RS   Record Separator (IS)
US   Unit Separator (IS)
DEL  Delete

CC: Communication control
FE: Format effector
IS: Information separator

# APPENDIX B

## Interface standards

### IEEE 696 (S-100)

The original interface called the S-100 bus was proposed by the makers of the Altair computer. It was rapidly adopted by other manufacturers — but most introduced their own variations. A few years ago the Institute of Electronic and Electrical Engineers (IEEE) in the United States started work on a definitive standard for the bus. This expanded the original idea, and provided pin allocations so that the new generation of 16-bit microprocessors would run on it. The IEEE standard allows up to 16 16-bit processors to run simultaneously — and consequently has a good interrupt handling capability. Figure B1 shows the pin allocations, with brief descriptions of each pin usage.

Fig B.1
IEEE-696 bus pin list

| PIN NO. | SIGNAL & TYPE | ACTIVE LEVEL | DESCRIPTION |
|---|---|---|---|
| 1 | +8 VOLTS (B) | | Instantaneous minimum greater than 7 volts, instantaneous maximum less than 25 volts, average maximum less than 11 volts. |
| 2 | +16 VOLTS (B) | | Instantaneous minimum greater than 14.5 volts, instantaneous maximum less than 35 volts, average maximum less than 21.5 volts. |
| 3 | XRDY (B) | H | One of two ready inputs to the current bus master. The bus is ready when both these ready inputs are true. See pin 72. Vectored interrupt line 0. |
| 4 | VI0*(S) | L | Vectored interrupt line 0. |
| 5 | VI1*(S) | L | Vectored interrupt line 1. |
| 6 | VI2*(S) | L | Vectored interrupt line 2. |
| 7 | VI3*(S) | L | Vectored interrupt line 3. |
| 8 | VI4*(S) | L | Vectored interrupt line 4. |
| 9 | VI5*(S) | L | Vectored interrupt line 5. |
| 10 | VI6*(S) | L | Vectored interrupt line 6. |

| PIN NO. | SIGNAL & TYPE | ACTIVE LEVEL | DESCRIPTION |
| --- | --- | --- | --- |
| 11 | VI7*(S) | L | Vectored interrupt line 7. |
| 12 | MNI*(S) | L | Non-maskable interrupt. |
| 13 | PWRFAIL*(B) | L | Power fail bus signal. |
| 14 | DMA3*(M) | L | Temporary master priority bit 3. |
| 15 | A18 (M) | H | Extended address bit 18. |
| 16 | A16 (M) | H | Extended address bit 16. |
| 17 | A17 (M) | H | Extended address bit 17. |
| 18 | SDSB*(M) | L | The control signal to disable the 8 status signals. |
| 19 | CDSB*(M) | L | The control signal to disable the 5 control output signals. |
| 20 | GND (B) | | Common with pin 100. |
| 21 | NDEF | | Not to be defined. Manufacturer must specify any use in detail. |
| 22 | ADSB*(M) | L | The control signal to disable the 16 address signals. |
| 23 | DODSB*(M) | L | The control signal to disable the 8 data output signals. |
| 24 | o (B) | H | The master timing signal for the bus. |
| 25 | pSTVAL*(M) | L | Status valid strobe. |
| 26 | pHLDA (M) | H | A control signal used in conjunction with HOLD* to co-ordinate bus master transfer operations. |
| 27 | RFU | | Reserved for future use. |
| 28 | RFU | | Reserved for future use. |
| 29 | A5 (M) | H | Address bit 5. |
| 30 | A4 (M) | H | Address bit 4. |
| 31 | A3 (M) | H | Address bit 3. |
| 32 | A15 (M) | H | Address bit 15 (most significant for non-extended addressing.) |
| 33 | A12 (M) | H | Address bit 12. |
| 34 | A9 (M) | H | Address bit 9. |
| 35 | DO1(M)/DATA1(M/S) | H | Data out bit 1, bidirectional data bit 1. |
| 36 | DO0(M)/DATA0(M/S) | H | Data out bit 0, bidirectional data bit 0. |
| 37 | A10 (M) | H | Address bit 10. |
| 38 | DO4(M)/DATA4(M/S) | H | Data out bit 4, bidirectional data bit 4. |
| 39 | DO5(M)/DATA5(M/S) | H | Data out bit 5, bidirectional data bit 5. |
| 40 | DO6(M)/DATA6(M/S) | H | Data out bit 6, bidirectional data bit 6. |
| 41 | D12(S)/DATA10(M/S) | H | Data out bit 2, bidirectional data bit 10. |
| 42 | D13(S)/DATA11(M/S) | H | Data out bit 3, bidirectional data bit 11. |
| 43 | D17(S)/DATA15(M/S) | H | Data out bit 7, bidirectional data bit 15. |
| 44 | sM1 (M) | H | The status signal which indicates that the current cycle is an op-code fetch. |
| 45 | sOUT (M) | H | The status signal identifying the data transfer bus cycle to an output device. |
| 46 | sINP (M) | H | The status signal identifying the data transfer bus cycle from an input device. |
| 47 | sMEMR (M) | H | The status signal identifying bus cycles which transfer data from memory to a bus master, which are not interrupted acknowlede instruction fetch cycle(s). |
| 48 | sHLTA (M) | H | The status signal which acknowledges that a HLT instruction has been executed. |
| 49 | CLOCK (B) | | 2 MHz (0.5%) 40-60% duty cycle. Not required to be synchronous with any other bus signal. |
| 50 | GND (B) | | Common with pin 100. |
| 51 | + 8VOLTS (B) | | Common with pin 1. |
| 52 | −16VOLTS (B) | | Instantaneous maximum less than −14.5 volts, instantaneous minimum greater than −35 volts, average minimum greater than −21.5 volts. |
| 53 | GND (B) | | Common with pin 100. |
| 54 | SLAVE CLR*(B) | L | A reset signal to reset bus slaves. Must be active with POC* and may also be generated by external means. |
| 55 | DMA0*(M) | L | Temporary master priority bit 0. |
| 56 | DMA1*(M) | L | Temporary master prioirity bit 1. |
| 57 | DMA2*(M) | L | Temporary master priority bit 2. |
| 58 | sXTRQ*(M) | L | The status which requests 16-bit slaves to asset SIXTN*. |
| 59 | A19 (M) | H | Extended address bit 19. |
| 60 | SIXTN*(S) | L | The signal generated by 16-bit slaves in response to the 16-bit request signal sXTRQ*. |
| 61 | A20 (M) | H | Extended address bit 20. |
| 62 | A21 (M) | H | Extended address bit 21. |
| 63 | A22 (M) | H | Extended address bit 22. |
| 64 | A23 (M) | H | Extended address bit 23. |
| 65 | NDEF | | Not to be defined signal. |
| 66 | NDEF | | Not to be defined signal. |
| 67 | PHANTOM*(M/S) | L | A bus signal which disables slave devices and enables phantom slaves—primarily used for bootstrapping systems without hardwrae front panels. |
| 68 | MWRT (B) | H | pWR*—sOUT (logic equation). This signal must follow WR* by not more than 30 ns. |

| PIN NO. | SIGNAL & TYPE | ACTIVE LEVEL | DESCRIPTION |
|---|---|---|---|
| 69 | RFU | | Reserved for future use. |
| 70 | GND (B) | | Common with pin 100. |
| 71 | RFU | | Reserved for future use. |
| 72 | RDY (S) | H | See comments for pin 3. |
| 73 | INT*(S) | L | The primary interrupt request bus signal. |
| 74 | HOLD*(M) | L | The control signal used in conjunction with pHLDA to co-ordinate bus master transfer operations. |
| 75 | RESET*(B) | L | The reset signal to reset bus master devices. This signal must be active with POC* and may also be generated by external means. |
| 76 | pSYNC (M) | H | The control signal identifying BS1. |
| 77 | pWR*(M) | L | The control signal signifying the presence of valid data on DO bus or data bus. |
| 78 | pDBIN (M) | H | The control signal that requests data on the DI bus or data bus from the currently addressed slave. |
| 79 | A0 (M) | H | Address bit 0 (least significant). |
| 80 | A1 (M) | H | Address bit 1. |
| 81 | A2 (M) | H | Address bit 2. |
| 82 | A6 (M) | H | Address bit 6. |
| 83 | A7 (M) | H | Address bit 7. |
| 84 | A8 (M) | H | Address bit 8. |
| 85 | A13 (M) | H | Address bit 13. |
| 86 | A14 (M) | H | Address bit 14. |
| 87 | A11 (M) | H | Address bit 11. |
| 88 | D02(M)/DATA2(M/S) | H | Data out bit 2, bidirectional data bit 2. |
| 89 | D03(M)/DATA3(M/S) | H | Data out bit 3, bidirectional data bit 3. |
| 90 | D07(M)/DATA7(M/S) | H | Data out bit 7, bidirectional data bit 7. |
| 91 | D14(S)/DATA12(M/S) | H | Data out bit 4 and bidirectional data bit 12. |
| 92 | D15(S)/DATA13(M/S) | H | Data out bit 5 and bidirectional data bit 13. |
| 93 | D16(S)/DATA14(M/S) | H | Data out bit 6 and bidirectional data bit 14. |
| 94 | D11(S)/DATA9(M/S) | H | Data out bit 1 and bidirectional data bit 9. |
| 95 | D10(S)/DATA8(M/S) | H | Data out bit 0 (least significant for 8-bit data) and bidirectional data bit 8. |
| 96 | sINTA (M) | H | The status signal identifying the bus input cycle(s) that may follow an accepted interrupt request presented on INT* |
| 97 | sWO*(M) | L | The status signal identifying a bus cycle which transfers data from a bus master to a slave. |
| 98 | ERROR*(S) | L | The bus status signal signifying an error condition during present bus cycle. |
| 99 | POC*(B) | L | The power-on clear signal for all bus devices; when this signal goes low, it must stay low for a least 10 msecs. |
| 100 | GND (B) | | System ground. |

(B) = Bus signals

(S) = Slave signals

(M) = Master signals

Preliminary—Subject to Revision

When looking at S-100 bus based equipment it is essential that **all** the boards follow the pin allocation at least! The standard also defines the minimum and maximum time for signals on the bus, and their interrelationship with one another. These are not considered here — but it is reasonable to assume that those manufacturers who use the correct pin allocations and claim to support the bus, do so properly. It is worth checking this with the retailer.

## RS232C

The RS232C standard was specified by the Electronics Industry Association (EIA) and defines both the electrical and physical specifications for bit-serial transmission. It also defines the handshaking signals used to control standard telephone connection equipment and standard modems (modulator-demodulator).

The main signal lines are transmit data and receive data. With ground these are the three wires necessary to configure any system. The bit rate is defined in bauds, or bits/second. The standard rates are:

50, 75, 110, 150, 300, 600, 1200, 2400, 4800, 9600, and 19,200.

Teletypes usually use 110, 150, or 300 baud, whereas video display units use 600 or 1200, in small systems.

The voltage on the lines varies between plus and minus 12 v, although the voltage can go down as low as 3 v and still work reasonably well. A 25-pin connector is used, and the connections are shown in Figure B2. Only the primary fifteen connections are shown, the other ten being used for data and control paths for a second serial channel running at much lower speed. Although the second channel is hardly ever used, it is useful for providing the information for the modems connected at each end of the communication link.

Fig B2.

| Pin Number | RS232C name | Description |
| --- | --- | --- |
| 1 | AA | Protective ground |
| 2 | BA | Data transmitted from terminal |
| 3 | BB | Data received from modem |
| 4 | CA | Request to send |
| 5 | CB | Clear to send |
| 6 | CC | Data set ready |
| 7 | AB | Signal ground |
| 8 | CF | Carrier detector |
| 9 | | |
| 10 | | unassigned |
| 11 | | |

| | | |
|---|---|---|
| 12 | SCF | Secondary received line signal detect |
| 13 | SCB | Secondary clear to send |
| 14 | SBA | Secondary transmitted data |
| 15 | DB | Tx. timing (from modem) |
| 16 | SBB | Secondary received data |
| 17 | DD | Rx. timing (from modem) |
| 18 | | unassigned |
| 19 | SCA | Secondary request to send |
| 20 | CD | Data terminal ready |
| 21 | CG | Signal quality detector |
| 22 | CE | Ring detector |
| 23 | CH/CI | Data rate selector |
| 24 | DA | Tx. timing (from terminal) |
| 25 | | unassigned |

When used with modems on domestic telephone links the lines designated "request-to-send", "clera-to-send", "data-terminal-ready" are used to control the modem link.

Sometimes manufacturers specify a V24 interface instead of RS232C. This is essentially the same, the only differences being in the pulse shape. Another standard is the 20 mA current loop. This again is a serial transmission standard, but the voltage range can be up to $\pm$ 80 v. In this case the current passing through the circuit is held constant at 20 mA.

## IEEE-488

The IEEE-488, or general purpose, interface bus — GPIB — was developed some eight years ago around a standard proposed by Hewlett-Packard in the United States. There are now around 1000 products using the bus — mostly in instrumentation. A typical system consists of a controller (e.g. the PET) and up to 14 devices (e.g. printers, recorders, etc.). Each peripheral device is designated a "listener" or a "talker". Listeners are usually printers, x-y plotters etc., whereas talkers are counters or meters. It is possible to have devices that are both listeners and talkers and the PET floppy disk is an ideal example. It is very important that the peripheral used is identified as a listener, talker or both and the GPIB is very specific in identifying whether the message is for an interface unit or an actual device. The ATN line allows the PET to set up all the relevant devices into their listen or talk modes by addressing specific devices one after the other, and using the status control lines before releasing the devices to begin the operating cycle using the full 8-bit data bus.

The 16 signal lines in the passive interconnecting GPIB cable are grouped into three sets, according to their function — Figure B3. Eight DATA lines carry coded messages in bit-parallel, byte-serial form to and from devices with each byte being transferred from one TALKER to one or more listeners. Data flow is bi-directional in that the same lines are used both to input program data and to output measurement data from an individual device. Data is exchanged asynchronously, enabling compatibility among a wide variety of devices. All interface messages (to set up, maintain, and terminate an orderly flow of device-dependent messages) are 7-bit coded. Device-dependent messages may be from 1 to 8 bits; however, the codes containing printable characters of the ASCII (American Standard Code for Information Interchange) code set are most commonly used and messages containing numbers are typically presented in scientific notation (FORTRAN-type) format.

Three DATA BYTE TRANSFER CONTROL (handshake) lines are used to effect the transfer of each byte of coded data oon the eight DATA lines.

The five remaining GENERAL INTERFACE MANAGEMENT lines ensure an orderly flow of information within the GPIB system. One of these is called the "attention" line.

Several listeners can be active simultaneously, but only one talker can be active at a time. Whenever a talk address is put on the data lines (while attention is low), all other talkers are automatically unaddressed.

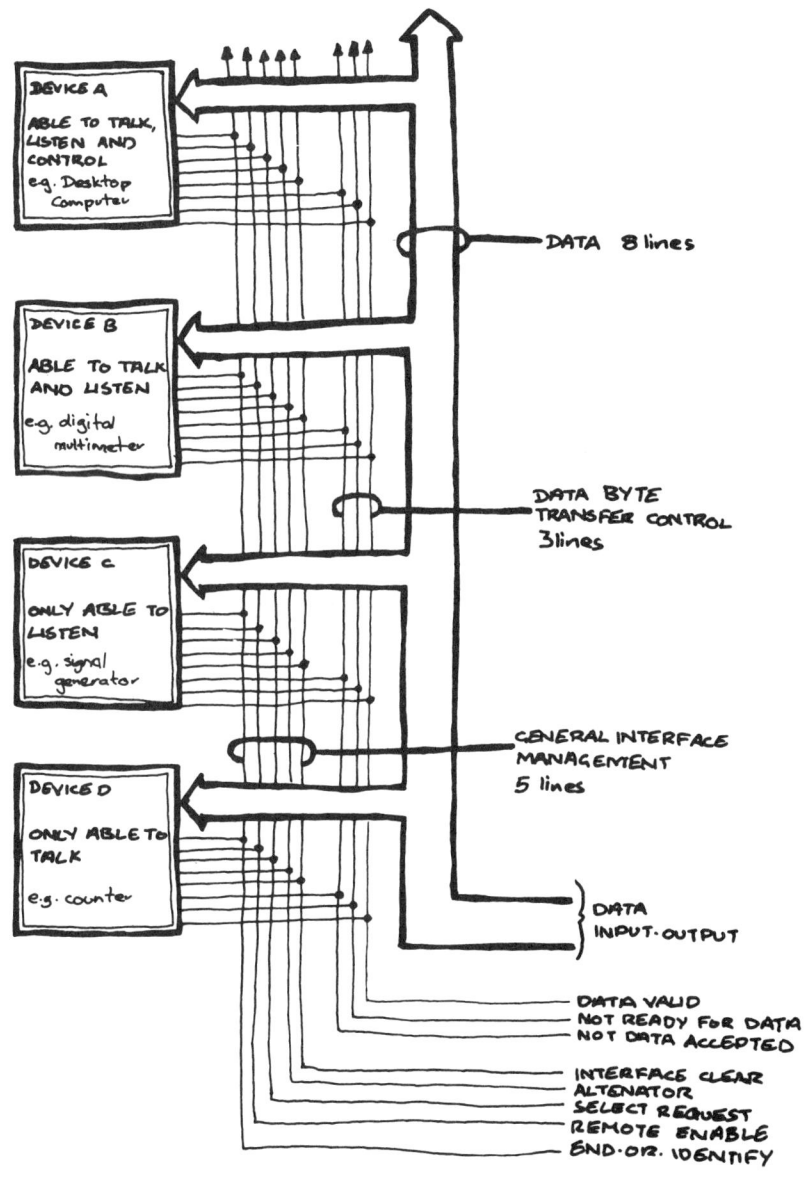

FIG B3. INTERFACE CONNECTIONS AND BUS STRUCTURES

## The Centronics Parallel Interface

The majority of parallel printer interfaces adopt the Centronics standard for data exchange.

The interface is implemented on a 36 pin connector – the pin assignment is as shown in Figure B.4.

The data is transferred via lines 2-9 while signals at pins 1, 10 and 11 control the interchange of data.

To transfer the eight bit byte from source to destination (nominally from computer to printer) the data is first placed on lines 2-9. Line 1 (data strobe) is then taken low to signal that the data is ready. When the printer has received the data it will pull line 10, acknowledge, low.

These 10 signal lines (eight data and two control) are all that are needed for a basic parallel interface.

Of the other lines, the most significant is probably the busy, pin 11, signal. Often printers will not output characters until a full line has been received (a carriage return of line feed signal is detected). The printer then becomes 'busy' and some software will detect this condition and cause a computer to perform other tasks during the time that the printer is 'tied up'.

The function lines 12 and 13 are fairly self-explanatory.

For the most reliable data transfer, the connecting cable used should be of a twisted pair type – even so cable lengths should be limitedd to about two metres.

| PIN | SIGNAL | PIN | SIGNAL | PIN | SIGNAL |
|---|---|---|---|---|---|
| 1 | DATA STROBE | 13 | PRINT ENABLE and NOT OUT OF PAPER | 25 | — |
| 2 | DATA BIT 1 | | | 26 | — |
| 3 | DATA BIT 2 | 14 | GROUND | 27 | — |
| 4 | DATA BIT 3 | 15 | — | 28 | — |
| 5 | DATA BIT 4 | 16 | GROUND | 29 | — |
| 6 | DATA BIT 5 | 17 | CHASSIS GROUND | 30 | — |
| 7 | DATA BIT 6 | 18 | +5V | 31 | — |
| 8 | DATA BIT 7 | 19 | — | 32 | — |
| 9 | DATA BIT 8 | 20 | — | 33 | GROUND |
| 10 | ACKNOWLEDGE | 21 | — | 34 | — |
| 11 | BUSY | 22 | — | 35 | — |
| 12 | PAPER OUT or PRINT OFF | 23 | — | 36 | — |
| | | 24 | TWISTED PAIR GROUND | | |

Fig B.4

# APPENDIX C

## Manufacturers/Distributors

**Acorn**
ACORN COMPUTERS LTD
4a Market Hill, Cambridge CB2 3N1
COMPUTER SYSTEMS: Atom, BBC A and B, Electron

**Apple**
APPLE COMPUTER INC
10260 Blandley Da Cupertino, Cal 95014, USA
*Dist:* APPLE COMP. (UK),
Finlay Road, Hemel Hempstead, Herts HP2 7PS
COMPUTER SYSTEMS: Apple II/IIe

**Atari**
ATARI CONSUMER DIVISION
1265 Borregas Ave, PO Box 427,
Sunnyvale, Cal 94086, USA
*Dist:* ATARI INTERNATIONAL (UK),
185 Ealing Road, Alperton, Middlesex
COMPUTER SYSTEMS: Atari 400, 800, 600XL, 800XL

**Camputers**
CAMPUTERS
33a Bridge Street, Cambridge CB2 1UW
COMPUTER SYSTEMS: Camputers Lynx

**Commodore**
COMMODORE BUSINESS MACHINES
675 Ajax Ave, Slough, Berks
COMPUTER SYSTEMS: CBM/PET, VIC20, 710, VIC64

**Dai**
DATA APPLICATIONS INTERNATIONAL
16B Dyer Street, Cirencester, Glos GL7 2PF
COMPUTER SYSTEMS: DAI PC-1

**Dragon**
DRAGON DATA
Queensway, Swansea Industrial Estate,
Swansea SA5 4EH
COMPUTER SYSTEMS: Dragon 32

**Eaca**
EACA INTERNATIONAL LTD
8-11 Fls. 13 Chong Yip St, Kwun Tong,
Kowloon, Hong Kong
*Dist:* LOWE ELECTRONICS
Chesterfield Rd, Matlock, Derby DE4 3HE
COMPUTER SYSTEMS: Genie I, II, Colour Genie

**Elan Computers Ltd**
31-37 Hoxton St, London N1 6NJ.
COMPUTER SYSTEMS: Elan Enterprise 64

**Epson**
EPSON UK
Dorland House, 388 High Road, Wembley,
Middlesex HA9 6UH
COMPUTER SYSTEMS: HX20

**Grundy**
GRUNDY BUSINESS SYSTEMS LTD
Somerset Rd, Teddington, Middlesex TW11 8TD
COMPUTER SYSTEMS: Newbrain

**Hewlett-Packard**
HEWLETT PACKARD LTD
Nine Mile Ride, East Hampstead, Wokingham,
Berks RG11 3LL
COMPUTER SYSTEMS: HP 85/85, 75C

**Jupiter**
JUPITER CANTAB
Cheshunt Bldg, Bateman Street, Cambridge CB2 1LZ
COMPUTER SYSTEMS: Jupiter Ace

**Lucas**
LUCAS LOGIC LTD
Welton Rd, Wedgnock Industrial Estate,
Warwick CV34 5PZ
COMPUTER SYSTEMS: Nascom 1, 2, 3

**MicroDecision**
MORROW DESIGNS
5221 Central Ave, Richmond, CA 94804, USA
*Dist:* INTERAM COMPUTER SYSTEMS
46 Balham High Road, London kSW12 9AQ
COMPUTER SYSTEMS: MicroDecision

**Multitech**
*Dist:* SIRTEL UK LTD
Fengate, Peterborough PE1 5XB
COMPUTER SYSTEMS: Multitech MPF II

**NEC**
NEC CORPORATION
NEC Building, 33-1 Shiba 5-chome, Minato-ku, Tokyo 108, Japan
*Dist:* NEC House, 164/166 Drummond St, London NW1 3HP.
COMPUTER SYSTEM: PC 8000

**Oric**
ORIC PRODUCTS INTERNATIONAL
Coworth Park, London Rd, Ascot, Berks SL5 7SE
COMPUTER SYSTEMS: Oric 1

**Osborne**
OSBORNE COMPUTER CORP
2650 Corporate Ave, Hayward, CA 94545, USA
*Dist:* OSBORNE (UK)
38 Tanners Drive, Blakelands North, Milton Keynes, Bucks MK14 5LL
COMPUTER SYSTEMS: Osborne I, Executive

**Positron**
POSITRON COMP. LTD
Unit 16, Deacon Trading Estate, Newton-le-Willows, Lancashire
COMPUTER SYSTEMS: Positron 900

**Powertran**
POWERTRAN INTERNATIONAL
Hollom Down Farm, Lopcombe, Salisbury, Wilts SP5 1BP
COMPUTER SYSTEM: Cortex

**Research Machines**
RESEARCH MACHINES LTD
209 Cowley Road, Oxford
COMPUTER SYSTEMS: LINK 480Z

**Rockwell**
ROCKWELL INTERNATIONAL
Microelectronic Devices, PO Box 3699, Anaheim, Ca 92803, USA
*Dist:* PELCO (ELECTRONICS) LTD
Regency Square House, 26-27 Regency Square, Brighton, Sussex BN1 2FH
DATATEXT
Namyth Rd, Southfield Ind. Estate, Glenrothes, Fife KY6 2SD
COMPUTER SYSTEMS: AIM 65

**Sanyo**
MARUBENI (UK) LTD
8 Greycaine Rd, Greycaine Estate, Watford WD2 4UQ
COMPUTER SYSTEMS: MBC 1000

**Sinclair**
SINCLAIR RESEARCH LTD
25 Willis Road, Cambridge, CB1 2AQ
COMPUTER SYSTEMS: ZX81, Spectrum

**Sharp**
SHARP CORPORATION
Osaka, Japan
*Dist:* SHARP ELECTRONICS (UK) LTD
107 Hulme Hall Lane, Manchester M10 8HL
COMPUTER SYSTEM: Sharp MZ80K/B

**Shelton**
SHELTON INSTRUMENTS LTD
74/77 White Lion Street, London N1 0JD
COMPUTER SYSTEMS: Sig-Net 10025

**Sord**
SORD COMPUTER SYSTEMS INC
Isoma No 2 Bld 42-12 Nishi Shunizoiwa, 4-chrome, Katsushika-ku, Tokyo, Japan 124
*Dist:* SORD (UK) LTD
Samuel House, 6 St Albans Street, Haymarket, London SW1Y 4SQ
COMPUTER SYSTEMS: M5

**Tandy**
TANDY CORP
Fort Worth, Texas 76102, USA
*Dist:* TANDY CORP (UK)
Bilston Road, Wednesbury, West Midlands WS10 7IN
COMPUTER SYSTEM: TRS 80/I, 80/II, Color

**Tangerine**
TANGERINE COMPUTER SYSTEMS LTD
Forehill, Ely, Cambs.
COMPUTER SYSTEMS: Microtan 65

**TI**
TEXAS INSTRUMENTS LTD
Monton Lane, Bedford
COMPUTER SYSTEMS: TI 99/4A, CC-40

# APPENDIX D

## Clubs and User Groups in the UK

The ACC has compiled an up to date list of all Clubs and User Groups in the UK. I have added a few extra that I've come across. The list is in alphabetical order of county, for locally based Clubs, and micro type for User Groups.

The ACC is the national coordinating body for all clubs and groups in the UK and if you want to start one, or find your club not on this list (August 1983) then contact:

Derek Fordred,
ACC,
72 Mill Road,
Hawley,
Dartford,
Kent

or send it to Personal Computer World, who act as coordinators on ACC's behalf. The list is ACC copyright by the way.

# APPENDIX D

# COMPUTER CLUBS

i) LOCAL CLUBS – ENGLAND

---

Avon

---

NAILSEA MULTI-USER CLUB
Valerie Boyde-Shaw

0272 851337

£7.50 per annum

BERKELEY NUCLEAR LABORATORIES (C.E.G.B.)
Neil Walker,
53 Wolfridge Ride,
Alveston,
Bristol BS12 2PR

0454 414262

BRUNEL COMPUTER CLUB
Mr R. Sampson,
4 The Coots,
Stockwood

Meets alternate Wednesdays 1900-2200. At St. Werburgh Community Centre.

BRUNEL TECHNICAL COLLEGE COMPUTING CLUB
S.W. Rabone,
18 Castle Road,
Worle,
Weston-Super-Mare,
Avon BS22 GJW

0934 513068

Meets alternate Mondays 1900-2230. At Woodsprings Inn Function Rooms.

The club is divided into two sections skilled & unskilled, share alternate Wednesdays.

BRISTOL COMPUTING CLUB
Leo Wallis,
6 Kilbernie Road,
Bridge Farm Estate,
Bristol BS14 0HY

0272 832453

£4.00 per annum
Meetings 3rd Wednesday monthly

---

Bedfordshire

---

BEDFORD AMATEUR COMPUTER CLUB
R. Bird,
7a High Street,
Great Barford,
Bedford MK44 3LB

(0234) 870763

Meets at Bedford Star Rowing Club at 8pm on 1st & 3rd Tuesday of every month. Talks, discussions, or visits on 1st Tuesday. 3rd Tuesday is an informal meeting. Subs are £3.00, reductions for students.

CHILTERN HOME COMPUTER CLUB
Stephen Betts,
42 Walace Drive,
Eaton Bray,
Beds LU6 2DF

0525 220922

LUTON COMPUTER CLUB
J.P. Fletcher
1, Trowbridge Gardens,
Luton,
Beds. LU2 7JY.

MILTON KEYNES MICROCOMPUTER USER'S GROUP (MKMUG)
Brian Pain

0908 564271

Meetings every Tuesday 7.30 pm. Sir Frank Markham School, Woughton Centre, Cnaffron Way, Milton Keynes.

---

Berkshire

---

SOUTH OXFORD COMPUTER CLUB
Mike Magnay,
'Ganymede',
Wantage Road,
Rowstock,
Didcot,
Oxon OX11 OJU
0235 834402

Covers Wantage, Abingdon, Didcot, Wallingford, and Newbury. Meets 1st Tuesday monthly at the Star, East Ilsley. Contacts: Malcolm – (0235) 816949 Paul (0235) 815305 Rockey – (0635) 34456

THAMES VALLEY AMATEUR COMPUTER CLUB
Brian Quarm,
25 Roundway,
Camberley,
Surrey GU15 1NR

Staines 51388 Ext. 253 (day), Camberley 22186 (home).

Meetings held on 1st Tuesday of month at the Griffon, Caversham.

---

Buckinghamshire

---

AYLESBURY COMPUTER CLUB
Ken Knight,
22 Mount Street,
Aylesbury
Bucks HP20 2SE
0296 5181

£5.00. 60 members, meets weekly on Fridays at 7.30 pm. Quarrendon Y.C. meets on 2nd Wednesdays monthly at A. Coll F.E. Montly Newsletter, Basic programming, Machine code, Hardware. ZX, and BBC Machines.

CHILTERN MICROCOMPUTER CLUB
Mr. W. Tibbitts,
Ellwood,
Deanway,
Chalfont St. Giles,
Bucks

Meets 1st Wednesday of each month at The Garden Centre, School Lane, Chalfont St. Giles.

Mr. Hearne, The Paddocks, Back Lane, Chalfont St. Giles.

---

*Denotes that club is a member of the Association of London Computer Clubs

IVER COMPUTER CLUB
John Haigh,
141 Leas Drive,
Iver,
Bucks

Meets bi-montly on 2nd & 4th Thursdays. First time on May 12th at 7.30 pm in the Huntsmoor Room in Iver Village Hall.

## Cambridgeshire

CAMBRIDGE MICROCOMPUTER CLUB
Derek Tripp,
3 Spurgeons Avenue,
Waterbeach,
Cambridge CB5 9HN

Cambridge 861804

Meets 3rd Wednesday monthly at Portland Arms, Cambridge. 0223 860084 (home).

PETERBOROUGH PERSONAL COMPUTER CLUB
Andrew Pike,
920 Bourges Boulevard,
Peterborough PE1 2AN

(0733) 44342 (after 5 pm).

£5 pa subscription. Meets fortnightly on Monday evenings at Crosfield Electronics Social Club.

## Cheshire

ALSAGER COMPUTER CLUB
Mr. M. Smith,
4 Mill Hill Drive,
Sandbach,
Chesire

Sandbach 2929

Meets fortnightly on Tuesday at 7.30 pm at Alsager Public Library. Meetings alternately formal and informal.

ALTRINGHAM COMPUTER ENTHUSIASTS
Martin Hickling,
39, Barrington Road,
Altringham,
Cheshire WA14 1HZ

061 941 4547

Meets fortnightly, N. Cestrian Grammar School, Dunham Road.

CREWE COMPUTER USERS CLUB
Bram Knight
Nantwich 623375

Meets 3rd Thursday of each month at 8 pm, The Oakley Centre, West Street, Crewe.

HOLMES CHAPEL MICRO CLUB
Margaret Baker,
1 Helton Close,
Holmes Chapel,
Crewe,
Cheshire

0477 34238

Meets 1st and 3rd Tuesday at Red Lion Hotel, Holmes Chapel.

ICI MICRO USERS CLUB
Keith Heron,
32, Norfolk Road,
Congleton,
Cheshire

932 5499

Fortnightly meetings free to ICI personnel.

KINDER PEEK COMPUTER CLUB
Mr. G.M. Flanagan,
11 Sundown Close,
New Mills,
Stockport,
Cheshire SK12 3DH

New Mills 44051

Meetings at New Mills School every other Monday. Regular newsletter with for sale/wanted section. Acorn, Sinclair, Commodore, Z80 sub-groups. Other contact John Eary 36 Parkway, New Mills SK12 4DU (New Mills 43870). Membership £2 per quarter (£1 for juniors under 11 years).

MCC (MID-CHESHIRE COMPUTER CLUB)
Dave Clare,
Winsford 51374.

Meets 2nd Friday of the month, in Winsford main Library at 7.30 pm.

NORTHWEST COMPUTER CLUB
John Lightfoot,
13 Ashton Drive,
Frodsham,
Warrington,
Cheshire WA6 7PU

0728 31519

Fortnightly meetings.

25p attendance fee, no subs.

## Cleveland

CLEVELAND MICRO COMPUTER USERS GROUP
J. Telford,
13 Weston Crescent,
Norton,
Cleveland

£2.00 for under-18's on 2nd Tuesday of month. £3.00 for 18-21's. £5.00 for over-21's on 3rd Tuesday. Newsletter.

DARLINGTON COMPUTER CLUB
L. Boxell,
8 Vane Terrace,
Darlington DL3 7AT

0325 67766

STOCKTON AMATEUR COMPUTER CLUB
60 Croft Road,
Eaglescliffe,
Stockton-on-Tees,
Cleveland TS16 0DY

0642 784819

Meet each Monday at 7.00 pm at Stockton YMCA. Subs 30p per week.

## Cornwall

**CORNWALL AREA COMPUTER CLUB**
M.F. Grove,
35 Causeway Head,
Penzance,
Cornwall

**ST. AUSTELL COMPUTER CLUB AND COMPUTER TOWN**
N.G. Day,
2, Glendale Cl.,
St. Austell,
Cornwall PL25 3DD

Contact N.G. Day for latest details. CTUK proposed for youngsters.

## Derbyshire

**GLOSSOP COMPUTER CLUB**
John Dearn,
2 Spinney Close,
Glossop,
Derbyshire

**DERBY MICROCOMPUTER SOCIETY**
Mike Riordan,
172 Blagreaves Road,
Littleover,
Derby

0332 769440

Meets fortnightly at Church Hall, Shepherd St. Littleover.

## Devon

**EXETER & DISTRICT AMATEUR COMPUTER CLUB**
Doug Bates,
2 Station Road,
Pinhoe,
Exeter EX1 3SA

General meetings 2nd Tuesday monthly. Specialist meetings 3rd or 4th Tuesdays monthly.

Adults £7.50 per annum.

**ITT CLUB**
J.D. Parker,
41, Gibson Road,
Whiterock,
Paignton,
Devon TQ4 7AQ

Churston 843964

**PLYMOUTH & DISTRICT AMATEUR COMPUTER CLUB**
Stuart Bell
31 Victoria Place,
Plymouth,
Devon PL2 1BY

0752 559192

Subscription £5.00 per annum. Meetings:
1st Wednesday in month – Beginners.
2nd Wednesday in month – Software.
3rd Wednesday in month – Beginners.
4th Wednesday in month – Club and speaker.

**TOTNES & S. DEVON COMPUTER CLUB**
Frank Watson & Andrew Page,
Dart Inst. Community Studies,
Dart,
Totnes,
Devon TQ9 6JE

0803 862271

## Dorset

**BOURNEMOUTH AREA COMPUTER CLUB**
Peter Hibbs,
54 Runnymede Avenue,
Bournemouth,
Dorset BH11 9SE

Bournemouth 576547

3rd Wednesday monthly at Kinson Community Centre. £5 pa (£2 pa Juniors).

**PURBECK COMPUTER USERS CLUB**
31 North Street,
Wareham,
Dorset BH20 1AD

## Durham

**DURHAM COMPUTER CLUB**
L. Boxall,
8 Vane Terrace,
Darlington

0325 67766

Business and Word Processors at 7.30 on Fridays and Scientific and Recreational on Saturdays at 10 am.

## Essex

**BRENTWOOD AMATEUR COMPUTER CLUB**
R.L. Sadler,
18 Wanescot Road,
Brentwood,
Essex CM15 9HD

Proposed new club.

**CANVEY COMPUTER CLUB**
Dean Williams,
17 Mornington Road,
Canvey Island,
Essex SSB BAT

New Club. Minimum age 14 yrs. Any Machine. Hope to start a newsletter.

**COLCHESTER COMPUTER SOCIETY**
A.H. Potten,
14 Foxmead,
Rivenhall,
Witham,
Essex CM8 3HD

Witham 516335

Meets at Severalls Hospital Social Club, Colchester.

COLCHESTER MICROPROCESSOR GROUP
INFORMATION CENTRE
University of Essex,
Near Colchester

Annual sub £5.00 (full time students) £1.00 2nd and 4th Wednesdays at the University at 7.30 pm.

Membership is open to all just contact the information centre on the eve of meeting.

GENIUS COMPUTER CLUB
30 Webber House,
North Street,
Barking,
Essex

Annual sub £1.00 for ZX81, £1.50 for Spectrum.

NAMEBUG
Nigel Ballard,
27 Crowhurst Road,
Colchester,
Essex

0206 72899

Meets second Thursday of each month in Witham.

ROMFORD CLUB
Mr. D. Norden,
138c, Church Road,
Harow Wood,
Romford,
Essex

SOUTH EAST ESSEX COMPUTER SOCIETY
Robin Knight,
128 Little Wakering Road,
Little Wakering,
Southend-on-Sea,
Essex

0702 218456

Monthly meetings with lectures. Open to members over 14. Hockey Club Hall, Roots Hall, Nr. Southend-on-Sea Football Club Stadium. Wednesdays 7.30 pm. Bar available.

STANWAY SCHOOL COMPUTING CLUB
G. Floyd,
c/o Physics Dept.
Stanway School,
Stanway,
Colchester,
Essex

School pupils only at the moment.

---

East Sussex

---

BRIGHTON, HOVE & DISTRICT COMPUTER CLUB
J. Smith,
30 Leicester Villas,
Hove,
E.Sussex BN3 5SQ

Meets every 2nd Wednesday at the Southwick Community Centre from 7.30 till 10.00. The club has members of all ages with a wide variety of machines and interests.

MICRO ENTHUSIASTS
G.M. Dinnage,
16 Malvern Street,
Hove,
Sussex BN3 3YR

WORTHING & DISTRICT MICROCOMPUTER CLUB
T.M. Pearson,
142, King Edward Avenue,
Worthing
0903 206685

Alternate Sundays 11 am to 1 pm Datex Micros, Tarring Road, Worthing.

---

Gloucestershire

---

CHELTENHAM AMATEUR COMPUTER CLUB
M. Hughes,
36 Riverview Way,
Cheltenham,
Gloucs.

0240 75213

Meetings are held on 3rd Tuesday of every month at 7.30 pm. £3.00 meetings are held at Prestbury Scout H.Q., The Burrage, Prestbury, Cheltenham.

---

Hampshire

---

COMMODORE COMPUTER CLUB (GOSPORT)
Brian Cox,
Bury Houuse,
Bury Road,
Gosport,
Hants

Fareham 280530

First meeting on Friday May 6th at 7.30 pm.

FAREHAM AND PORTSMOUTH AMATEUR COMPUTER CLUB
Alan J. Smith,
c/o 7, Francis Close,
Lee-on-The-Solent,
Gosport,
Hants PO13 8HB

0705 550907

Membership £4.00 pa.

PORTSMOUTH CO-OPERATIVE COMPUTER CLUB
Adrian May,
27 Victoria Road North,
Southsea,
Hants

0705 820339

Meets every Sunday from 7 pm to 10 pm Devonshire Square, Southsea.

Other contacts: Christian Penfold, 52 Owen Road, Eastney, Portsmouth, Hants 0705 827427.

RAF ODIHAM COMPUTER CLUB
c/o Officer I/C,
Royal Air Force,
Odiham,
Nr. Basingstoke,
Hants.

SOUTHAMPTON AMATEUR COMPUTER CLUB
Paul Blitz,
24 Chigwell Solent Close,
Chandlers Ford,
Eastleigh,
Hants

04215 69050

Meets 7.30 pm on 2nd Wednesday each month at Medical Science Building, Bassett Crescent, East Southampton. £5.00 pa. £3.50 students and OAP's.

Newsletter and special interest groups. Several User Groups – Sinclair, TRS80, S100/SIG80. Also Junior/Novice Group meets fortnightly on Saturday mornings.

Herefordshire

HEREFORD AMATEUR COMPUTER CLUB
Stuart Edinborough,
2 Warwick Walk,
Bobblestock,
Hereford HR4 9TG

Home 0432 269700 Work 0594 269700

Proposed new club.

Hertfordshire

HARPENDEN MICROCOMPUTER GROUP
R.S. Welch,
7 Tylers,
Harpenden,
Herts AL5 5RT

05827 3398

Informal meetings are held on alternate Mondays.

Meets at the Silver Cup, Harpenden. Subscription: £2.50 pa.

Humberside

GRIMSBY COMPUTER CLUB
Jensen Lee,
29 Park View,
Cleethorpes

0472 42559 (day)

Meets alternate Mondays at St. James Hall, Grimsby. Membership is £8.00 per year, reductions for schoolchildren, OAP's and Father/son joint membership. Periodical newsletter is published. Family nights, and courses. Further details from above & Ian Fell (Grimsby 49248) after 6 pm.

SCUNTHORPE & DISTRICT MICROPROCESSOR SOCIETY
G. Hinch,
21 Old Crosby,
Scunthorpe,
South Humberside DN15 8PU

0724 61076

N. Lindsey Tech. Coll. and Royal Legion Club.

Kent

CANTERBURY ACC
L.S. Fisher,
21, Manwood Avenue,
St. Stephens,
Canterbury,
Kent CT2 7AH

Cant 65948

Proposed new club.

GRAVESEND COMPUTER CLUB
c/o The Extra Tuition Centre,
39 The Terrace,
Gravesend,
Kent DA12 2BA

0474 50677

Meets 1st and 3rd Tuesday of every month at 7.30 pm in School room Extra Tuition Centre, 39 The Terrace, Gravesend. We have 50 members. Various machines.

MEDWAY AMATEUR COMPUTER & ROBOTICS ORGANISATION
L.G. Mason,
21 The Beeches,
Walderslade,
Chatham,
Kent ME5 0NS

0634 63036 (Mr. P. Cameron)

Meets monthly.

Sub £3.00.

*NORTH KENT AMATEUR COMPUTER CLUB
Kevin Viney,
95 Crofton Road,
Orpington,
Kent BR6 8HU

Orpington 22443

Meetings on 1st Thursday of each month 7.30 to 9.40, at Charles Darwin School, Lecture Theatre, Jail Lane, Biggin Hill, or Biggin Hill Public Library, (main reading room) Church Road, Biggin Hill.

£3.00 for adults (including spouse) and £1.00 for students. Sec. Ian House, 28 Canadian Avenue, Catford, London SE6 3AS

ORPINGTON COMPUTER USER CLUB
R.A. Pyatt,
23 Arundel Drive,
Orpington,
Kent BR6 9JF

Orpington 20281

Meets each Friday at 8 pm in the large hall, Christ Church, Charterhouse Road, Orpington. Free refreshments at 9 pm.

SEVENOAKS SCHOOL COMPUTER CLUB
G. Sommerhoff,
Technical Centre,
Sevenoaks School,
Sevenoaks,
Kent

Sevenoaks 456490

Building Robot arm.

TONBRIDGE AND TUNBRIDGE WELLS ACC
Ray Szatkowski,
1 Cromer Street,
Tonbridge,
Kent

0732 355960

Meets 1st & 3rd Thursday each month. Details from above, and Colin Turner: Tun. Wells 21120 Chris Wallwork: Tun.Wells 37682

Lancashire

BLACKBURN MICRO COMPUTER CLUB
Roger Longworth,
12 Shap Close,
Accrington,
Lancs

BOLTON COMPUTER CLUB
David Atherton,
16 Douglas Street,
Atherton,
Manchester M29 9FB

0942 876210

Meets Thursday Rm E4/E24 Bolton Institute of Higher Ed., Deene Road, Bolton. Subs £1.00 plus 20p per meeting. 70 members. Other contact Ray Munford, Bolton 493682.

BURNLEY COMPUTER CLUB
Clive Tallon,
27 Basnett Street,
Burnley,
Lancs BB10 3EQ

Tel: 0282 25103 (Eves) or 34683

Meets Tuesday 7.30 pm to 11.00 pm Carleton Hotel, Standish Street, 60+ members. General Club includes, ZX81 & Spectrum TRS80 Dragon 32 Apple RML 380Z VIC20 Pet etc.

CHORLEY COMPUTER CLUB
Chris Hicks,
131 Market Street,
Chorley,
Lancashire

025 72 78376

Every other Tuesday, 8 pm Townley Arms, Chorley.

LANCASTER & MORECAMBE COMPUTER CLUB
Sarah Blackler,
17 Belle Vue Terrace,
Greaves Road,
Lancs

0524 33553

NORTH LANCASHIRE USER GROUP
John Robinson,
12 Harold Avenue,
Blackpool

Also Julian Morgan, Blackpool 47514. Covers Blackpool, The Fylde and Preston.

RIBBLE VALLEY COMPUTER CLUB
Ian Thornton-Bryar,
25 Southfield Drive,
West Bradford,
Clitheroe,
Lancs BB7 4TU

0200 25933

SOUTH CHADDERTON COMPUTER CLUB
Mr. J. Jakeman,
26 Mardle Street,
Dorker,
Oldham,
Lancs

061 6826120

Meets Thursday 7 pm – 9.30 pm, Turf Lane Centre, Turf Lane, Chadderton.

General Club including Apple, Pet, ZX81, Spectrum, Jupiter, Vic, BBC.

---

Leicestershire

---

EAST LEAKE COMPUTER CLUB
Andrew Jones,
59, Bateman Road,
East Leake,
Loughborough,
Leics LE12 6NN

Ring for details.

HAWKER SIDDELEY COMPUTER CLUB
R.W. Wrathall,
6 Naseby Drive,
Loughborough,
LE11 0WU

THE LEICESTER PERSONAL COMPUTER CLUB
Ms Jill Olorenshaw,
c/o Arden Data Processing,
Municipal Buildings,
Charles Street,
Leicester

0533 22255

£2.00 per annum. (£1 for under-16's). Meet 7 pm 2nd Monday of every month. The meetings are held at Leicester University.

Mr. D. Foden, 11 Gaddesby Lane, Rearsby, Leics.

LOUGHBOROUGH AMATEUR MICRO SOCIETY
(L.A.M.S.)
Hosegrove Computer Science Dept.
Loughtborough University

Meetings held at Loughborough University.

---

Lincolnshire

---

LINCOLN COMPUTER CLUB
John Clifford,
448 Newark Road,
Lincoln LN6 8RX

0522 2160

Meets 1st & 3rd Wednesday of each month, Blanding's Public House, High Street, Lincoln.

Part of Lincolnshire Microprocessor Society.

LINCOLNSHIRE MICROPROCESSOR SOCIETY
Eric Booth,
Senior Common Room,
Bishop Grosseteste College,
Newport,
Lincoln

0522 27347

SKEGNESS COMPUTER CLUB
J. Gordon,
66 Drummond,
Skegness

Skegness (0754) 3327

Meets fortnightly at Country Hotel, South Parade. Subs £4.00 per annum.

---

London

---

*BRENT/BARNET USERS GROUP
Joseph Fox,
4 Harman Close,
London NW2 2EA

£3 per annum.

Bi-montly newsletter. No fixed meeting place as yet.

Last SUNDAY in month.

*EAST LONDON AMATEUR COMPUTER CLUB
Fred Linger,
82 The Drive,
Ilford,
Essex IG1 3JA

01-554 3288

Meets 7 - 10 pm on 2nd & 4th Tuesday montly. Harrow Green Library, Leystonstone E11. Beginners welcome. Micromouse, Newsletter. £4.00 per annum.

Peter Wright, 01-529 1663

EAST LONDON COMPUTER CLUB
John Grieve,
North East London Polytechnic

01-553 4761

Meets every Friday at 7.30 pm in term time, North East London Polytechnic, Romford Road Precinct, Stratford E15

*CROYDON MICRO COMPUTER CLUB
Eleanor Cranstoun,
Flat 7,
10 Lancaster Road,
South Norwood,
London SE25 4AQ

01-771 3525

1st & 4th Tuesdays of month from 7 pm. BASIC, Assembler, Robotics groups. Croydon Reference Library, Katherine Street.

Computertown UK in Junior Library, Saturday 9.30 to 12.30. Vernon Gifford, 01-653 3207, 111 Selhurst Road, London SE26 6LH.

IMPERIAL COLLEGE MICROCOMPUTER CLUB
Tim Panton,
c/o I.C. Union Office,
Prince Consort Road,
London SW7 2BB

Every Tuesday, Dept. of Computing Room 145. Level 1. 7.30 pm.

*ITN COMPUTER CLUB
Jim Cartwright,
01-637 2424

Meetings at ITN House, Wells Street, monthly.

Also Peter Grain.

*LAMBETH COMPUTER CLUB
Robert J. Baker,
54 Brixton Road,
London SW9 6BS

LONDON SCHOOL COMPUTER USERS CLUB
Burlington Danes School,
Dane Building,
DuCane Road,
Hammersmith,
London W12 UTY

Newsletter.

*METROPOLITAN POLICE AMATEUR COMPUTING CLUB
S. Farley,
Tel: 01-725 2428

Meets: 1st Thursday of Month at 7 pm. Ring for details.

*NORTH LONDON COMPUTER CLUB
Robin Bradbeer,
Polytechnic of North London,
Holloway Road,
London N7 8DB

01-607 8344

£25.00, £5.00 OAPs, students, unemployed, 250 + members, 4 evenings a week in term. 1 eve/wk vacations. Use of Poly Labs and DEC10. Newsletter. PET, VIC, User Groups. S/ware, commercial/homebrew, women's group, ZX, BBC. General meetings open to all on 4th Wednesday each month. Saturday am Computertown UK.

*PADDINGTON COMPUTER CLUB
Peter Hill,
01-723 5762

First meeting 17th May at 6.00 pm at Paddington College, 25 Paddington Green, London W2

*POST OFFICE HQ MICROCOMPUTER CLUB
Vernon Quaintance,
British Telecom Enterprises,
BP&S/CCS2.2,
Room 315/317,
Cheapside House,
138 Cheapside,
London EC2V 6JH

01-726 4716

Open to Post Office & British Telecom Staff in London. All machines & interests are covered. Membership of over 100. Meetings 2nd Thursday of each month from 12.15 in Room 314S, River Plate House, 12-13 South Place, off Moorgate.

*QUEEN'S CRESCENT COMPUTER CLUB
01-485 4551

Meets every Tuesday 7.30 pm to 9.00 pm at Queens Crescent Library, 165 Queens Crescent, London NW5

*SOUTH EAST LONDON MICROCOMPUTER CLUB
Peter Phillips,
61 Craigerne Road,
London SE3

01-853 5829

80 members. £5.00. Alternate Wednesdays at 7.45 pm. Newsletter. Thames Polytechnic, Greens End, Woolwich.

SOUTHGATE MICROCOMPUTER CLUB
Mr. K. Pretorious,
15 The Vineries,
Resevoir Road,
Oakwood,
London N14 4BH

01-882 2282

Meets alternate Thursday at 7.30 pm to 9.00 pm (term time only) in Room B106, Southgate Technical College. Beginners and Gurus welcome.

THE SOBAT COMPUTER CLUB (LEYTON)
T. Kayani,
Berridge House,
Hillfield Road,
London NW6

01-556 5423 at weekends.

Membership is free. Meetings fortnightly at Leyton, Ilford, or East Ham. Newsletter. Anyone is welcome (including beginners). Building up a software library. Specialised information, access to several micros. Most of club members are Atom/BBC users.

*WANDSWORTH COMPUTER CLUB
Howard Cooke,
West Hill Library,
West Hill,
London SW18

01-874 1144

First free meeting on Monday 21st February at 7 pm at West Hill Library. Other meetings 5th March Earlsfield Library, Magalan Road, 14th March, York Gardens Community Centre, Lavender Road, SW11

Manchester

MANCHESTER COMPUTER CLUB
David Wade,
28 Hazel Road,
Altrincham,
Cheshire WA14 1JL

061-941 2486

Covers Greater Manchester Area. 1st and 3rd Thursdays.

Computer Science Building, Manchester University, Oxford Road, Manchester.

SMALL BUSINESS COMPUTER USERS CLUB (N. MANCHESTER)
K. Wadsworth,
061-740 7232 after 5 pm.

New club will meet on every last Tuesday from April, subs £7.50 per annum.

SOUTH TRAFFORD MICROCOMPUTER CLUB (SOUTH MANCHESTER)
Ian White,
16 Leicester Avenue,
Timperley,
Altrincham WA15 6HR

061-969 2080

Meets fortnightly. Wide range of computers. Monthly newsletter.

Merseyside

MERSEYSIDE 380Z AND BBC ATOM USERS GROUP
Alan Pope,
Paal Enterprise,
37 Stuart Road,
Crosby,
Liverpool L23 0QE

MERSEYSIDE MICROCOMPUTER GROUP
Fred Shaw,
14 Albany Avenue,
Eccleson Park,
Prescot,
Merseyside L34 2QW

051-426 5436

Computer Education Soc. M. Trotter 051-652 1596. SC/MP Special Interest Group B. Perrigo 051-677 6716. PET, 6800 and 77/68, Apple. BBC Atom.

SOUTHPORT COMPUTER CLUB
Ian Britstone,
28 Weld Road,
Southport,
Merseyside

0704 64524

Weekly meetings.

THE HARDWARE EXCHANGE
D. Edwards,
PO Box 13,
Birkenhead,
Merseyside LS42 4RL

181

WIRRAL COMPUTER CLUB
Gary Metcalfe,
24 Marlston Avenue,
Irby,
Wirral,
Merseyside

WIRRAL MICROCOMPUTER USERS GROUP
J. Phillips,
14 Helton Close,
Nocturum,
Birkenhead,
Merseyside L43 9HP

051-652 0268

Meets Mondays at Birkenhead Technical College.

---

Middlesex

---

*BRIGADIER COMPUTER CLUB
Steve Ward,
28 Brodie Road,
Enfield,
Middx EN2 0EU

01-363 3786

Meets on 1st and 3rd Mondays at Brigadier Youth Centre, Brigadier Hill, Enfield from 7.30 pm to 10.00 pm. Membership £2.00 plus 25p per night. Caters for novice and expert alike.

*HARROW COMPUTER GROUP
Bazyle Butcher,
16 St. Peter's Close,
Bushey Heath,
Watford,
Hertfordshire WD2 3LG

01-950 7068

Alternate Wednesdays at Harrow College of Higher Education. Room W24 at 7 pm. Membership is free. Library of American magazines held for loan.

When the college is closed, meetings are in the 'PLOUGH', Kenton.

*RICHMOND COMPUTER CLUB
Bob Forster,
18a The Barons,
St. Margarets,
Twickenham,
Middlesex

01-892 1873 after 7 pm

2nd Monday at Richmond Community Centre, Sheen Road. 35p per meeting, 8 pm.

Members have use of a good range of equipment. Just turn up – wide, variation of machines.

*SUNBURY COMPUTER CLUB
S.N. Taylor,
8 Priory Close,
Sunbury-on-Thames,
Middlesex TW16 5AB

Sunbury 86649

Meets last Tuesday of each month at 8 pm, St. Benedicts Church Hall, Napier Road, Ashford. Bring Machine. Every other Tuesday at Grey Horse Public House, Staines Road East, at 8 pm. No machines. 40p per meeting, £4.00 per annum. (under 18 please ask cost)

*WEST LONDON PERSONAL COMPUTER CLUB
Graham Brain,
81 Rydal Crescent,
Perivale,
Middlesex UB6 8DZ

01-997 8986

Meet first Tuesday of each month at 7.45 pm. Back room of the Fox and Goose Pub, Hanger Lane, Alperton TRS80, Forth, Nascom, Young persons, Homebrew, Sorceror, ZX81. Annual subs: £5.00 16 and over or £2.50 under 16's and OAP's. Special interest groups, demos.

Neil 01-997 9437

*WORCESTER PARK COMPUTER CLUB
Library 337 1609
Windsor Road Library

---

Norfolk

---

ANGLIA COMPUTER USER GROUP
Jan Rejzl,
128 Templemere,
Sprowston Road,
Norwich NR3 4EQ

EAST ANGLIA COMPUTER USER GROUP
Jan Rejzl,
88 St. Benedicts Street,
Norwich NR2 4AB

0603 29652

Meets 2nd and 4th week in the month on Wednesdays at 7 pm, at Crome Community Centre, Telegraph Lane, Norwich.

SPECTRUM USERS GROUP
M. Osborne,
8 Elvington,
Kings Lynn,
Norfolk

---

Northamptonshire

---

SOUTH NORTHANTS COMPUTER USERS GROUP
Simon Clark,
83 Watling Street,
Towcester,
Northants NN12 7AG

(0327) 52191

Meets weekly, Wednesdays at 7.30 pm, Anchor House, Moat Lane, Towcester. 50p per meeting, no age limit. Various machines, General Forum for discussions.

---

North Yorkshire

---

YORK COMPUTER CLUB
K. Thomas (Chairman),
Green Lea,
Ripon Road,
Harrogate,
North Yorkshire HG1 2BY

0904 38239

Meetings every Monday at 8 pm. The Enterprise Club, Nunnery Lane. Club Literature Package.

WORKSOP COMPUTER CLUB
Mr. Andrews,
Worksop 487327

First meeting Worksop Library Lecture room on Tuesday June 14th. More information contact above.

Nottinghamshire

ASHFIELD COMPUTER CLUB
Deric Daines,
c/o 18, Cutting Avenue,
Sutton-in-Ashfield

Mansfield 553198

Notts
Derrick Daines, 0380 56198

1st and 3rd Thursdays at Carsic Junior School. £3.00. St. Mary's Road, S. in A.

EASTWOOD TOWN MICRO COMPUTER CLUB
Ted Ryan,
15 Queens Square,
Eastwood,
Nottingham NG16 3BJ

Langley Mill 65011

Meetings: Wednedays 5.45 at Devonshire Drive Junior School, Fridays 5.30 or 6.30 at Eastwood Volunteer Bureau (or Upper School, Mansfield Road, or Sunnycroft Scout HQ Derby Road.) One night per month CTUK (usually 1st Wednesday). Other contacts: Roger Hellins – Langley Mill 69281 Robert Clifford – Ripley 812459

NOTTINGHAM MICROCOMPUTER CLUB
Mr. D. Harvey,
68 Roseleigh Avenue,
Nottingham NG3 6FH

(0602) 608491

1st Tuesday each month (except August and January). Friends Meeting House, 25-27 Clareden Street, Nottingham. User group meetings also take place at other times.

Oxfordshire

MICROSOC (OXFORD UNIVERSITY MICRO GROUP)
R.P. Steele,
St. John's College,
Oxford University.

Meets Clarendon Laboratory, Parks Road, Oxford. Weekly during university terms. Machines: Acorn Atom, RML 380Z, DEC PDP11 (RSX).

OXFORD PERSONAL COMPUTER CLUB (OPeCC)
Len Phelps,
Southport Cottage,
Sutton Courtenay,
Nr. Abingdon,
Oxon OX14 4AN

Sutton Courtenay 438

40 Members. £8.00 including ACC membership. Fortnightly meetings in central Oxford. Speakers and workshops. Courses.

Shropshire

LUDLOW AND DISTRICT MICROCOMPUTER CLUB
David Pauli,
32 High Street,
Leintwardine,
Craven Arms,
Shropshire

(05473) 287

Meets 7.30 pm 2nd Monday of each month at the Diocesan Education Centre, Lower Galdeford, Ludlow.

TELFORD COMPUTER CLUB
H.D. Briggs,
53 Gilpin Road,
Admaston,
Telford,
Shropshire TFS 0BG

Telford 595959

Meets at Telford I.T.E.C. Halesfield 14, Telford. Mondays, run in conjunction with Telford Electronics Club.

Somerset

YEOVIL COMPUTER CLUB
D.G. Carrington,
2 Romsey Road,
Yeovil,
Somerset BA21 5XN

South Yorkshire

BARNSLEY CO-OPERATIVE COMPUTER CLUB
James Bridson,
c/o 39 Keresforth Hall Road,
Barnsley,
South Yorks S70 6NF

Barnsley 41753

Meetings held last Tuesday of every month at 7.30 pm, CO-OP Social Club, Pogmore, Barnsley. Membership fee £1.00 put into a share account refundable when leaving the club, no attendance fee.

Machines used are Tandy/Genie, Atoms, Sharp, BBC, Apple.

DONCASTER AMATEUR COMPUTER SOCIETY
John Wilkinson,
316 Bawtry Road,
Doncaster,
S. Yorkshire

£1.00 entrance fee. £5.00 per year over 18 and £2.50 per year for under-18's. Meets at YMCA, Wood Street on 1st Wednesday of each month.

John Wilkinson on 0302 868379 (6-9 pm)

SOUTH YORKSHIRE PERSONAL COMPUTER GROUP
Paul Sanderson (Chairman)
3 Vernon Road,
Totley,
Sheffield S17 3QE

0742 351895

Meets 2nd Wednesday at 7.30 pm, in General Lecture Theatre, St. Georges Building, Mappin Street, Sheffield. Experts and beginners welcome.

Visitors always welcome. Membership £4.00 per year.

---

Staffordshire

---

ABACVS
Les Ellington,
18 Underwood Close,
Parkside,
Stafford

0785 41153

TAME VALLEY COMPUTER CLUB
c/o Bob Overton,
57 Maitland,
Glascote Heath,
Tamworth,
Staffs B79 8JG

Meets fortnightly. Contact the above for more details.

THE AMATEUR COMPUTER CLUB OF NORTH STAFFS
J. Roll,
16 Hill Street,
Hednesford,
Staffordshire WS12 5DS

05438 4363

20 members. £3.00. 3rd Wednesday of the month.

---

Suffolk

---

HAVERHILL MICROCOMPUTER CLUB
Andrew Holliman,
5 Trinity Close,
Balsham,
Cambridge CB1 6DW

West Wratting 583

Meets at St. Mary's Church Hall, Camps Road, Haverhill. Castle Manor Adult Centre, Haverhill, Suffolk.

Memb. Sec. Adrian Burr, 13 Helions Road, Steeple Bumpstead, Suffolk. Steeple Bumpstead 211

SUFFOLK MICROCOMPUTER CLUB
Adrian L. Theobald,
42 Newbury Road,
Ipswich,
Suffolk IP4 5EX

Meets 1st Thursday each month at 15 Lower Brook Street. Sub. £5.00 per annum.

THE NEWMARKET HOME COMPUTER GROUP
John Smyth,
5 New River Green,
Exning,
Newmarket,
Suffolk

Exning 8100

---

Surrey

---

ASHTEAD COMPUTER CLUB
P.G. Palmer,
6 Corfe Close,
Ashtead,
Surrey

Ashtead 77418

Last Thurs Month.

EWELL MICRO CLUB
Dave De Silva,
316 Kingston Road,
Ewell,
Surrey KT19 0SU

01-393 1469

ZX81/Spectrum/Software.

FARNHAM COMPUTER CLUB
Adam Sharp,
14 Thorn Road,
Boundstone,
Farnham,
Surrey

Membership £2.00 per year. Meets 2nd Wednesday of month in Farnham 6th Form College, Morley Road, Farnham, Surrey. For details please contact the above.

GUILDFORD AREA MICROCOMPUTER USERS GROUP
Mr. M. Bawtree,
Royal Grammar School,
Guildford,
Surrey GU1 3BB

Guildford 502424

SURREY MICROPROCESSOR SOCIETY (SUMPS)
Mike Patrick,
28 West Drive,
Cheam,
Surrey

01-642 8362

40 members. £5. Twice a month.

Also Ron Halley-Williams 01-661 9975.

*SUTTON LIBRARY COMPUTER CLUB
David Wilkins,
22 Chestnut Court,
Mulgrave Road,
Sutton,
Surrey SM2 6LR

01-642 3102 (evenings)

Sub. Adults £6 pa, students/pensioners £4 pa, extra family £2 pa. Contact: Jennifer Woeller 01-661 5031 (Sutton Library). Meetings 1st Friday of month at 6.15 pm, and 3rd Tuesday at 8.15 pm. Specialist groups for beginners, Acord, Sinclair. Projected groups for Oric, Dragon, m/c.

WEST SURREY COMPUTER CLUB
Chris Karney,
0483 68121 x 497

Paddock Room,
Green Man Public House,
Burpnam,
Guildford

1st Thursday of each month.

---

Tyne & Wear

---

SURREY CLUB
John Bone,
2 Claremont Place,
Gateshead,
Tyne and Wear NE8 1TL

(0632) 770036

Supporters Annual Sub – £1.00. Meetings on Saturdays 10 am to 4 pm at 2 centres. Science & Engineering Museum – 3rd flr. study area. Convenor – Ron Dixon. YMCA Building, South Shields. Convenor – Pam Collier (0632) 564905. Admission 30p (20p for CT Supporters).

NEWCASTLE-UPON-TYNE PERSONAL COMPUTER SOC.
Peter Scargill (Secretary),
21 Percy Park,
Tynemouth

0632 573905

Geff Cass (Chairman)
John Walton (Treasurer)

Meets first Tuesday each month in Room D103, Newcastle Polytechnic. 100+ members. Sub £6.00. Groups include PET, TRS80, and S100. The S100 group meets weekly. NPCS helps to support Computertown NE (meets weekly). Contact (0632) 77036 John S. Bone, 2 Claremont Place, Gateshead, NE8 1TL.

---

Warwickshire

---

KENILWORTH COMPUTER CLUB
Jo Gedrych,
4 Crackley Hill,
Kenilworth CV8 2FP

Kenilworth 56385

---

West Midlands

---

ACOCKS GREEN COMPUTER CLUB
Mike Bedford-White,
16 Westfield Road,
Acocks Green,
Birmingham B27 7TL

021-707 3100

Meets Wednesday nights 7.00 pm to 9.00 pm at Stone Hall Education Centre. Subs £6.00, concession £2.50. New group all micro users welcome.

BIRMINGHAM COMPUTER CLUB
Dr. M. Bayliss,
125 Berryfield Road,
Sheldon,
Birmingham B26 3UU

021-743 7197

CANNOCK COMPUTER SOCIETY
Terry Sale,
20 Redwood Drive,
Chase Terrace,
Walsall WS7 8AS

Meets fortnightly from Wednesday 15th December. Cannock Computer Systems, Old Penkridge Road, Cannock.

Subscription will be £3.00 for adults, £1.00 for students, small charge each meeting for refreshments, various computers will be catered for.

COVENTRY COMPUTER CIRCLE
Chris Baugh,
9 Hillman House,
Smithford Way,
Coventry CV1 1FZ

0203 25802

Free Membership.

COVENTRY COMPUTER CLUB
Jack Hewitt,
3a Boswell Drive,
Coventry,
West Midlands

Coventry 615543

Meets Wednesday nights at 7.30 pm to 10.00 pm at Walsgrove Junior School, Boswell Drive, Coventry.

HANDSWORTH/BALSALL HEATH COMPUTER CLUB
Dennis Pain,
12 Cannon Hill Road,
Balsall Heath,
Birmingham B12 9NN

I.C.L. BIRMINGHAM BRANCH MICRO-CLUB
c/o W.B.A. Ecclestone,
26, Browns Lane,
Tamworth,
Staffs

WALSALL COMPUTER CLUB
Alison Hunt,
'Lael',
58 Princes Avenue,
Walsall,
West Midlands WS1 2DH

Meets 2nd and 4th Mondays, Park Hall Community School, Park Hall Road, 6.45 to 9.45 pm.

WEST MIDLANDS AMATEUR COMPUTER CLUB
John Tracey,
100 Booth Close,
Brierley Hill,
Kingswinford,
West Midlands

0384 70097

£4.00. 2nd and 4th Tuesday at Elmfield School, Love Lane, Stourbridge.

£3.00. Full-time students.

## West Sussex

**ARUN MICROCOMPUTER CLUB**
P.W.H. Cherriman,
c/o Wick Amenity Centre,
Wick Farm Road,
Littlehampton,
W. Sussex BN17 7BL

Littlehampton 7607

Meets 1st Monday, at 8.00 pm and 3rd Sunday 6.00 pm.
Subs £3.00 for 6 months + £1.00 joining fee.

**MID-SUSSEX MICROCOMPUTING CLUB**
Jeff Hayden,
2 Hillary Close,
East Grinstead,
West Sussex RH19 3XQ

0342 24655

**WEST SUSSEX MICROCOMPUTER CLUB**
J.M. Clarke,
31 Hyde Heath Court,
Pound Hill,
West Sussex

0293 884207

Open to those with or without facilities. Subs £6.00, £3.00 for students (includes newsletter). Various machines, includes Nascoms & Vics. Discussions & problem solving, talks & exhibitions part of mid Sussex computer club.

## West Yorkshire

**GREENHEAD GRAMMAR SCHOOL COMPUTER CLUB**
Brian Smith,
Greenhead Road,
Keithley,
West Yorks BN20 6EB

Keithley 62828

School internal club. Interested in control and robotics.

**KIRKLEES COMPUTER CLUB**
Chris Townsend,
760/4 Manchester Road,
Linthwaite,
Huddersfield

(0484) 657299 24hr

Meets every Monday in Huddersfield. Full program. Everyone welcome. Info pack.

**LEEDS MICROCOMPUTER USERS GROUP**
David Parsons,
22 Victoria Walk,
Horsforth LS18 4PL

(0532) 585480

Meets fortnightly on Thursday evenings in Leeds. New members welcome.

**PENNINE & DISTRICT COMPUTER CLUB**
Douglas Bryant,
26 Mill Hey,
Haworth,
West Yorkshire

0274 569660

Club premises open 10 am to 10 pm Saturday, and Sunday at 26 and 51 Mill Hey, Haworth, West Yorks. Tel. (0535) 43007

Systems books, magazines, members shop.

**POCKET COMPUTER USERS CLUB**
Andrew Faint,
13 Sutherland Avenue,
Leeds LS8 1BY

Membership (UK) £5.00 per annum, (overseas) £7.50. Newsletter 'Output'.

**SHIPLEY COLLEGE COMPUTER GROUP**
Paul Channell,
0274 595731
Yorkshire

Wednesdays – Hardware/Advanced.

Between 7.00 & 9.00 pm. Tuesdays – software.

Sorcerer, 6800.

**WEST YORKSHIRE MICROCOMPUTER GROUP**
Phillip Clark,
c/o Suite 204,
Crown House,
Armley Road,
Leeds LS12 2ES

0532 450667

Meets 2nd Tuesday of month.

Varied Diary has been drawn up.

## Wiltshire

**CHIPPENHAM AND CALNE**
Matthew Jones,
Pinhills,
Calne SN11 0LY

Proposed new club. All machines, languages. Help for newcomers.

## Worcestershire

**WORCESTER AND DISTRICT COMPUTER CLUB**
D.J. Stanton,
55 Vauxhall Street,
Rainbow Hill,
Worcester WR3 8PA

0905 22704

Meets 2nd Monday of month. Old Pheasant Inn, New Street, Worcester.

## ii) Channel Islands

JERSEY COMPUTER ASSOCIATION
Michael Murphy,
PO Box 441,
St. Helier,
Jersey,
Channel Islands

0534 78399 (working hours)

Subs £16.00 to £2.00 per annum. Various Machines. Local Information Service being set up.

GUERNSEY MICROCOMPUTER USERS GROUP
Tony Thorne (Chairman),
Summerfield House,
Vale,
Guernsey

(0481) 44955

Graphics, training, etc. Seminars and shows.

## iii) Wales

ABERGELE COMPUTER CLUB
W.F. Jones,
77, Millbank Road,
Rhyl,
Clwyd.,
N. Wales

All micro and Business users welcome. Subs £5.00 Adult, £2.50 Junior (under 16, 18 and under if still at school). Meets Thursday 7.30 – 10 Abergele Council Offices.

COLWYN COMPUTER CLUB
D. Bevan,
c/o 20 Abergele Road,
Colwyn Bay,
Clwyd LL29 7PA

Meetings are held at 7 pm, at the Greenlawns Hotel, Colwyn Bay.

GWENT AMATEUR COMPUTER CLUB
Rothery Harris,
16 Alanbrook Avenue,
Newport,
Gwent,
Wales NPT 6QJ

0633 852924

£3.50 pa. Every Thursday 7.30 pm St. Mary's Inst. Stow Hill. Tel. 0633 852924 eve.

MILFORD CENTRAL COMPUTER CLUB
Harry Evans,
Milford Central School,
Prioryville,
Milford Haven,
Dyfed

043 784 571

Open to school children over 11yrs in area, meets every lunch hour and evening. Pets, BBC, and access to two floppy disc drives.

PENCOED AMATEUR COMPUTER CLUB
Philip Williams,
38 Bryn Rhedyn,
Pencoed,
Bridgend,
Mid Glamorgan CF35 6TL

05473 287

Meets fortnightly on Saturday from 3 pm to 5 pm at Pencoed Library, in Reference Room. Subs £5.00 and £3.50 for OAP's and Students.

PONTYPOOL COMPUTER CLUB
Graham Loveridge,
Pontypool 2827

Meets every Friday, at The Settlement, Rockhill Road, Pontypool, Gwent.

SWANSEA & SOUTHWEST WALES AMATEUR COMPUTER CLUB
Paul Griffiths,
1 Prescelli Road,
Penlan,
Swansea SA5 8AF

0792 583897

20 members. Last Friday of month.

## iv) Scotland

BISHOPTON COMPUTER CLUB
Alasdair Law,
10 Dunglass Road,
Bishopton,
Renfrewshire

Bishopton 3137

Meets monthly on Sunday afternoons. Contact the above for further details.

CENTRAL SCOTLAND COMPUTER CLUB
James Lyon,
78 Slamannan Road,
Falkirk,
Scotland FK1 5NF

0324 22430

1st & 3rd Thursdays at Falkirk College of Technology Grangemouth Road, Falkirk.

FIFE COMPUTER USERS CLUB
Murray Simpson,
31 Tom Steward Lane,
St. Andrews,
Fife KY16 8YB

0334 72485

Membership £5.00 adults, £3.00 under 18's and unemployed. Newsletter called Micro 81. Fortnightly club meetings and special events sponsored by the club. Hope to organise a Fife Computer Fair.

GRAMPIAN AMATEUR COMPUTER SOCIETY
A.J. Morrison,
21 Beech Road,
Westhill,
Skene,
Aberdeenshire AB3 6WR

0224 741387

Yearly subscription: £10 members: £4 16-18 years: £1 under 16. Meets 2nd Monday every month.

New premises are: 35 Thistle Lane, Aberdeen.

User Groups and Special Interests catered for.

KEMNAY COMPUTER CLUB
S.J. Stubbs,
15, The Glebe,
Kemnay, Inverurie,
Aberdeenshire

Kemnay 3070

Meets weekly. H/ware interest group. Free membership. 15 members.

MOTHERWELL COLLEGE COMPUTER CLUB
M. Singh,
Dept. of Elec. Engineering,
Dazell Drive,
Motherwell ML2 1DD

PERTH & DISTRICT AMATEUR COMPUTER SOCIETY
Alastair MacPherson,
154, Oakbank Road,
Perth PH1 1HA

0738 29633

3rd Tuesday at Hunters Lodge Motel, Bankfoot at 7.30 pm.

RAF KINLOSS
Steve Barthorpe,
18 Trenchard Crescent,
Kinloss,
Forres,
Moray IV36 0UP

SCOTTISH AMATEUR COMPUTER SOC. SACS
Mike Anthony,
46, Moredun Park Gardens,
Edinburgh EH17 7JR

031337 5611

SKY AND LOCHALSH COMPUTER SOCIETY
C.J. Manvell,
25 Breacais Isol,
Isle of Sky IV42 8QA

STONEHAVEN COMPUTER CLUB
Ross Martin,
Belmont House,
Belmont Brae,
Stonehaven,
Kincardineshire,
Scotland

STRATHCLYDE COMPUTER CLUB
Secretary: B. Duffy,
24 Lomond Drive,
Condorrat,
Cumbernauld,
Scotland G4 0NW

(02367) 33800

Meets 3rd Wednesday of every month. Wolfson Centre, 106 Rottenrow, Glasgow.

WELLINGTON SCHOOL COMPUTER CLUB
P.C.G. Pascoe,
Wellington School,
Osnaruck BFPO 36

## v) Ireland

BANGOR COMPUTER CLUB (N. IRELAND)
Derek Blanc,
c/o Queen's University,
Belfast,
Northern Ireland

CORK AMATEUR COMPUTER CLUB
T. Moriarty,
'Tiger Bay',
Rochestown,
Douglas,
Cork,
Eire

021-293651 (home) 021-582433 (work)

Talks and demonstrations. Hardware, programming, and games.

## Specialist System User Groups

**1802**

COSMAC USERS CLUB
James Cunningham,
7 Harrowden Court,
Harrowden Road,
Luton,
Bedfordshire LU2 0SR

0582 423934

35 Members. RCA 1802.

ELF.

## 6502

6502 USERS CLUB
Walter Wallenborn,
21 Argyll Avenue,
Luton,
Bedfordshire LU3 1EG

0582 2697

Monthly meetings in Hitchin. Contact Joe Manifold for dates.

Joe Manifold,
16 Bunyan Close,
Pirton,
Hitchin,
Herts

6502 USERS CLUB (SOUTHERN REGION)
Steve Cole,
70 Sydney Road,
Gosport,
Hants

Regular Newsletter.

Welcomes all 6502 users.

Acorn, Aim, Apple, Atari, Atom. Kim, Microtan, Pet, Sym, Superboard.

## 6800/6809

*68 MICROGROUP
Jim Anderson,
41 Pebworth Road,
Harrow,
Middx

01-422 4724

£5.00 with a further charge of £1.00 per meeting. 3rd Tuesday of every month, Regents Park Library, Robert Street, N.W.1 at 7.30. Library and bi monthly Newsletter. Newsletter articles and letters to Joe Johnson, 19 Mary Anne Gardens, London SE8

6809 USER GROUP
Mr. W. Gibbons,
Clarence Lodge,
Hurdon Road,
Launceston,
Cornwall PL 15 9DB

Bi-monthly newsletter, proposed sub £5.00 details from bove.

## 77/68

77/68 USERS GROUP
40 Bartholomew Street,
Newbury,
Berkshire

0635 30505

500 members. £1.50. Newsletter.

Free membership for the first year if you buy the 77/68 instruction manual.

## APPLE

APPLE MUSIC SYNTHESIS GROUP
Dr. David Ellis,
22 Lennox Gardens,
London SW1

Enclose a SAE.

Interested in Alf and Mountain Hardware, Alpha Synatauri and Soundchaser systems.

ASHTEAD USER GROUP (APPLE)
M. Lawrence,
15 Petters Road,
Ashtead,
Surrey

Ashtead 73906

Meets 1st Monday of every month. Contact above for details.

BIRMINGHAM & REGION APPLE GROUP (BRAG)
Mel Golder,
021 426 2275

New Club part of BASUG.

Other contact: Mike Bayliss 021 743 7197

BRITISH APPLE SYSTEMS USER GROUP (BASUG)
John Sharp,
BASUG,
PO Box 174,
Watford WD2 6NF

(09273) 75093

Meets 1st Tuesday evening & 3rd Sunday afternoons monthly at the Old School, Branch Road, Park Street, St. Albans. (A5 about 2 miles south of city centre) Incorporates UK Apple User Group.

Publishes magazine called 'Hard Core'. Fee £12.50 + £2.50 (joining). D. Bolton, 0727 72917

BRITISH APPLE USERS AND DABBLERS (BAUD)
Geoff Smythe,
Datalink Microcomputer Systems Ltd.
10 Waring House,
Redcliffe Hill,
Bristol BS1 6TB

0272 213427

BUCKINGHAMSHIRE/BERKSHIRE AREA
Steve Proffitt,
The Granary,
Hill Farm Road,
Marlow Bottom,
Bucks

01-759 5511 ext 7298 day

Setting up Apple Users Group.

062 84 73074 evenings or weekends.

## ATARI

*ATARI COMPUTER ENTHUSIASTS (ACE)
A.P. Miles,
8 Cosdach Avenue,
Wallington,
Surrey SM6 9RA

01-647 1713

Meetings monthly, maybe fortnightly soon, Friday or Saturday evening. Software and hardware discounts. Working on Adventure-type program.

ATARI USER GROUP
Ken Ward,
45 Coleburn Road,
Lakenham,
Norwich,
Norfolk NR1 2NZ

Norwich 661149

BIRMINGHAM USER GROUP (ATARI 400/800/1200)
Mike Reynolds-Jones,
66 Cyril Road,
Smallheath,
Birmingham 10

021-773 2849

Annual subs £5.00 Juniors (under 16) £1.00. Free membership for Wives/Husbands. Entrance fees 25p members, non members 50p. Meetings weekly at the 'Malaga Grill', The Matador, Bull Ring, Birmingham, meetings start at 7.30 pm. Software Library, Guest Speakers, BASIC programming courses.

CARSHALTON ATARI USER GROUP
Paul Deegan,
01-642 5232

SILICA ATARI 400/800 USERS' CLUB
Secretary: Richard Hawes,
1-4 The Mews,
Hatherley Road,
Sidcup,
Kent DA14 4DX

01-301 1111

UK ATARI COMPUTER OWNERS CLUB
PO Box 3,
Rayleigh,
Essex

## ACORN ATOM/BBC

ACORN ATOM USER GROUP
Peter Frost,
18 Frankwell Drive,
Coventry CV2 2FB

£4.00. Program library.

Quarterly Newsletter. Some local groups. Technical help where possible.

BEEBUG (BBC USERS GROUP)
David Graham or Sheridan Williams,
Dept 1,
P.O. Box 50,
St. Albans,
Herts

National club for BBC users – about 6000 members. Membership £4.90 6 months, £8.90 1 year.

BOTTISHAM ACORN USERS GROUP
P.M. Rank,
27 Bell Road,
Bottisham,
Cambridge CB5 9DF

Emphasis on BBC Micro.

John Harris, 0233 811487.

BOURNEMOUTH BBC USER'S GROUP
Norman Carey,
26, Felton Road,
Parkstone,
Poole,
Dorset

Poole 749612

Meets 1st and 4th Wednesday 7.30-10.30, Landsowne Computer Centre, 5 Holdenhurst Road, Bournemouth.

CARDIFF BBC MICROCOMPUTER CLUB (CBBC)
Geoff Barker,
Penarth 701023

Meets alternate Wednesday evenings in Applied Science Lecture Theatre, University College, Newport Road, Cardiff. Sixty members, hope to provide forum for owners.

GCHQ BBC MICRO USER GROUP
D.W. Adam,
16 Court Road,
Prestbury,
Cheltenham,
Glos.

LASERBUG (BBC NATIONAL GROUP)
4 Station Bridge,
Woodgrange Road,
Forest Gate,
London E7 0NF

02812 3064

LIVERPOOL BBC & ATOM GROUP
Nik Kelly,
56, Queens Drive,
Walton,
Liverpool L4 6SH

051 525 2934

Meets 1st Wednesdays of every month at Old Swan Technical College, Room C33, 7.30 pm to 9.30 pm. Meets 3rd Thursday of every month at Birkenhead Tech. College, 1st Floor, Science & Maths Dept. 7.30 pm to 9.30 pm. Acorn Atoms welcome.

MANCHESTER ACORN USER GROUP
John Ashurst,
192 Verdure Close,
Failsworth,
Manchester

061 681 4962

Meets every Tuesday (except school holidays) at AMC, Crescent Road, Crumpsall, Manchester 8.

**MEDWAY ACORN USER GROUP**
Clem Rutter,
c/o St. John Fisher School,
Ordnance Street,
Chatham,
Kent

0634 42811 (day) 0634 373459 (evenings)

Meets at St. John Fisher School usually last Monday of every month. Weekly pub session, Thursdays 9 pm New Fox & Hounds, Chatham. Atoms, BBC's, System 1, visits from lonely 6502's.

**NORTH LONDON BBC MICRO USERS GROUP**
Dr. Leo McLaughlin,
Dept. of Chemistry,
Westfield College,
Kidderpore Avenue,
London NW3

01-435 0109

Meets on Tuesday at 7 pm at The Prince of Wales, 37 Fortune Green Road.

**POT-BUG (BBC MICROCOMPUTER USER GROUP)**
Mike Forster,
8 St. Georges Prave,
Hugh Lane,
Eurslem,
Stoke-on-Trent

Stoke-on-Trent 818499

Meets twice a month at Burslem Leisure Centre, Burslem, Stoke-on-Trent, 7.30 pm to 10.00 pm, meetings usually second and last Wednesdays of the month, membership fees £3.00 and 45p per meeting. Mainly BBC Micros all others welcome. Demos and discussions on the BBC Micro.

**PRESTON AREA BBC MICROCOMPUTER USER GROUP**
Mr. D. Coulter,
8 Briar Grove,
Ingol,
Preston

Preston 725793

Meet at 7.30 pm in room F2, Preston Polytechnic.

**TYNE & WEAR BBC USER CLUB**
Ian Waugh,
13 Briardene Drive,
Wardley,
Tyne & Wear NE10 8AN

## CASIO

**FX500-P USERS ASSOCIATION**
Max Francis,
38 Grymsdyke,
Great Missenden,
Bucks HP16 0LP

## COLOUR GENIE

**NATIONAL COLOUR GENIE USER'S GROUP**
Geoffrey Hillier,
5a Gregory Street,
Lenton,
Nottingham NG7 2LR

Nottingham 783938

Chairman:- Marc Leduc. Send large sae to above for further details.

**NATIONAL COLOUR GENIE USERS CLUB**
Lowe Computers Ltd.
Chesterfield Road,
Bentley Bridge,
Matlock,
Derbyshire DE4 5LE

Matlock (0629) 4995/4057

Regular magzine 'Chewing Gum'.

## COMMODORE

**PET USERS EDUCATION GROUP**
Dr. Chris Smith,
Dept. of Physiology,
Queen Elizabeth College,
Campden Hill Road,
London W8 7AH

20 members. Newsletter. CAI.

**INDEPENDENT COMMODORE PRODUCTS USER GROUP (NATIONAL)**
Membership Secretary,
30 Brancoates Road,
Newbury Park,
Ilford,
Essex IG2 7EP

**ICPUG (AYR)**
John Shankland,
2 Strathdoon Place,
Ayr,
Strathclyde,
Scotland

041-332 9969

**ICPUG (BARNSLEY)**
Bob Wood,
13 Ward Green,
Barnsley,
South Yorkshire

0246 811585

**ICPUG (BASILDON)**
Walter Green,
151 The Hatherley,
Basildon,
Essex

**ICPUG (BIRMINGHAM)**
J.A. McKain,
P.P.I. Limited,
177 Lozells Road,
Birmingham

021 544 0202

**ICPUG (BLOXHAM)**
John Temple,
'Kirabanda',
Rose Bank,
Bloxham,
Oxon

ICPUG (BOURNEMOUTH & POOLE)
Douglas M. Shave,
97 Canford Cliffs Road,
Poole,
Dorset BH13 7EP

ICPUG (BURNLEY)
John Ingham,
72 Ardwick Street,
Burnley,
Lancashire

ICPUG (BURY ST. EDMUNDS)
Alan Morris,
30 Kelso Road,
Bury St. Edmunds,
Suffolk

Bury St. Edmunds 61870

ICPUG (CARRICKFERGUS)
David Bolton,
19 Carrickburn Road,
Carrickfergus,
County Antrim,
Northern Ireland BT38 7ND

ICPUG (CHELMSFORD)
A.G. Surridge,
97 Shelley Road,
Chelmsford,
Essex

ICPUG (CHELTENHAM)
Mrs. Alison Schofield,
78 Hesters Way Road,
Cheltenham,
Gloucester

0242 580789/27588

Meets last Thursday of each month at 19.30 Cheltenham Ladies College, Archway Entrance, St. Georges Street, Cheltenham.

ICPUG (CLWYD)
John Poole,
6 Ridgeway Close,
Connah's Quay,
Clwyd CH5 4LZ

ICPUG (COVENTRY)
Will Light,
22 Ivybridge Road,
Stvyechale,
Coventry,
Warwickshire

0202 413511

PET USER GROUP (CRAWLEY)
Richard Dyer,
33 Parham Road,
Ilfield,
Crawley RH11 0ET

ICPUG (CROMER)
J. Blair,
7 Beach Road,
Cromer,
Norfolk

ICPUG (DERBYSHIRE & DISTRICT)
Raymond Davies,
105 Normanton Road,
Derby DE1 2GG

0332 41025 (day) 0332 514016 (eve)

Meets every other Monday at 7 pm to 9 pm at Davidson Richards Ltd., 14 Duffield Road, Derby.

ICPUG (DEVON)
Matthew Stibbe,
The Lawn,
Lower Woodfield Road,
Torquay,
Devon

ICPUG (DYFED)
Simon Kniveton,
Penpompren Hall,
Talybont,
Dyfed

Talybout 303

ICPUG (ESSEX)
Carol Taylor,
101 Courtlands Avenue,
Cranbrook,
Ilford,
Essex

01-554 5246

Meets at Grange Remedial Centre, Woodman Path, Hainault at 8 pm.

ICPUG (GLASGOW)
A.J. Quin,
Dept. of Environment Studies,
Glasgow College of Building & Printing,
60 North Hanover Street,
Glasgow G1 2BP
Scotland

041-332 9969

ICPUG (GLOUCESTER AND BRISTOL AREA)
Mrs. Janet Rich,
Rose Cottage,
20 Old Court,
Springhill,
Cam,
Gloucester GL11 5PF

0453 47708

Informal meetings last Friday each month at above address.

ICPUG (HAMPSHIRE AREA)
Ron Geere,
109 York Road,
Farnborough,
Hants

Meets 3rd Wednesday of the month 70 Reading Road, Farnborough, Hants.

ICPUG (KILMARNOCK)
John Smith,
19 Brewlands Road,
Symington,
Kilmarnock KA1 5RW

0563 83047

ICPUG (KINGS LYNN)
Peter Petts,
Bramley Hale,
Wretton,
Kings Lynn,
Norfolk PE33 9QS

Stoke Ferry 500692

ICPUG (LLANDYSSUL)
F.J. Townsend,
The Hill,
Rhydowen,
Llandyssul,
Dyfed SA44 4QD

05455 5291

ICPUG (LIVERPOOL)
Tony Bond,
27, Ince Road,
Liverpool L23 4UE
Lancs

051 924 1505

Informal meetings 2nd Thursday, The Merchant Taylor School for Boys, Crosby. 19.00 to 23.00.

ICPUG (MAIDSTONE)
Ron Moseley,
Rosemont,
Lord Romney Hill,
Weavering,
Maidstone,
Kent

0622 37643

Meets on 1st Wednesdays of each month at 19.45 for 20.00.

ICPUG (MANCHESTER AREA)
David Jowett,
197 Victoria Road,
Thornton Cleveleys,
Blackpool FY5 3ST

0253 869108

Meets 3rd Thursday of each month at Arnold School, Blackpool.

ICPUG (NEWTON MEARNS)
Dr. Jim MacBrayne,
27 Paidmyre Crescent,
Newton Mearns,
Glasgow,
Scotland

041 639 5696

ICPUG (NORTHAMPTON)
Peter Ashby,
215 Lincoln Way,
Corby,
Northamptonshire

05363 4442

ICPUG (NORTHEAST-DURHAM)
Jim Cocallis,
20 Worcester Road,
Newton Hall Estate,
Durham

0385 67045

Meets at Lawson School, Burnley.

PET, CBM, CIV-20, CBM64/MAX, 500, 700
Second Monday for software tuition. Third Monday for hardware tuition. These are in addition to normal activities. Meetings start at 7 pm.

ICPUG (N. HERTS)
B. Grainger,
73 Minehead Way,
Stevenage,
Herts SG1 2HZ

0438 727925

Meets last Wednesday of month. Provident Mutual Assurance, Purwell Lane, Hitchin, Herts.

ICPUG (NORTHUMBERLAND)
Graham J. Saunders,
Starling House,
22 Front Street,
Guide Post,
Northumberland

0670 823242

ICPUG (RHYL)
Frank Jones,
77 Millbank Road,
Rhyl,
Clwyd

0745 54820

ICPUG (SLOUGH)
Brian Jones,
Dept. of Maths and Computing,
Slough College of Higher Education,
Wellington Street,
Slough

Slough 34585 ext. 81

*ICPUG (SOUTH EAST)
Mick Ryan,
164 Chesterfield Drive,
Sevenoaks,
Kent TN13 2EH

0732 53530

Meet 3rd and 4th Thursday at Charles Darwin School, Jail Lane, Biggin Hill, at 7.30 pm. Bi-monthly Newsletter.

ICPUG (SE-CANTERBURY)
J. Bickerstaff,
48 Martin Down Lane,
Whitstable,
Kent CT5 4PR

0227 272702

Meets 1st Tuesday at The Physics Lab. Canterbury University. Subs £5.00 pa.

ICPUG (SOUTH HANTS)
Tony Cooke,
7 Russell Way,
Petersfield,
Hampshire GU31 4LD

Slough 34585 ext. 81

ICPUG (STAFFORDSHIRE)
57 Clough Hall Road,
Kidsgrove,
Stoke on Trent,
Staffordshire

ICPUG (STOURPORT-ON-SEVERN)
M.J. Merriman,
12 York Street,
Stourport-on-Severn

Meets on last Thursday of month at above address.

ICPUG (TEDDINGTON)
G. Squibb,
108 Teddington Park Road,
Teddington,
Middlesex

01-997 2346

ICPUG (WATFORD)
Stephen Rabagliati,
c/o Institute of Grocery Distribution,
Grange Lane,
Letchmore Heath,
Watford,
Herts

Meets on 2nd Monday of each month at above address.

ICPUG (WITNEY)
Ian Blyth,
40 Wilmot Close,
Witney,
Oxon

Witney 5171 home, Witney 3671 work.

ICPUG (WOLVERHAMPTON)
J. Bowman,
6 The Oval,
Albrighton,
Wolverhampton,
West Midlands

Monthly meetings, free program library, & advice.

**COMP-80**

COMP-80 USERS GROUP
Philip Probetts,
50 Cromwell Road,
Wimbledon,
London SW19 8LZ

01-540 3713

£6.50 UK £8.00 Overseas.

**COMPUCOLOR**

COMPUCOLOR USERS GROUP (UK)
Bill Donkin,
19 Harwood Avenue,
Bromley,
Kent BR1 3DX

01-460 2626 (eve)

Has contacts with US and Canadian groups.

Quarterly Newsletter, Hardware and Software advise. Program Library and exchange.

**COMPUKIT**

COMPUKIT USER CLUB
S.H. Grisvenor,
11 Bernard Road,
Oldbury,
Warley,
West Midlands

021-422 3298

COMPUKIT USER CLUB
Adrian Waters,
117 Haynes Road,
Hornchurch,
Essex RM11 2HX

Hornchurch 40490

COMPUKIT USER CLUB
P. Crabb,
21 Jones Close,
Yatton,
Avon

(0934) 834808

**DAI**

DAI UK USER GROUP
Dave Atherton,
16 Douglas Street,
Atherton,
Manchester M29 9FB

0942 876210

Subs £2.00 per annum. Produces a Newsletter and gives advice.

**DEC**

DECUS UK & IRELAND
Tracey Pardoe,
DECUS, PO Box 53,
Reading,
Berks RG2 0TW

Membership is free. Personal Computer Special Interest Group.

PDP8 USERS GROUP
Nigel Dunn,
21 Campion Road,
Widmer End,
High Wycombe,
Buckinghamshire

0494 714483

50 members. Spares. Newsletter. Software, 6100.

Full information on all 8 Hardware.

PDP11 USERS GROUP
Pete Harris,
119 Carpenter Way,
Potters Bar,
Hertfordshire EN6 5QB

0707 52091

30 members. Information service only. Also 01-248 8000 ext 7065.

## DRAGON

THE DRAGONS DEN
D. Buckingham,
83 Neville Road,
Limbury,
Luton,
Beds

New Group
National Dragon 32 User Club

DRAGON INDEPENDENT OWNERS ASSOCIATION
Doug Bourne,
School House,
Nevern Road,
Rayleigh,
Essex

Membership £8.00 per annum. Monthly newsletter.

SCOTTISH DRAGON CLUB
D.J. Anderson,
Top Flat,
1 Walker Street,
Edinburgh EH3 7JY

031-225 5285

Membership £8.00 includes membership card. Newsletter, discounts and free games tape.

## HEATHKIT/ZENITH

HEATHKIT USER GROUP
John Smithson,
Heath (Gloucester) Ltd.
Bristol Road,
Gloucester GL2 6EE

0452 29451

£4.00. Worldwide membership. Newsletter 'Remark'.

Technical advice.

## HEWLETT-PACKARD

HP-85 USER GROUP
Margaret Corbett,
10 Nichols Green,
Montpelier Road,
Ealing,
London W5 2QU

## INTEL

UK INTEL MDS USERS GROUP
Lewis Hard,
c/o S.P.A.C.E. Limited,
The Old Coach House,
Court Row,
Upton-on-Severn,
Worcs WR8 0NS

06846 3626

100 Members. Annual meeting. Newsletter.

## ITHACA

ITHACA S100 USERS GROUP
Dave Weaver,
41 Dore Avenue,
North Hykeham,
Lincoln LN6 8LN

25 members. Discount.

Information and software exchange.

## JUPITER ACE

JUPITER ACE USERS CLUB
Remsoft,
18 George Street,
Brighton BN2 1HR

0273 602354

Annual sub £7.00. 3 Newsletters advice on add-ons, special offers on software and hardware.

MATTEL INTELLIVISION TV GAME GROUP
Warrington 62215 after 4 pm. Warrington.

To organise meetings and competitions.

## NASCOM

INTERNATIONAL NASCOM MICROCOMPUTER CLUB
INMC,
80 Oakfield Corner,
Sycamore Road,
Amersham,
Buckinghamshire HP6 5EQ

2000 members. £5 Program library. Newsletter. 80-bus News for Nascom & Gemini users.

NAS-TUG (NASCOM THAMES VALLEY U.G.)
Mike Rothery,
37, Eton Wick Road,
Eton Wick,
Windsor,
Berks

Windsor 56106

MERSEYSIDE NASCOM USERS GROUP
T. Searle,
14 Hawkeshead Close,
Maghull,
Liverpool L31 9BT

Now independent. 150 members. Meets 1st Wednesday of month at 7.30 pm at Mona Hotel, James Street, Liverpool.

PROGRAM POWER
R.G. Simpson,
5 Wensley Road,
Leeds LS7 2LX

0532 683186

BIRMINGHAM NASCOM USER GROUP
Martin Sidebotham,
021-744 3093

Meets last Thursday of each month (except December) at 8 pm, Davenports Social Club, Granville St., Birmingham behind the Brewery, off Bath Row, near Birmingham Accident Hospital.

## NEWBRAIN

NEW BRAIN USER GROUP
Angela Watkiss,
4 Ninnings Lane,
Rabley Heath,
Welwyn,
Herts AL6 9TD

Stevenage 812439

## OHIO

OHIO SCIENTIFIC UK USER GROUP
Tom Graves,
19a West End,
Street,
Somerset BA16 0LQ

0458 45359

£5. Newsletter.

OSI UK USER GROUP
Richard Elen,
12 Bennerley Road,
London SW11 6DS

## ORIC

ORIC-1 USER GROUP
Edmund Boncran,
14a Vicars Hill,
Ladywell,
London SE13 7JH

01-690 5408 (eves/weekends)

## OSBORNE

BRITISH OSBORNE OWNERS' GROUP
Dr. Jonathan Angelsea,
Flat 19, Rowan House,
Mitton Road,
Handsworth,
Birmingham B20 2JR

Annual sub £18.00, 50% discount on additional members from the same address. Newsletter to be published on 1st July. More details from above.

## RESEARCH MACHINES

380-Z WEST MIDLANDS USER GROUP
Spencer Instone,
59 Avenue Road,
Leamington Spa CV31 3PF

0926 38751

NORTH EAST RML 380Z USERS GROUP
M. Hatfield,
Computer Unit,
Northumberland Building,
The Polytechnic,
Newcastle-upon-Tyne NE1 8ST

0632 26002 ext 268 office hours

Meets monthly at Micro-Electronics Education Centre of The Polytechnic, Coach Lane Campus. Also R. Reed.

RESEARCH MACHINES NATIONAL USER GROUP
c/o Clare Moat,
RML,
Mill Street,
Osney,
Oxford OX2 0BW

0865 49866

## SC/MP

SMALL PROCESSOR USER GROUP
Roger Knight,
Dept. of Meteorology,
University of Reading,
Earley Gate,
Whitenights,
Reading RG6 2AY

Large amount of data and designs.

Newsletter.

## SHARP

NATIONAL MZ80K/A USER GROUP
N. Brown,
48 Brander Road,
Leeds
Yorkshire LS9 6PR

New group aims to produce quarterly newsletter giving advice, tips, program listings and members letters. Members library. Membership free. All enquiries SAE please, stating machine.

SHARP MZ80K USER GROUP
Joe Seet,
16 Elmhurst Drive,
Hornchurch,
Essex RM11 1PE

04024 42905

SHARP PC1211 USERS CLUB
Jonathan Dakeyne,
281 Lidgett Lane,
Leeds LS17 3AQ

£5. Newsletter.

SHARP USER CLUB
Computer Centre,
Yeovil College,
Yeovil,
Somerset BA21 4AE

Extensive library and facilities. Details of meetings and magazines available (sae please). Other computers are RML, BBC Model 'B'. Magazines published, £3.00 in UK, £6.00 elsewhere. Further information from above address, written correspondence only.

SHARP USER GROUP
Graham Knight,
108 Rosemount Place,
Aberdeen,
Scotland

0224 630526

£3.00 sub includes MZ-80K Space Invaders Cassette. Newsletter.

## SIRIUS

THE SIRIUS USER GROUP
Edward Hasted,
12 Chesterfield Street,
London W1X 7HF

01-403 3800 (office), 01-499 1670 (evenings)

Regular and regional and national meetings. Quarterly newsletter. Comprehensive software reviews. Software library. Talks on Sirius and general computing skills. More information on request.

## SORCERER

EUROPEAN SORCERER CLUB
Colin Morle,
32 Watchyard Lane,
Formby,
Liverpool L37 3JU

07048 72137

£7.50 UK £10.00 Europe £15.00 Overseas. Newsletter. Contact Colin Morle for a sample Newsletter.

EXIDY SORCERER USER GROUP
Andy Marshall,
44 Arthurs Bridge Road,
Woking,
Surrey GU21 4NT

04862 66084

£5. Program exchange. Newsletter.

SPRINGFIELD COMPUTER CLUB
Stephen Cousins,
1 Aldeburgh Way,
Springfield,
Chelmsford,
Essex CM1 5PB

0245 50155

1st Friday of month. Sorcerer.

## TANGERINE

TANGERINE HOMEBREW
A.C.L. Coates,
35, Mogg Street,
St. Warburghs,
Bristol BS2 9UB

TANGERINE USERS GROUP
Bob Green,
1 Marlborough Drive,
Worle,
Avon BS22 0DQ BH3 7JR

0934 21315

National Tangerine User Group
Hardware and Software supplier

Also international section, recently formed for users of Microtan 65, and Oric-1.

## TEXAS INSTRUMENTS

BRITISH TI USERS CLUB
Philip Rowley,
2 Woodside Crescent,
Clayton,
Newcastle-under-Lyme,
Staffordshire ST5 4BW

£5.50. Newsletter. Program exchange.

NATIONAL TI 58/59 USER GROUP
R.M. Murphy,
Dept. of Electronic Engineering,
University College,
Singleton Park,
Swansea,
South Wales.

£5.50. Program exchange. Newsletter. £3.50 if you include a program with your sub.

TEXAS TI99 CLUB (MANCHESTER)
T. Grimshaw,
21 Allingham Street,
Longsight,
Manchester

061 224 0374

TI 99/4 TIHOME (USER GROUP)
P.M. Dicks,
157 Bishipsford Road,
Morden,
Surrey

01-640 7503

Sends out a monthly newsletter. Access to a software library.

TI 99/4A USERS CLUB
Mrs. Ann Flynn,
53 Georgian Close,
North Road,
Drogheda,
Co. Louth,
Eire

TI/99 4A USER GROUP
I. Youldon,
0532 401408

Meets at 30 Gipton Wood Road, Leeds 8 every Monday at 7 pm.

9900 USERS GROUP (TIMUG)
Chris Cadogan,
Department of Computer Science,
University of Manchester,
Manchester M13 9PL

20 members. Software & Data libraries.

## TRITON

TRITON USER GROUP
Nigel Stride,
Transam Ltd,
12 Chapel Street,
London NW1

01-402 8137

1200 members. £4.00. Software exchange. Newsletter.

## TRS-80

EAST MIDLANDS TRS-80 USERS GROUP
(NOTTINGHAM)
Mike Costello,
17 Langbank Avenue,
Rise Park,
Nottingham NG5 5BU

Nottingham 751753

Newsletter. 50p. Send for a free sample copy enclose large sae.

EDUCATIONAL USER'S GROUP FOR TRS-80 & VIDEO GENIE
Dave Futcher,
Head Teacher,
Beaconsfield First and Middle School,
Beaconsfield Road,
Southall,
Middlesex

01-574 3506

HULL & DISTRICT TRS-80/BEEB USERS GROUP
R.V. Souter,
25 Carr Lane,
Willerby,
Hull HU10 6JP

0482 654117

Meets 2nd Tuesday of month, & Thursday 16 days later at Psychology Dept. of Hull University, at 8 pm. Tuesday meeting a talk or demonstration. Thursday meeting free for members to do as they wish, other contact:– J. Lawrence, 2a Hall Road, Hull HU6 8SA Telephone:– 0482 493886

ISLE OF WIGHT TRS80 CLUB
M. Collins,
11 Star Street,
Ryde,
Isle of Wight

0983 614589

Meets last Friday of every month at 7.30 pm, London Hotel, Ryde.

MERSEYSIDE TRS-80/VIDEO GENIE USERS CLUB
Peter Tootill,
101 Swanside Road,
Liverpool L14 7NL

051-220 9733

Meetings 2nd Thursday of each month at 7.15, Stem Offices, Crown Street, (near Myrtle St. Jn.).

NATIONAL TRS-80 AND GENIE USERS GROUP
(WATGUG)
Brian Pain,
40a High Street,
Stony Stratford,
Milton Keynes

0908 566660/564271

800 Members. £6/six months (including 6 issues Newsletter). Monthly Newsletter (aprox 40 pages). Independent advice; local and specialist sub-groups. Workshops (London, Birmingham, Manchester, Glasgow, etc). Computerised Bulletin Board. Software library (free to members).

NATIONAL TRS-80 USER GROUP – BIRMINGHAM & WEST MIDLANDS AREA
Michael Gibbons,
1 New Street,
Castle Bromwich,
Birmingham B36 9AP

021 747 2260

Meets 1st Friday of every month at Adam & Eve Pub 1st Floor, Bradford Street, Birmingham. £5+B12. We have about 40 members, cater for TRS-80 & Video Genie. Mem. fee £2.50/year, 25p/meeting, 1st free. Newsletter, software library, advice column. Associated with the National TRS-80 group.

SCOTTISH TRS-80 USERS' GROUP
Dick Mackie (Chairman),
3 Warrender Park Crescent,
Edinburgh EH9 1DX

031-229 6032

Second Thursday each month at 7.30 pm. Mansion House Hotel, Milton Road, Edinburgh. All TRS-80, Genie & Dragon Users all welcome, present membership around 30. Software Library, Newsletter for members.

TOPIC
David Washford,
1 Alexandra Road,
Bournemouth,
Dorset BH6 5JA

0202 423064 (evenings) 0202 671122 (day)

Tandy Owners Programming & Information Club

Other contact Derek Higbee Ringwood 6720.

TRS-80/GENIE USERS GROUP (NOTTINGHAM)
Geoffrey Hillier,
5a Gregory Street,
Lenton,
Nottingham NG7 2LR

Nottingham 783938

Meets 1st & 3rd Wednesdays of each month from 7.30 pm at Wilford Moderns Rugby Club House. Club magazine called LPRINT.

TRS-80 LEVEL 1 USER GROUP
N. Rushton,
123 Roughwood Drive,
Northwood,
Kirby,
Merseyside L33 9UG

£5.00. Bi-monthly newsletter. Software library. For Model 1 and Model III owners using Level 1 BASIC.

TRS-80 MEDICAL AND LABORATORY USERS
Dr. N. Robinson,
The Residency,
Northwick Park Hospital,
Harrow,
Middlesex

Free quarterly newsletter detailing members' interests.

TRS-80 NORTHWEST GROUP
Melvyn Franklin,
40 Cowlees,
Westhoughton,
Bolton BL5 3EG

0942 812843

£5.00. Newsletter 6 issues. Meetings last Wednesday monthly except December. Lancs Aero Club, Barton Aerodrome. Plus Manchester sub group, meets 1st & 3rd Mondays.

TYNE AND WEAR TRS-80 USER GROUP
Dr. S. Tetlow,
3 Highbury Close,
Springwell,
Gateshead NE9 7PU

Washington 462532

TRS-80 USERS GROUP LONDON BRANCH
J. Wellsman,
292 Caledonian Road,
London N1

01-607 0157

2nd Friday each month.

WEST HERTS 80 USER GROUP
Terry Bradbury,
20 Spruce Way,
St. Albans

Meets at St. Stephen's Parish Centre, Station Road, Bricket Wood, St. Albans, Herts at 7.30 pm to 10.30 pm on Tuesday evenings fortnightly (on odd numbered calendar weeks) visitors welcome TRS-80/Video Genie.

Other contact:- Reg Smith, 24 Sempill Road, Hemel Hempstead.

**UK101**

UK 101 USER GROUP
Adrian Waters,
9 Moss Lane,
Romford,
Essex RM1 2QB

Romford 64954

Newsletter and software library. Technical service. Membership per 6 months £4.60 inc VAT. £5.00 overseas.

**ZX81/SPECTRUM**

COLCHESTER SINCLAIR USER GROUP
Richard Lawn,
102 Prettygate Road,
Colchester,
Essex

Colchester 61066

Meets fortnightly.

EDINBURGH ZX C. C.
John Palmer,
56, Meadowfield Drive,
Edinburgh

031 661 3183

Meets 2nd & 4th Wednesday of month Claremont Hotel, Claremont Crescent, Edinburgh 7.30 – 10.30. ZX '80, '81, Spectrum club 70+ members. Tutorial groups, bring your machine and show it, bimonthly newsletter, workshops. Subs £5.00 pa or £3.00 juniors, students, OAPs and unemployed.

EDUCATIONAL ZX80/81 USERS GROUP (EZUG)
Eric Deeson,
Highgate School,
Balsall Heath Road,
Highgate,
Birmingham B12 9DS

An offshoot of MUSE. Caters specifically for education uses and users of Sinclair micros. Has over 1000 members. (EZUG). Annual sub. £2.50. Europe – £6.00 or $12 elsewhere.

GUILDFORD ZX81(80) USERS GROUP
A. Bond,
54 Farnham Road,
Guildford,
Surrey GU2 5PE

Guildford 62035

Meets regularly on Fridays. Club magazine.

LIVERPOOL ZX USER'S CLUB
Keith Archer,
17, Sweeting Street,
Liverpool L2 4TE

051 236 6109

Meets Wednesday evenings 7.00 pm – ring for details.

NATIONAL ZX USER'S CLUB
Tim Hartnell,
44-46 Earls Court Road,
London W8 6EJ

Publishes monthly magazine INTERFACE. For sample copy and club details, send £1.00 to the above address.

THE 81 CLUB
Mike Hayes,
54, Oakley Place,
Grangetown,
Cardiff

Cardiff 371732

Telephone service and software library.

Wolverhampton ZX81/ZXSPECTRUM User Group

Meets Mondays at 6.30 pm in the Dinner Hall of Dunsdale School, Wombourne, Wolverhampton.

ZX80/ZX81 USERS CLUB
David Blagden,
PO Box 159,
Kingston-upon-Thames,
Surrey KT2 5UQ

Technical support
Newsletter. Low cost ZX80/81 software in members software bank. Send a sae for further information.

ZX AMATEUR RADIO USER GROUP
Paul Newman G4INP,
3, Red House Lane,
Leiston,
Suffolk IP16 4JZ

Newsletter to cater for Radio Hams.

## SOFTWARE SPECIFIC USER GROUPS

### CP/M

CP/M IRL. IRISH CP/M USERS' GROUP
Doug Notley,
Gardner House,
Ballsbridge,
Dublin 4

Dublin 686411

Meets monthly in Dublin area. £5.00. Newsletter, CP/M. MAG.

CP/M USER GROUP (UK)
David Powys-Lybbe,
11 Sun Street,
Finsbury Square,
London EC2M 2QD

01-247 0691

£7.50 per annum single membership other rates of membership please enquire. Newsletter. Software Library. Help service.

### DOSPLUS (TRS)

UK DOSPLUS USER GROUP
Peter Toothill,
101 Swanside Road,
Liverpool L14 7NL

### FORTH

FORTH INTEREST GROUP UK
K.C. Goldie-Morrison,
15 St. Albans Mansion,
Kensington Court Place,
London W8 5QH

01-937 3231

£7.00 per year entitles you to 6 copies of the Newsletter. Meets 1st Thursday of each month, Room 408, South Bank Polytechnic. Bi-monthly newsletter, 'FORTHWRITE'. Help in implementing FIG Forth.

FORTH USERS GROUP
David Husband,
2 Gorleston Road,
Branksome,
Poole,
Dorset BH12 1NW

(0202) 764724

Forth Users club, particularly xFORTH and NasFORTH. Variety of machines covered. Some members using poly-FORTH. Subscription £7.50 per annum. Quarterly newsletter. Hope to hold meetings in Poole when venue arranged. Weekly radio-net news exchange.

### LOGO

BRITISH LOGO USER GROUP
Pam Valley,
British LOGO User Group,
c/o Shell Centre for Mathematics,
University of Nottingham

Quarterly Newsletter to be published, also a Annual Newsletter. More substantial items also. LOGO is for all levels of user.

### PASCAL

PASCAL USER GROUP (PUG)
Nick Hughes,
PO Box 52,
Pinner,
Middlesex HA5 3FE

01-866 3816

Membership is £9.00.

UCSD PASCAL UK USERS GROUP
Malcolm Harper,
Oxford University Computing Laboratory,
Programming Research Group,
45 Banbury Road,
Oxford OX2 6PE

USCD SYSTEM USERS SOCIETY
John Ash,
Dicoll Data Systems Ltd.,
Bond Close,
Kingsland Estate,
Basingstoke,
Hants RG24 0QB

Existing Special Interest groups. Industrial application, word processors. Real time, Business applications, and forward planning.

UK PILOT USER GROUP
Alec Wood,
Wirral Grammar School for Boys,
Crosslane,
Bebington,
Wirral,
Merseyside LG3 3AQ

sae for fact sheet on Pilot versions. Reference manual £5.00.

### UNIX

/USR/GROUP/UK
A.J. Lazzerinin,
Plexus Computers Inc.
Langley House,
Langley Mill,
Notts. NG16 4AN

(07737) 66141

Unix users group. Official chapter of /usr/group International. Formed to provide a forum for UNIX users, software suppliers, and manufacturers of UNIX-based hardware to discuss matters of mutual interest. (Mainly commercial, rather than technical or academic.)

**NON-SPECIFIC, NATIONAL and MISCELLANEOUS GROUPS**

ACC
Rupert Steele,
St. John's College,
Oxford OX1 3JP

Oxford (0865) 47671

(Membership Secretary)

£5.00, £2.50 under 18's and OAP's.

Peter Whittle (Chairman)
Phone (0865) 721180

The National Club. Bi-monthly newsletter 'Allumulator'. 6800, 6502, z80 and 2650 libraries. Co-ordinates all Computer Club activities in UK.

AMATEUR RADIO SPECIAL INTEREST GROUP
Peter Whittle,
G4BBU,
49 Bartlemas Road,
Oxford OX4 1XW

APEX (ASTROCOMPUTING PROGRAM EXCHANGE)
c/o M.V. Gavin,
79 Ardrossan Gardens,
Worcester Park,
Surrey

Subscription £2.00, Overseas £3.00 sterling. Magazine 3/4 issues a year.

ASSOCIATION OF LONDON COMPUTER CLUBS
c/o 187 Upper St.,
London N1 1RQ.

01-359 5045

An association covering the major London general Computing Clubs. Clubs marked '*' are members of the ALCC.

CENTRAL PROGRAM EXCHANGE
Mrs. Judith Brown,
The Polytechnic,
Wulfruma Street,
Wolverhampton WV1 1LY

Wolverhampton 28521/27371

Full membership Europe £25.00.
Full membership overseas £40.00.

Small users service Europe £10.00.
Small service Overseas £20.00.
Subscription provides 30 free programs per annum. 10 free programs for Small Users.

COMPUTER EDUCATION SOCIETY OF IRELAND
Dairmuid McCarthy,
7 St. Kevins Park,
Kilmacud,
Blackrock,
Co. Dublin

£3.00 Branches £1.00 extra. Brief is to monitor computer education 12. Cork. M. Moynihan, Colaiate an SpicraidNaomh, Bishopstown, Cork. J. Walsh, Sr. Lourda Keane Convent FCJ Laurel Hill, Limerick. H. Dobbs, Newtown School, Waterford. Sr Helen Lenehan, Presentation School, Kilkenny.

DENSPET
DENSPET
Rock House,
Ballycrog,
Westport,
Co. Mayo,
Eire

Group specifically for exchange or original programs for MTU 200 x 320 dot matrix hi-res PET add-on. Send sample of your work or £2.50 and receive sample in return plus newsletter sub and lists of available programs.

MEDICAL MICRO USERS GROUP
P.J.V. Dixon,
MEDICOM,
1-2 Hanover Street,
London W1

Aids location of medical programs. Newsletter.

MICRO-CONTACT
Peter Paton,
176 Todmorden Road,
Burnley,
Lancs BB11 3EU

(0282) 53241

New group to cater for all types of computer. Newsletter 6 times per year. Annual Subscription £3.00. Software Library of members contributions.

MICROMODELLER USER ASSOCIATION
Phillip Matthews,
Philip Morris House,
21 High Street,
Feltham TW13 4AD

Meetings to be held three times a year. Hope to produce a quarterly newsletter.

01-751 6388

MINI AND MICROCOMPUTER USERS IN EDUCATION (MUSE)
Lorraine Boyce,
Westhill College Teaching Centre,
Woeley Park Road,
Birmingham B29 6LL

021 471 3723

MUSE.

National organisation for coordinating activity in schools, teacher training colleges etc. Operates a software pricelist, insurance and provides a regular journal.

NATIONAL PERSONAL COMPUTER USERS ASS.
The Secretary,
NPCUA,
11 Spratling Street,
Manston,
Ramsgate,
Kent

£12.00 UK. £15.00 overseas. Secretary Eric Keeley (G8XWM).

NATIONAL WESTMINSTER PERSONAL COMPUTER SOCIETY
P.J. Moore,
National Westminster Bank PLC,
Trustee & Income Tax Dept.,
Birmingham Branch,
2nd Floor,
104/106 Colmore Row,
Birmingham B3 3AJ

021-236 6176 ext 382

60 members at present. National Westminster Group employees only.

SOCIETY OF GENEALOGISTS
David Hawgood,
26 Cloister Road,
London W3 0DE

01-993 2897

Quarterly newsletter. 800 members, various machines.

TRANSDUCER CLUB
D. Stockqueler,
66 Waterloo Road,
Penylan,
Cardiff

0222 495374

Club for those interested in robotics, Micros and micro hardware. Send 25p for sample newsletter and details.

**BULLETIN BOARDS**

BO-NET
Leon Heller and Brian Pain,
(0908) 566660

NATIONAL TRS80 USERS GROUP
Electronic mail. Software for downloading. Newsletter. TRS80 information. Hours: 7 days a week. 1900 to 2200.

CBBS-LONDON
P. Goldmann,
PO Box 100a,
Surbiton,
Surrey KT5 8HY

Operation times:
Sundays 1600 – 2200. Phone number 01-399 2136 (Data only). 300 baud, full-duplex. No charge. Message entry and retrieval, downloading of programs.

FORUM-80 LONDON
Leon Jay,
01-286 6207

Electronic mail, program downloading. Hours: Tuesday, Friday, Saturday, Sunday – 1900 to 2300.

FORUM 80 USERS GROUP
Frederick Brown,
421 Endike Lane,
Hull HU6 8AG

Hull (0482) 859169

Bulletin Board. No access charge. Open to any micro owner. Operates Tuesdays and Thursdays 1900 – 2200 and Saturday and Sunday 1200 – 2200. Program library for downloading programs (all in Microsoft BASIC). Program uploading for adding your own programs to library. Forum 80 Users Group (membership free) enables access to programs not in public domain.

FORUM-80 WEMBLEY
Victor Saleh,
01-902 2546

System hours: 7 days a week, 7 pm to 10 pm.

**INTERNATIONAL (WITH UK CONNECTIONS)**

**BELGIUM**

DAINAMIC
W. Hermans,
Heide 98,
3171 Westmeerbeek,
Belgium.

500+ members, mainly in Belgium, Holland, Germany and France. Publish a monthly newsletter with most of articles in English.

**CANADA**

CANADIAN SORCERER USER GROUP
Maurice Dow,
84 Camberley Crescent,
Brampton,
Ontario,
Canada L6V 3L4

416 451 9452

International Sorcerer Information Service Newsletter form, $15 Canadian funds, US Dollars elsewhere. Further information from above.

**DENMARK**

HADSTEN COMPUTER CLUB
Peter Mortensen,
Skovvangsvej 8,
DK-8370 Hadsten,
Denmark

**GERMANY**

AMATEUR RADIO & COMPUTER CLUB
Officer I/C,
Royal Air Force,
Gutersloh,
BFPO 47

**HOLLAND**

CP/M-GG
H. van Andel,
Trajanusplein 1,
4041 AK Kesteren,
Holland

Users meeting 3/4 times a year. CP/M Users Group software library. Newsletter 'Software Bus'. Software catalogue of public domain CP/M software. Publishes 'Introduction to CP/M' – Dfl. 16 to members.

FORUM-80 HOLLAND
Nico Karssemeyer,
010 313 512 533

Electronic mail. Program up/downloading. Shopping list. Hours: Tues-Sat 1800 to 0700 nightly. Continuous from 1800 Sat. to 0700 Tues.

## ITALY

ITALIAN ZX USER CLUB
c/o Arrigo Bondi,
via Molino Vecchio 10/F,
40026 Imola,
Italy

Quarterly magazine.

## NORWAY

MICROCOMPUTER USERS CLUB
c/o Synthetronics Microcomputers,
PO Box 151,
1322 Hoevik,
Norway

Program Exchange.

SARPSBORG & OMEGN DATA & ELECTRONIC CLUB
Tore Foss,
Bikely,
1745 Skjeberg,
Norway

Recently established for data and electronic users in general. Monthly magazines, technical service, meetings, excursions and courses. We are in the process of establishing a member-library.

## SPAIN

ZX CLUB SPAIN
Mr. C. Benito,
PO Box 3253,
Madrid,
Spain

Monthly Newsletter. Meets every day from 1300 to 1930. Program exchange. Free BASIC courses.

## USA

GROUP/380
Mokuri Cherlin,
PO Box 1131,
Mount Shasta,
CA 96067,
USA

$10 for individuals, $20 for organisations.

Program exchange. Access to computerised database listings. IBM 360/370 Mainframes.

## ZIMBABWE

GREEN SCREEN CLUB
B. Creighton,
Box 2900,
Harare,
Zimbabwe

Only club in Zimbabwe.

# APPENDIX E

## Magazines in English . . . UK/USA/Australia

### '68 MICRO JOURNAL

*'68 Micro Journal, 6131 Airways Blvd, Chattanooga TN 37421 $14,50 (12 issues)*

Aimed at users of the 6800 family microprocessors.

### 80 MICRO

*PO Box 981, Farmingdale, NY 11737 USA $24.97 (12 issues)*

Specialises in looking at Tandy (Radio Shack) computers. A recommended buy for anybody with a TRS80 or Video Genie computer.

### A + B COMPUTING

*ASP, 145 Charing Cross Rd, London WC2H 0EE. £11.10 (6 issues)*

A monthly aimed at BBC micro users. Quite good for news and programs.

### ACCumulator

*ACC, c/o 72 Mill Rd, Hawley, Dartford, Kent. £5 (6 issues).*

The bi-monthly newsletter of the ACC, the national computer club. Lots of technical articles and news sent in by members. Rather thin, but worth it.

## ACE INTERNATIONAL

*189 Fore St, Angel Place, London N18 2TU. Free (9 issues).*

A European-wide consumer electronics journal aimed at the retailer. Gives a good background to what's happening in the Far East and the US. Also available in French, German and Italian!

## ACORN USER

*Addison-Wesley Publishers Ltd, 53 Bedford Square, London WC1B 3DZ £15.00 (12 issues)*

Acorn Computer's own magazine for Atom and BBC microcomputers. The usual mixture of news, publicity blurb and occasional program listings.

## BEE BUG

*PO Box 109, High Wycombe, Bucks HP11 2TD £9.90 (12 issues)*

The best of the independent newsletters covering the popular BBC microcomputer.

## BUSINESS COMPUTER SYSTEMS

*PO Box 17452, Boulder, CO 80217 USA Free to qualified readers.*

For those really interested in the business computer market. Lots of technical articles and product information. Only for those really dedicated to the business market.

## BYTE

*Byte Publications Inc, 70 Main Street, Peterborough NH 03458 $43 (12 issues)*

The world's first magazine devoted exclusively to personal computing with a staggering, estimated world-wide circulation of 250,000 copies. It is orientated to hardware rather than software and it is aimed at the experience hobbyist or professional engineer rather than the novice. Since being taken over by McGraw Hill it is beautifully produced, professionally laid out, and averages 500 pages per issue.

## CALL APPLE

*1e Puget Sound Program Library Exchange, 6708 38th Ave, WW Seattle WA98136, USA*

Specialist magazine for Apple users. More hobby based than commercial.

## CLOAD MAGAZINE

*825 Marxmiller, Box 1267, Goleta CA 9301, USA*

Tandy's disc based magazine. Lots of useful programs and information about Tandy.

## COLOR COMPUTER

*New England Publications Inc, Highland Mill, Camden, ME 04843 USA $34 (12 issues)*

A nice glossy monthly magazine devoted to users of the Tandy Color computer. Full of good information, Could be useful to those Dragon owners who are capable of converting software to their system.

## COMMODORE COMPUTING

*167-169 Great Portland St, London W1 (10 issues)*

This started life as Commodore's in-house magazine but was sold off to the present owners. Standards of articles are rather patchy. Really only of use to dedicated PET users.

## COMPUTE

*Small System Services Inc, PO Box 5406, Greensboro, North Carolina 27403 $42.50 (12 issues)*

Subtitled the "6502 resource magazine for PET, APPLE, ATARI, KIM, SYM, AIM and OSE owners", this magazine is a combination of three popular newsletters that have been available for a number of years: 6502 User Notes, the PET Gazette and the PET User Notes. Compute is essential reading for anybody with a 6502 based machine.

## COMPUTER AIDED DESIGN

*PO Box 63, Westbury Hse, Bury St, Guildford, Surrey GU2 5RH*

Although this is not really for personal computer users, the news pages, and some of the less complicated articles, contain useful information for those involved with microcomputers.

## COMPUTER AND VIDEO GAMES

*EMAP Publications, 8 Herbal Hill, London EC1R 5JB £10.00 (12 issues)*

One of the UK's largest selling magazine. Originally aimed at the teeny-bopper market, this magazine has now settled down to a very easy reading style and is a must for those who just want to play games on their computer.

## COMPUTER ANSWERS

*62 Oxford St, London W1A 2HG £10 (12 issues)*

A monthly magazine directed at those computer users who want to improve or replace their existing systems. Lots of questions and answers which have been aggressively packaged. Useful for those who know what questions they want to ask!

## COMPUTER BUSINESS EUROPE

*EEC Publications, 196-200 Balls Pond Road, London N1. Free (12 issues)*

CBE is a jointly owned venture with CW Publications in America. It is aimed more at the computer retailer than the computer user. It has a rather patchy style and is generally considered to be inferior to MicroScope. Free to those who qualify.

## COMPUTER CHOICE

*Business Press International, Quadrant House, The Quadrant, Sutton, Surrey SM2 5AS.*

IPC's answer to What Micro? Aimed at the under £200 machine market. Too new for comment.

## COMPUTER MANAGEMENT

*196-200 Balls Pond Road, London N1.*

Originally this magazine was aimed at managers of large computer systems, but has now moved into the personal computer field. Useful reading for those who are involved in the management of organisations using a number of microcomputers.

## COMPUTER MUSIC JOURNAL

*People's Computer Company, Menlo Park CA 94024 $11.00 (4 issues)*

This is devoted to "high quality musical applications of digital electronics". A wide ranging magazine covering not only the theoretical aspects of digital signal processing but also the more mundane topics like reviews of particular musical instruments. Its articles are quite successful attempts to make comprehensible material from what can be a difficult field.

## COMPUTER SYSTEMS

*Techpress Publishing Company Ltd, Walton House, 94 High Street, Bromley BR1 1JW. £25 (12 issues).*

Another free magazine, if qualified. However, the subscription is worth it if you're looking for a magazine that takes a more detailed look at applications.

## COMPUTER TALK

*Quadrant Hse, The Quadrant, Sutton, Surrey SM2 5AS*

A weekly "freebie" for those involved on the software side of computing. Lots of useful gossip. You may have to wait to get on to its circulation list, if you are a qualified reader.

## COMPUTER UPDATE

*The Boston Computer Society Inc, Three Center Plaza, Boston, MA 02108 USA $40.00 (6 issues)*

The glossy bi-monthly 'newsletter' of the Boston Computer Society. The subscription price includes membership. At least six meaty articles about the world-wide personal computer scene written by well-known correspondents.

## COMPUTER WEEKLY

*Quadrant Hse, The Quadrant, Sutton, Surrey SM2 5AS £25.00*

Another free magazine for those who are qualified readers, but you can subscribe if you are not. Lots and lots of news with some interesting articles about the industry in general. Although it has a rather boring style the information is there if you are prepared to dig.

## COMPUTERS AND ELECTRONICS

*PO Box 2774, Boulder, CO 80302 USA $15.97 (12 issues)*

Originally called Popular Electronics this was the magazine that put the very first microcomputer, Altair, on its January 1975 cover. Credited with giving the founders of Microsoft the idea for their now ubiquitous BASIC. Aimed at the do-it-yourself hobbyist, with articles about building computers from kits etc.

## COMPUTING

*53-55 Frith St, London W1A 2HG £20.00*

VNU's competitor to IPC's Computer Weekly. A far glossier publication and a jazzier style. Required reading for all those who take their personal computing seriously. Free to qualified readers and members of the British Computer Society. Worth subscribing to if you can't get on the free list (it's cheaper to become an associate member of the BCS!).

## COMPUTING TODAY

*ASP Ltd, 145 Charing Cross Rd, London WC2 0EE £12.70 (12 issues)*

Originally a supplement to the fine constructional magazine Electronics Today International, Computing Today was expected to fill the need for a good, solid personal computer constructional magazine. It is now, though, the typical blend of introductory articles for the beginner with software listing mainly in BASIC and machine code.


## CREATIVE COMPUTING

*PO Box 5214, Boulder CO 80321 $29.00 (12 issues)*

Its subtitle — "the magazine computer applications and software" reflects its contents very accurately. Aimed at the personal user, it has the usual mixture of introductory articles, product reviews and news about the industry. It is a very good source of games software and has regular columns devoted to the APPLE, PET and TRS-80 etc.


## DATALINK

*53 Frith St, London W1A 2HG*

Another free weekly, for those euphemistically called systems analysts! If you can't get on to the free list then don't bother.


## DATA PROCESSING

*PO Box 63, Westbury Hse, Bury St, Guildford, Surrey GU2 5BH*

A free monthly, again for those 'qualified', which originally started life as a magazine for those involved with large computer systems. It is now moving towards the personal computer field, especially office systems.

## DESKTOP COMPUTING

*PO Box Farmingdale NY 117737 USA $25.00 (12 issues)*

To quote a well known American editor "Desktop was started in 1981 as the plain language computer language magazine for business. The language was so plain, it was virtually unreadable. Although a recent change is editors has improved readability somewhat, the magazine is still struggling to find a niche."

## DRAGON USER

*Sunshine Publications, Hobhouse Court, 19 Whitcombe St., London WC2. £12 (8 issues)*

The only monthly magazine for Dragon users. The usual mix of games, news and ads.

## DR DOBB'S JOURNAL OF COMPUTER CALISTHENICS AND ORTHODONTIA

*People's Computer Company, Box E, 1263 El Camino, Menlo Park, CA 94025 $42 (12 issues)*

Apart from Byte, probably the most famous of the computer hobbyist magazines. Its specializes in systems software and its articles will invariably include the full documentation and source code. This is by any standards a good quality journal.

## EDUCATIONAL COMPUTING

*EMAP Publications, 8 Herbal Hill, London, EC1R 5JB £10.00 (11 issues)*

The first UK magazine specifically devoted to the use of computers in education. Since its recent change in format, it has endeavoured to cater for the interests of the further and higher education sector. It is primarily orientated to the secondary school market, with a fair number of its contributors being practising teachers. There is obviously a market for a specialist educational computer magazine; however, it is variable in the quality of its articles.

## ELECTRICAL & ELECTRONIC TRADER

*Quadrant Hse, The Quadrant, Sutton, Surrey SM2 5AS. Free (46 issues)*

Although this magazine is aimed at the electrical retailers it has regular sections on personal computers and is good background reading for anybody in the retail trade. Free if qualified.

## ELECTRONICS & COMPUTING

*EMAP Publications Ltd, 155 Farringdon Rd, London EC1R 3AD £9.50 (12 issues)*

Aimed specifically at the home do-it-yourself constructor. Each month it has a couple of useful projects, but you really need to know what you are doing. It's not really aimed at the beginner.

## ELECTRONIC DESIGN

*Hayden Publishing Co. Inc., 50 Essx St, Rochelle Park NJ 07662 USA. Free (32 issues)*

One of the major US publications in the electronics field. Usually has lots of information on new computer systems. Required reading for those involved on the engineering applications side.

## ELECTRONICS (INTERNATIONAL)

*McGraw Hill Publications, 34 Dover St, London W1X 4BR*

An American publication, with a European edition, this magazine is aimed at the professional engineer but its new section contains lots of good information for those using personal computers in an engineering environment.

## ELECTRONICS – THE MAPLIN MAGAZINE

*Maplin Electronic Suppliers Ltd, PO Box 3, Raleigh, Essex £2.80 (4 issues)*

Full of do-it-yourself projects for the home electronics fanatic. At least seven projects each quarter, most of them based around the Sinclair and Atari computers.

## GAMES COMPUTING

*ASP, 145 Charing Cross Rd, London WC2H 0EE. £12.25 (12 issues)*

Argus's answer to the incredibly successful Computer & Video Games. Too new for comment.

## HOME COMPUTING WEEKLY

*Argus Specialist Publications Ltd, 145 Charing Cross Rd, London WC2 0EE 35p weekly*

A fairly thin (less than 50 pages) weekly news sheet mainly consisting of games programs for all popular computers.

## IBM USER

*EEC Publications, 196-200 Balls Pond Road, London N1. £12 (12 issues)*

This magazine originally started life as a monthly journal for user of IBM mainframe computers. It has now moved into looking at the IBM pc as well.

## ICPUG NEWSLETTER

*ICPUC, c/o 30 Brancaster Road, Newbury Park, Ilford, Essex 1G2 7EP. £7.50 (6 issues)*

This is the newsletter of the Independent Commodore Products User Group, and usually contains 150 odd pages of useful info that's impossible to get elsewhere. Well worth the money that also gives you free (!) membership of the group. (A similar publication is produced by ICPUG South East – see in Club section).

## IEEE MICRO

*IEEE Computer Society, Los Alamitos, CA 90720 $23.00 (4 issues)*

One of the Institute of Electrical and Electronic Engineers magazines published by their Computer Society. Aimed at computer specialists.

## I/O

*Atari International (UK) Inc., Atari House, Railway Terrace, Slough, Bucks. £6.00 (6 issues)*

The Atari-run national User Group magazine. Full of good ideas for the users of a machine that is sometimes neglected by others on the bookstalls. Rather thin for the price (approx 24pp).

## INCIDER

*PO Box 911, Farmingdale, NY 11737. USA $24.97 (12 issues)*

A specialist magazine for Apple users. No different from any other single computer orientated magazine.

## INFOMATICS

*53-55 Frith St, London, W1A 2HG £10.00*

A free monthly magazine, again for those qualified with lots of news and articles aimed at the large office user. There is a companion daily newsheet, which is relatively expensive, called Infomatics daily bulletin. This is required reading for those new freaks who need to know everything yesterday!

## INFOWORLD

*375 Cochituate Rd, Box 837, Framingham MA 01701 USA $95.00 (51 issues)*

The original trade paper for the microcomputer industry, Infoworld is now moving into the consumer publication market. This weekly newspaper was originally called the Intelligent Machine's Journal. Now owned by Computerworld Publications, publisher of the world's largest trade journal. Infoworld is the only publication that gives programs standardised ratings in its software reviews, which are probably the best of any computer magazine.

## INTERFACE AGE

*McPheters Wolfe & Jones, 16704 Marquardt Ave, Cerritos, CA 90701 $35 (12 issues)*

A typical mixture of introductory articles, product reviews and news about the industry. It has a strong orientation with regular articles for the small businessman. Until recently of uneven quality but now much more consistent. Each year it publishes indexes to the software and hardware available in the USA.


## LASERBUG

*10 Dawley Ride, Colnbrook, Slough, Berks SL3 0QH £12.00 (12 issues)*

A cheap and cheerful independent magazine for BBC microcomputer users. Lots of program listings and software and hardware tips.


## LIFELINES

*TM Lifelines Pub. Co., 1651 3rd Ave, NY, NY 10028 USA $50 (12 issues)*

Probably the best users guide to CP/M software available. It is particularly good at finding bugs in software using this operating system.


## LOAD RUNNER

*EEC Publications, 196-200 Balls Pond Road, London N1 4 AQ. 40p/issue (26 issues)*

Billed as the galaxy's first computer comic, this colourful picture mag. is aimed at the 8-12 year olds. An interesting idea that seems to have caught on.

### MICRO: 6802/6809

*MicroInk Inc, PO Box 6502, Chelmsford MA 01824 $33 (12 issues)*

The 6502 is reputed to be the most widely used micro in the world. It is used in the KIM, PET, APPLE, ACORN, etc. The 6809, a development of the 6502, is used in the Tandy Colour Computer and the Dragon 32. There are two good quality journals specifically aimed at 6502 users. This one and Compute complement each other in that Micro concentrates more on software and interfacing techniques than Compute. It also carries a bibliography of 6502/6809 articles which is reasonably comprehensive.

### MICRO BUSINESS

*Business Press International, Quadrant House, The Quadrant, Sutton, Surrey SM2 5AS. £10 (12 issues)*

A new monthly aimed at the retailer. Free if you're in that category. Has its work cut out to match MicroScope.

### MICRO-DIGEST

*Kluwer Technische Tijdschriften BV, PO Box 23, 7400 GA Deventer, The Netherlands £21.00 (10 issues)*

A European-wide trade magazine which is published in four languages. Lots of useful information of the European microcomputer industry.

### MICRO DISCOVERY

*Micro Digest Inc., 5152 Katella Avenue, Suite 102, Los Alamitos, CA 90720 USA. $35 (12 issues)*

Subtitled "The Non-Technical Magazine of Personal Computing" this is probably one of the best mags. Looking *behind* the news etc, with ten or more articles a month. Reminiscent of the badly missed Computer Age.

## MICROCOMPUTER PRINTOUT

*7A Harpton Parade, Yateley, Camberley GU17 7TD £11.40 (12 issues)*

This magazine originally started life exclusively devoted to the PET. It has now moved on, been taken over by a publishing conglomerate, and other than its irreverent style, its contents are virtually indistinguishable from any of the other monthlies. It still has a good 'insider' contacts with a number of manufacturers, and frequently publishes industry scoops. Julian Allison's column always worth reading.

## MICROCOMPUTING

*Wayne Green Inc, 80 Pine St, Peterborough NH 03458 $62 (12 issues)*

One of the best value for money magazines for the hobbyist. Each issue has a large number (over 20) of good solid articles for the hobbyist or small businessman. It has regular columns on most common microcomputers. Wayne Green's rather idiosyncratic view of life pervades the magazine.

## MICRODECISION

*VNU Publications, 62 Oxford St, London £9.60 (12 issues)*

Another monthly from VNU, aimed at the commercial personal computer user. Lots of articles on networking etc.

## MICROPROCESSORS AND MICROSYSTEMS

*IPC Science and Technology Press Ltd, PO Box 63, Westbury Hse, Bury St, Guildford, Surrey GU2 5BH £55 (10 issues)*

Not really a hobbyist magazine but designed for practising engineers. However it features a wealth of practical information and is worth looking at if you're an experienced hobbyist.

## MICROSCOPE

*Sportscene Specialist Press Ltd, 14 Rathbone Place, London W1P 1DE £35.00 (26 issues)*

By far the best magazine aimed at the microcomputer trade. Lots of up-to-date news and very interesting articles looking behind the UK microcomputer industry. It is produced by the publishers who created PCW in its current, successful, format.

## MICRO SOFTWARE AND SYSTEMS MAGAZINE

*Newtech Publishing Ltd, 7 Banstead Rd, Purley, Surrey, CR2 3ER Free (10 issues)*

Another free magazine for computer dealers, systems and software manufacturers, consultants and those professional micro users who purchase software or hardware. Mainly consists of good in-depth reviews of the more popular software packages.

## MICROSYSTEMS – THE CP/M AND S100 USERS'S JOURNAL

*Microsystems, PO Box 789-M, Morristown NJ 07960 $10 (6 issues)*

A bi-monthly journal aimed specifically at those using the CP/M operating system and the S100 bus.

## MIND YOUR OWN BUSINESS

*106 Church Rd, London SE19 2UB*

This is really a magazine looking at the whole field of office and small business technology, but it is now rapidly moving into the personal computer field, and most of the articles are orientated towards the impact of the microcomputer in these areas.

## MINI-MICRO SYSTEMS

*Cahners Publishing Co, 221 Columbus Ave, Boston, MA 02116 $65.00 (14 issues)*

Another free monthly for those professionally involved with microcomputers. Usually contains about 400 pages of news and interesting articles, mainly aimed at the professional user.

## NATGUG NEWS

*c/o Morris Walk, Newport Pagnell, Bucks MK16 8QD. £12 (12 issues)*

The monthly newsletter of the National TRS-80 and Genie Users' Group. Lots of good info in tightly packed A4 news sheet, usually about 40 pages thick. Free membership of group with newsletter subscription!

## NIBBLE

*MicroSPARC Inc., 10 Lewis St., Lincoln, MA 01773, USA. $47.50 (8 issues)*

Another American magazine for the Apple user.

## PC

*PO Box 598, Morris Plains, NJ 07950. USA $27.00 (12 issues)*

A new magazine aimed at the IBM personal computer user. Its tenth issue was over 500 pages in size and is required reading for any IBM pc user.

## PC USER

*EMAP, 57A Hatton Garden, London EC1N 8JP £18.00 (12 issues)*

A British attempt to emulate the success of the two American journals in this field. Rather thin and expensive in comparison.

## PC WORLD

*PO Box 6700, Bergenfield, NJ 07621. USA $24.00 (12 issues)*

Founded by most of the original staff of PC, PC World had over 400 pages in its first issue. Virtually identical to PC this magazine is also required reading for those involved with the IBM.

## PERSONAL COMPUTER NEWS

*VNU Business Publications, 62 Oxford St, London W1A 2HG £23.00 (51 issues)*

The weekly stable mate of PCW. By far the best of the three weekly publications aimed at the personal computer user. A colourful, glossy publication averaging 90-100 pages, PCN is packed full of hardware and software reviews, news and thankfully few program listings.

## PERSONAL COMPUTER WORLD

*VNU Publications, 62 Oxford St, London 1DE £9.00 (12 issues)*

Europe's first magazine for personal computing has re-established itself as unquestionably UK's premiere magazine in this field. It now has a nice balance between hardware and software features while its news column by Guy Kewney is consistently entertaining and informative. PCW's main strength however lies in the quality of its regular contributors: Malcolm Peltu's book reviews, Sheridan William's computer clinic, Sue Eisenbach's features etc. Now approaching the size of the US monthlies.

## PERSONAL COMPUTING

*Hayden Publishing Inc, 50 Essex St, Rochelle Park, NJ 07662 $32.00 (12 issues)*

Since the takeover by Hayden Publishing, Personal Computing has aimed for a more business orientated reader. Each issue features a theme eg. word processing, database management systems etc. Software listings, as usual, primarily in BASIC.

## PERSONAL COMPUTING TODAY

*145 Charing Cross Rd, London WC2H 0EE 35p per week*

A weekly magazine, available on bookstalls and newsagents, aimed at the home computerist. Cheap and cheerful, but not very informative.

## POPULAR COMPUTING

*PO Box 307, Martinsville, NJ 08836 $11.97 (12 issues)*

This magazine, an offshoot of Byte, was started as a non-technical magazine for beginners. This didn't pay and it is now more sophisticated and manages to keep a good balance, focusing more on home computing applications than some of the other American magazines.

## POPULAR COMPUTING WEEKLY

*Sunshine Publications Ltd, Hobhouse Crt, 19 Whitcombe St, London WC2 £19.95 (50 issues)*

A rather thin (less than 30 pages) weekly magazine containing little news and a few games and utility programs for the more popular micros.

## PORTABLE COMPUTER

*500 Howard St, San Fransisco, CA 94105, USA. $20 (6 issues)*

A new glossy from the States, that covers all aspects of the so-called "portable computers". More applications and news orientated, than meaty articles.

## PRACTICAL COMPUTING

*IPC Electrical Electronic Press Ltd, Quadrant Hse, The Quadrant, Sutton, Surrey SM2 5AS £14.00 (12 issues)*

It was predicted that Practical Computing would become the premiere British personal computer magazine. It does not appear to have attracted such good quality contributors as its main competitor (Personal Computer World). It has regular columns devoted to the ZX80/81, TANDY, APPLE, PET and the 6502 microprocessor.

## PURSER'S MAGAZINE

*PO Box 466, El Dorado, CA 95623, USA $4 (annual)*

A specialist magazine that lists software available for the Apple and Tandy computers. Lots of potted software reviews. Quite useful if you're interested in that sort of thing.

## RADIO & ELECTRONICS WORLD

*Publishers Broadcast Ltd, 117a High St, Brentwood, Essex CM14 4SG 75p per issue*

Although this magazine is really aimed at the electronics enthusiast, there are many articles of a do-it-yourself nature for the home constructor of computer add-ons.

## ROBOTICS AGE

*Robotics Publishing Corp, 5147 Angeles Crest Hwy, La Canada, CA 91011 $15 (4 issues)*

A useful magazine for those wishing to build their own robots, or take part in one of the many "Micromouse" competitions. Can be a bit technical.

## SINCLAIR PROGRAMS

*196-200 Balls Pond Road, London N1. £6.60 (6 issues)*

Spin off from Sinclair User, this bi-monthly magazine is full of games for Sinclair computers. If you're not too bored by pushing keys then this is a cheap way of getting hold of software.

## SINCLAIR PROJECTS

*196-200 Balls Pond Road, London N1. £6.60 (6 issues)*

The only magazine devoted soley to add-ons for Sinclair computers. 'Projects' has six or seven articles each issue graded from absolute beginner to quite difficult. A useful magazine for those Sinclair users who feel that they are quite good with a soldering iron and want to save some money.

## SINCLAIR USER

*196-200 Balls Pond Road, London N1. £9.00 (12 issues)*

A good monthly magazine aimed at the owners of Sinclair computers. Lots of interesting news and articles and some program listings.

## SIRIUS COMPUTING

*Paradox Group Ltd, 39-41 North Road, London N7 9DB £9.00 (6 issues)*

A very comprehensive magazine for Sirius users. Covers all aspects, both hardware and software. Required reading for Sirius users.

## SMALL BUSINESS COMPUTERS MAGAZINE

*PO Box 789-M, Morristown, NJ 07960. USA $28.00 (6 issues)*

A not very enterprising bi-monthly from America. The poor relation of its sister publication Creative Computing.

## SOFT

*Sportscene Specialist Press Ltd, 14 Rathbone Place, London W1P 1DE £12.00 (12 issues)*

A new magazine covering every aspect of microcomputing software. Although too new for comment, its first issue contains several excellent in-depth reviews – seems well worth the money.

## SOFTALK

*Softalk Publishing Inc, PO Box 60, North Hollywood, CA 91603 USA $24.00 (12 issues)*

A software magazine aimed at Apple users.

## SOFTWARE

*Quadrant Hse, The Quadrant, Sutton, Surrey SM2 5AS 12 issues (free)*

Another IPC free monthly, which concentrates on micro and mini applications software.

## SOFTWARE AND MICROSYSTEMS

*IEE, PO Box 8, Southgate House, Stevenage, Herts SG1 1HQ £30 (6 issues)*

This is a fairly technical magazine produced by the Institution of Electrical Engineers. It is not really recommended for the casual reader but has very good technical articles for those who take their computing seriously.

## SOFTWARE NEWS

*26 Radcliffe Close, Old Brompton Rd, London SW5 9HX*

This publication was also originally aimed at the professional large computer user. It is now moving in to the personal computing market.

## SYNC

*c/o 27 Andrew Close, Stoke Golding, Nuneaton CV13 6EL £10 (6 issues)*

The original American publication for Timex Sinclair users. Sync obviously has an American view of the Sinclair scene and makes fascinating reading for British readers.

## SYSTEMS INTERNATIONAL

*Quadrant Hse, The Quadrant, Sutton, Surrey SM2 5AS*

A free monthly originally designed for large systems users. It has an interesting European view of the computer industry with occasional articles of interest to the personal computer user.

## SYSTEMS AND SOFTWARE

*Hayden Publishing Co., 50 Essex St, Rochelle Pk, NJ 07662 12 issues (free)*

Another free monthly for those who can convince that they should be on the mailing list! Not much different from any other general purpose freebie.

## TIMEX SINCLAIR USER

*49, LaSalle Ave, Buffalo, NY 14214 USA $29.95 (12 issues) or EEC Publications, 196-200 Balls Pond Road, London N1. £20 (12 issues)*

The American edition of Sinclair User. Complements its progenitor in giving an American viewpoint.

## TRS-80 MICROCOMPUTER NEWS

*PO Box 2910, Fort Worth, Texas 76113 USA. $15 (12 issues)*

Tandy's in-house produced magazine. Full of good information for all Tandy's computers. May be available in single issues from Tandy stores in the UK.

## VIC COMPUTING

*39-41 North Rd, London, N7 9DP*

A bi-monthly aimed at Vic users. Rather patchy editorial style. For the enthusiast only.

## WHAT MICRO?

*62 Oxford St, London W1A 2HG £8.00 (12 issues)*

Nothing more than an extended buyers guide to all sorts of computer hardware. Not very inspiring but a useful source of information for those wanting to purchase a personal computer.

## WHAT'S NEW IN COMPUTING

*Morgan Grampian Hse, 30 Calderwood St, London SE18 6QH*

Another free monthly which basically consists of nothing more than a collection of press releases!

## WHICH COMPUTER?

*8 Herbal Hill, London EC1R 5JB £12.00 (12 issues)*

The original British computer magazine aimed at the business market. Which Computer? has now settled down into a style which makes it invaluable reading for anybody involved with personal computers in a business environment.

## WHICH MICRO AND SOFTWARE REVIEW

*Petersham Hse, 57a Hatton Garden, London EC1N 8JD £10.00 (12 issues)*

Similar in conception to What Micro? Which Micro? is probably easier to read.

## WHICH WORD PROCESSOR?

*8 Herbal Hill, London EC1R 5JB*

A spin-off from Which Computer? This magazine looks at both hardware and software in the word processing field. It is gradually covering all aspects of office automation.

## WINDFALL

*Europress Ltd, Europa Hse, 68 Chester St, Hazel Grove, Stockport SK7 5NY £12.00 (12 issues)*

Specialist magazine aimed at Apple users. Very glossy production with many useful hints and good advice.

## YOUR COMPUTER

*IPC Electrical and Electronic Press, Quadrant Hse, The Quadrant, Sutton, Surrey SM2 5AS £8.00 (12 issues)*

Aimed at the teenage games playing market and published by the people that bring you Practical Computing. Good for Sinclair freaks and has lots of games listings.

## YOUR COMPUTER FOR BUSINESS AND PLEASURE

*The Federal Publishing Co. Prop. Ltd., 140 Joynton Avenue, Waterloo, NSW Australia. A$30 (12 issues)*

An interesting mag. from the Antipodes. Probably the best of an exceedingly varied bunch.

## ZX COMPUTING

*145 Charing Cross Rd, London WC2H 0EE*

Produced for Argos specialists publications by the same people that produce Interface for the national ZX users club. ZX Computing is really a collection of games program listings.

# APPENDIX F

**Bibliography of selected microcomputer books**

With over 2500 books in publication in English just about computers it is clearly a difficult task to pick some representative sample. However, I have endeavoured to do this with the help of Richard Ross-Langley, at Mine of Information. He provided the original bibliography in the first two editions, and I have built on that. In choosing the books below I have tried to list those I've seen, or heard about, as well as those recommended by Richard. I hope that you find it useful.

If you want to get hold of any of the books listed, or be kept up to date with new publications, then contact:

Richard Ross-Langley,
Mine of Information,
1 Francis Avenue,
St. Albans,
AL3 6BL

The prices are approximate. With the pound up and down like a yoyo against the dollar, it's impossible to state stable prices!

## GENERAL

**The Soul of a New Machine** by Tracy Kidder. (Allen Lane 1982) 256pp £7.50. This amazing book won the Pulitzer Prize in 1981 and concerns the design and building of a new data general minicomputer. It is a fascinating insight into the world behind the public face of computing.

**Running Wild – The Next Industrial Revolution** by Adam Osborne (Osborne 1979) 191pp. This book surveys the microelectronic revolution and provides examples of how it will affect business and industry, as well as the individual.

**Choosing a microcomputer** by Francis Samish (Granada 1982) 140pp £4.95. A rather thin look at the personal computer scene really orientated to the businessman.

**Information Technology – an introduction** by Peter Zorkoczy (Pitman 1982) 134pp £5.95. A very basic introduction to the whole field of IT. A good primer for school, college or even personal use.

**The Mighty Micro** by the late Christopher Evans (Gollancz 1980) 222pp, hardback £7. This intelligent and exciting analysis of the computer revolution was serialized on television.

**Computing is easy** by David Parker and Martin Hann (Newnes 1982) 112pp, £4.50 paperback. Really a BASIC programming book dressed up as an introductory text. Good for absolute beginners.

**The Making of the Micro** by the late Christopher Evans (Gollancz 1981 118pp £6. Illustrated history of the computer enhanced with irreverent anecdotes.

**Mindstorms: Children, Computers, Powerful Ideas** by Seymour Papert of M.I.T. (Harvester Press, 1980) £10. An eminent mathematician explains how to use computers in the classroom so that even maths is enjoyable: less teaching and more learning.

**The flame from Japan** by Takeo Miyauchi (Sord 1982) 104pp. The amazing story of the rise and rise of the Japanese micro company Sord. Absolutely fascinating.

**The Personal Computer Guide** by Tim Hartnell (Virgin 1982) 188pp £5.95. Tim really should stick to writing his very good books on programming. This book repeats a lot of information found in the magazines.

**The Beginner's Book** – Third Edition, by Adam Osborne (Osborne/McGraw Hill 1982) 230pp £10. Volume Zero in the Classic series "Introduction to Microcomputers" takes the hand of those who would rather not know. American bias.

**Computer Crunch** (introductory textbook) by Lew Hollerbach. (Wiley 1981) 137pp £4.40. A handy reference guide to the fundamentals of home business computing.

**Basic Concepts** – Second Edition, by Adam Osborne (Osborne/McGraw Hill 1980) 439pp £12.50. Volume I of the series, now a standard textbook in hundreds of courses in the USA. Hardware bias. Very good.

**Scelbi's Secret Guide to Computers** by Russell Walter (Scelbi 1980) 335pp £5. A short course involving the use of the BASIC computer language, pitched to appeal to schoolchildren.

**1001 Things to Do With Your Personal Computer** by Mark Sawusch (Tab 1980) 96pp £5. Full of ideas with sketchy programs to fire you into action.

**Business System Buyer's Guide** by Adam Osborne (Osborne/McGraw Hill 1981) 165pp £8. Practical handbook from the guru himself helps you evaluate the significant features of competing systems.

**The Personal Computer Book** – Third Edition, by Robin Bradbeer (Gower Publishing 1983) 250pp £6.95. A good introduction to low-price computing, includes a market survey and a recursive bibliography.


**The Computer Book** by Robin Bradbeer, Peter De Bono and Peter Laurie (BBC Publications 1982) £7.95. The best selling computer book of all time. Written to accompany the BBC series. A very good introductory textbook.


**Microcomputers in education** edited by Chris Smith (Ellis Horwood 1982) 206pp £10.50PB £16.50HB. The proceedings of the first PET Education conference. A useful intro to the subject for teachers and other educators.


## LEARNING BASIC

**BASIC made easy** by Don Cassel and Richard Swanson (Reston 1980) 240pp £11.90. A very traditional text really designed for business or academic users.


**Making BASIC work for you** by Claude DeRossi (Reston 1979) 176pp £7.60. Another traditional text based around mainframe users. Some good illustrative programs though.


**Illustrating BASIC** by Donald Alcock (Cambridge University Press 1978) 134pp £3. Immensely popular hand-written script that keeps to a standard, portable subset of BASIC. Highly recommended.

**Armchair BASIC – An absolute beginner's guide to programming in BASIC** by Dave and Annie Fox (Osborne 1983) 264pp £7.50. This book is based upon the Foxs' teaching experience in California's first public access computer centre. A very informal presentation. A good first reader.

**BASIC With Style** by Nagia & Ledgard (Hayden 1978) 134pp £5. In the Programming Proverbs series – for those who like to get it right. Sound advice with humour.

**Advanced BASIC** by James Coan (Hayden 1977) 184pp £8. Applications and problems with a strongly mathematical bias. If you are determined to learn Basic in the same way, try BASIC BASIC by the same author.

**Data File Programming in BASIC** by LeRoy Finkel & Jerald Brown (Wiley 1981) 338pp £11.50. Teaches file handling in TRS-80, Microsoft and Northstar dialects of BASIC.

**A Bit of BASIC** by Dwyer & Critchfield (Addison-Wesley 1980) 184pp £6. Includes the Eight-Hour Wonder Course and sections on the TRS-80 and Apple II. This is an updated, shorter version of BASIC and the Personal Computer by the same authors.

**The BASIC Handbook** – Second Edition, by David Lien (Compusoft 1981) 480pp £16.50. Encyclopaedia of dialects of BASIC to help you understand and convert other people's programs. Essential reference book for the hobbyist.

**Executive Computing** by John Nevison (Addison-Wesley 1981) 319pp £6.90. Chatty casebook shows the development of useful working programms in BASIC.

**The Little Book of BASIC Style** by John Nevison (Addison-Wesley 1978) 151pp £5. Subtitled "How to Write a Program YOU Can Read". Nineteen rules for neat presentation to reduce maintenance costs later.

**BASIC Programming** – Third Edition, by Kenneny & Kurtz (Wiley 1980) 333pp £10. A straightforward machine independent manual from the original founders of BASIC.

## BASIC PROGRAMS

**24 tested ready-to-run game programs in BASIC** by Ken Tracton (Tab Books 1978) 250pp £6.50. One of the first books full of games software and still one of the best. Written for the PET and the TRS-80.

**BASIC Computer Games** edited by David Ahl (Creative Computing Press 1978) 185pp £8. The classic from microcomputer maker DEC, adapted to Microsoft for this microcomputer edition.

**More BASIC Computer Games** edited by David Ahl (Creative Computing Press 1979) 185pp £6. Another 84 games to add to the repertoire of your micro.

**Some Common BASIC Programs** by Poole & Borchers (Osborne/McGraw Hill 1979) 195pp £12. Third edition of seventy-six tested programs in finance, maths and statistics.

**General Ledger – CBASIC** by Poole & Borchers (Osborne/Mcgraw Hill 1979) 1978pp £16. Documentation and listings for a business package ro tun under CP/M using CBASIC-2. Now on diskette in the CP/M User Library. American accounting standards.

**Stimulating Simulations** by C. W. Engel (Hayden 1979) 98pp £5. Twelve entertaining simulation programs including navigation, business and fantasy.

**Practical BASIC Programs** edited by Lon Poole (Osborne/ McGraw Hill 1980) 176pp £12. Forty documented programs in financial management and statistics, following on from "Some Common BASIC Programs".

(See also under individual micro headings)


## PASCAL

**A Practical Introduction to Pascal** by Wilson & Addyman (Macmillan 1978) 148pp £5. An excellent and inexpensive programmer's primer in a gentle British style.

**Introduction to Pascal Including UCSD Pascal** by Rodnay Zaks (Sybex 1980) 419pp £12.50. An attractive book with plenty of example programs.

**The Pascal Handbook** by Jacques Tiberghien (Sybex 1981) 482pp £15.70. Alphabetical encyclopaedia of Pascal and many of its dialects such as UCSD Pascal.

**Pascal User Manual and Report** – Second Edition, by Jensen & Wirth (Springer-Verlag 1975) 167pp £8. The international reference work on the Pascal language.

**Introduction to Pascal** by Welsh & Elder (Prentice-Hall 1979) 300pp £8.45. Sober textbook with 17 case study programs.

**The Byte Book of Pascal** – Second Edition, edited by Blaise Liffick (Byte/McGraw Hill 1979) 333pp £18. Collected reprints from BYTE magazine including the Tiny Pascal compiler.

**Pascal From Basic** by P. J. Brown. (Addison-Wesley 1982) 182pp £7.90. A useful book, although educationally suspect, for those who want to convert their Basic Knowledge into Pascal.

## FORTH

**Starting Forth** by Leo Brodie. (Prentice-Hall 1981) 384pp £20.65HB £15.25PB. Generally acknowledged to be the clearest introduction to the FORTH language.

**Complete Forth** by Alan Winfield. (Wiley 1983) 255pp £6.95. An introductory text with many programs that are claimed to run on different micros.

**Threaded Interpretive Languages** by Ronald Loeliger. (McGraw-Hill 1981) 251pp £18.50. A tutorial text which is a good introduction to this method of using and writing interpreters. Not for beginners.

## MICROCOMPUTER SYSTEM DESIGN

**Practical Microprocessor Systems** by Ian Sinclair (Newnes 1981) 139pp £6.00. An introductory book by a well known technical author. Concentrates on the SC/MP II, 6502 and Z80 processors.

**Interfacing Microprocessors and Microcomputers** by Owen Bishop (Newnes 1982) 145pp £4.95. A series of practical projects for the home constructor ranging from light sensors to light pens. Not really for beginners.

**Simple interfacing projects** by Owen Bishop (Granada 1982) 168pp £6.95. For those who can't get to grips with the more advanced style of his previous book above.

**Don Lancaster's Micro cookbook: Vol 1: fundamentals** by Don Lancaster (Prentice-Hall 1983) 400pp £13.55. The first volume of a straightforward introduction to microcomputers and microprocessors from one of the great American technical authors.

**The architecture of small computer systems** by Arthur Lippiatt (Prentice-Hall 1978) 192pp £5.95. An old and trusted friend for most micro engineers.

**Microprocessor Interfacing Techniques** by Lesea & Zaks (Sybex 1979) 420pp £13.05. Third edition covers peripherals, analogue circuitry, bus standards, trouble-shooting. Case study is a 32 channel miltiplexer (concentrator).

**Interfacing to S-100/IEEE 696 Microcomputers** by Sol Libes & Mark Garetz (Osborne/McGraw Hill 1981) 317pp £12.40. UP-to-date and detailed handbook for anyone interested in the technicalities of the S-100 bus.

**Complete Handbook of Robotics** by Edward Safford (Tab 1978) 358pp £6. A treasurehouse of information on mobility, sensors, power, servo, radio control etc.

**Communicating with Microcomputers** by Ian Witten (Academic Press 1980 163pp £7. Deliberately ambiguous title for this stimulating book, ranging from computer buses to speech synthesis and recognition.

**Microprocessors for Measurement and Control** by Auslander & Sagues (Osborne/McGraw Hill 1981) 310pp £12. Industrial case studies with specific solutions. Programs in Basic, Fortran, Pascal, C and assembly level coding for the 8080 and PDP-11.

**The S100 and other micro buses** by Elmer Poe and James Goodwin (Prentice-Hall 1981) 144pp £8.45. Twentyone of the most widely used buses examined.

**Osborne 4 & 8-Bit Microprocessor Handbook** by Osborne & Kane (Osborne/McGraw Hill 1981) 1226pp £16.50. Facts and independent opinions on many 4 and 8 bit microprocessor chips.

**Osborne 16-Bit Microprocessor Handbook** by Osborne et al (Osborne/McGraw Hill 1981) 791pp £16.50. Companion to the Osborne 4 & 8-Bit Microprocessor Handbook.

## SOFTWARE METHODS & MANAGEMENT

**Software Engineering for Micros** by T. G. Lewis (Hayden 1979) 156pp £6. Subtitled "The Electrifying Streamlined Blueprint Speedcode Method". How to get assembly language programs up and running quickly and reliably with a fascinating tailpiece on the possibilities for hardware assistance.

**Writing Interactive Compilers & Interpreters** by Peter Brown (Wiley 1981) 265pp £8. An amusing and very practical book for hobbyists.

**Fundamental Algorithms** by Donald Knuth (Addison-Wesley 1979) 634pp £11. One of the standard DP reference books now available in paperback. Very strong on storage allocation: trees, arrays, lists, queues.

**Microprocessor Programming for Computer Hobbyists** by Neill Graham (Tab 1977) 382pp £6. Handy reference book for data structures, searching, sorting and arithmetic routines.

**Successful Software for Small Computers** by Graham Beech (Sigma Technical Press 1980) 210pp £6. Teaches structural programming in Basic with solutions to common problems.

**Computer Language Reference Guide** by Harry Helms (Sams 1980) 109pp £5. Slim booklet that gives just the flavour of Algol, Basic, Cobol, Fortran, Lisp, Pascal and PL/I. Worth a quick skim at the library.

## CP/M

**Using CP/M: A Self-Teaching Guide** by Fernandez & Ashley (Wiley 1980) 243pp £12.90. Carefully structured for a quick understanding of the main points.

**Osborne CP/M User's Guide** – Second Edition, by Thom Hogan (Osborne/McGraw Hill 1982) 286pp £12.90. Thoroughly up-to-date textbook on CP/M, including DDT commands.

**CP/M Primer** by Murtha & Waite (Sams 1980) 96pp £12.70. Expensive and erratic, contains some pearls.

**CP/M assembly language programming** by Ken Barber (Prentice-Hall 1983) 226pp £11. A beginner's look at ED and ASM.

## UNIX/C

**The C Programming Language** by Kernighan & Ritchie (Prentice-Hall 1978) 228pp £16.95. Describes the main language behind the UNIX 16-bit operating system.

**UNIX System: The Bell System Technical Journal** edited for Bell Laboratories (Bell Labs 1978) 416pp £3.50. Twenty papers with UNIX as the central theme.

**UNIX: The Book** by M. Banahan and A. Rutter. (Wiley 1983) 212pp £7.50. A new introductory text that covers most of what you need to know to get started.

**The Unix System** by Stephen Bourne. (Addison-Wesley 1983) 368pp £11.90. Stephen Bourne is one of the people involved with the latest developments in UNIX and this book is probably the best introduction to the subject.

**Using the UNIX system** by Richard Gauthier (Prentice-Hall 1981) 312pp £21.55HB £13.55PB. A relatively straightforward if overpriced manual.

**A UNIX primer** by Ann and Nick Lomuto (Prentice-Hall 1982) 256pp £16.95. Written for the first time user with its main emphasis on problem solving.

## 16-BIT MICROS

**The 8086 Primer** by Stephen Morse (Hayden 1980) 205pp £9.90. Subtitled "An Introduction to its Architecture, System Design and Programming".

**8086/8088 16-Bit Microprocessor Primer** by Morgan & Waite. (McGraw Hill 1982) 364pp £13.90. A complete examination of 16-bit technology, featuring the Intel 8088 as used in the IBM pc, Sirius I and many other 16-bit computers.

**The 8086 Book** by Rector & Alexy (Osborne/McGraw Hill 1980) 610pp, £13.50. Describes the hardware, interfacing and programming of the 8086, and its close relative the 8088 as used in the IBM Personal Computer.

**Programming the Z8000** by Richard Mateosian (Sybex 1980) 297pp £12.90. Compact description of the Z8000 family with programming details and examples.

**68000 Assembly Language Programming** by Gerry Kane. (Osborne McGraw Hill 1981) 500pp £13.90. A comprehensive book providing the information needed to tap the full potential of the 68000's architecture. It covers 68000 Assembly language programming in great detail.

**Z8000 Handbook** by Bradley Fawcett (Prentice-Hall/Zilog 1982) 320pp £14.40. A complete description of the Z8000 series of chips.

**Z8000 cpu user's reference guide** by Zilog (Prentice-Hall/Zilog 1982) 304pp £11.85. The manufacturer's definitive handbook.

**MC68000 16-bit microprocessor user's guide** by Motorola (Prentice-Hall/Motorola 1982) 232pp £12.70. Ditto.

**iAPX 88 Book** by Intel (Prentice-Hall/Intel 1983) 318pp £11. Ditto.


## 8080/8085

**Introduction to 8080/8085 Assembly Language Programming** by Fernandez & Ashley (Wiley 1981) 303pp £9.75. This Self-Teaching Guide is good value for beginners.

**The 8080/8085 Microcomputer Book** by Intel (Wiley 1980) 603pp £13. Comprehensive and authorative source of facts and ideas.

**8080A microcomputer interfacing and programming** by Peter Rony. (Prentice-Hall 1982) 506pp £15.25. A revision of the best selling 8080A Bugbook.

## Z80

**The Z80 Microprocessor: Programming and Interfacing: Books 1 and 2** by Nichols & Rony (Sams 1979). Book 1 304pp £11, Book 2 496pp £14.40. Examples are based on the SGS-ATES Nanocomputer and therefore rather specialised.

**Z80 Instruction Handbook** by Nat Wadsworth (Scelbi 1978) 117pp £5.50. Pocket sized reference book on the Z80 architecture and instruction set.

**8080/Z80 Assembly Language: Techniques for Improved Programming** by Alan Miller (Wiley 1981) 318pp £9.90. A single reference source for the programmer and ten useful Appendices and a chapter on linking to CP/M.

**Z80 Software Gourmet Guide & Cookbook** by Nat Wadsworth (Scelbi 1979) 322pp £11. Contains useful assembly language routines including a floating-point package.

**Programming the Z80** Third Edition by Rodnay Zaks (Sybex 1982) 624pp £12.90. Latest reprint is nominally the third edition. Readable and well presented.

**Z80 Assembly Language Programming** by Lance Leventhal (Osborne/McGraw Hill 1979) 623pp £12.90. An accurate and reliable textbook with examples and algorithms.

**Z80 microprocessor advanced interfacing with applications in data communications** by Joseph and Elizabeth Nichols and K Musson. (Prentice-Hall 1983) 352pp £16.95. The title says it all.

## 6800/6809

**6800 Assembly Language Programming** by Lance Leventhal (Osborne/McGraw Hill 1978) 472pp £12. Describes the instruction set in detail, with examples and algorithms.

**6809 Assembly Language Programming** by Lance Leventhal (Osborne/McGraw Hill 1981) 563pp £13.50. The instruction set for this advanced 8-bit micro introduced, explained and demonstrated.

**6809 Companion** by Mike James. (1982) £2.60. History, architecture, addressing modes and instruction set all in full. Other chapters look at programming style and interrupt handling.

## 6502

**6502 Assembly Language Programming** by Lance Leventhal (Osborne/McGraw Hill 1979) 250pp £13.50. Probably the best book in its class: instruction set, examples, algorithms.

**6502 Assembly Language Subroutines** by Leventhal & Saville. (Osborne/McGraw Hill 1982) 600pp £12.50. This book provides code for more than 40 6502 subroutines. The authors describe general 6502 programming methods as well.

**Programming the 6502** by Rodnay Zaks (Sybex 1980) 387pp £11.20. Popular third edition, easy to read.

**6502 Applications Book** by Rodnay Zaks (Sybex 1979) 278pp £10.90. A stimulating source of ideas on using the 6502, 6522, 6530, 6532 I/O chips with the 6502.

**6502 Software Gourmet Guide & Cookbook** by Robert Findley (Scelbi 1979) 204pp £9. Assembly language routines including a floating-point package.

**6502 Software Design** by Leon Scanlon (Sams 1980) 272pp £11.50. Assembly language explained with examples using the AIM-65 computer.

**Advanced 6502 interfacing** by John Holland (Prentice-Hall 1982) 190pp £11. Covers most interfacing circuits.

## COMMODORE PET/CBM

**The PET and the IEEE-488 Bus (GPIB)** by Fisher & Jensen (Osborne/McGraw Hill 1980) 243pp £11. Describes how to interface the PET via the IEEE bus to the outside world.

**Programming the PET/CBM** by Raeto West (Level 1982) 500pp £16. The definitive reference book for all models.

**PET/CBM Personal Computer Guide** – Second Edition, by Osborne & Donahue (Osborne/McGraw Hill 1980) 506pp £12. Clear and comprehensive manual, includes the 8000 series.

**Library of PET Subroutines** by Nick Hampshire (Computerbits 1980) 141pp £10. About fifty valuable routines mostly in Basic for input, screen handling, disk sort algorithms etc.

**Learning to use the PET Computer** by Garry Marshall (Gower Publishing 1983) 100pp £4.95. A very basic introductory text by a well-known author.

**The PET Personal Computer for Beginners** by Seamus Dunn & Valerie Morgan (Prentice-Hall 1981) 242pp £5.95PB £8.95HB. One of the more useful books published for the PET.

**Getting Acquainted with your VIC 20** by Tim Hartnell (Interface 1982) 132pp £7.00. 60 ready-to-run programs back up a rather thin introductory section.

**Learning to Use the VIC 20 Computer** by Ron Geere (Gower Publishing 1983) 100pp £4.95. Another basic introductory text.

**Hands on Basic with a PET** by Herbert Pekham (McGraw-Hill 1979) 279pp £9.90. A very introductory book with lots of illustrations.

**PET Basic – Training your Pet Computer** by Ramon Zamora & Bob Aldrecht & William Scarvey (Reston 1981) 329pp £9.90. A complete and well written guide.

**The VIC Revealed** by N Hampshire (Computabits 1982) £10. To quote a well informed commentator "this book is 226 pages of vaguely useful background for anyone who has already done some machine code programming."

**Learn Computer Programming with the Commodore VIC** by L R Carter and E Huzan. (1981) £2.50. This book provides some of the reference material that is outside the scope of this book and is a good follow up text for the beginner.

**Commodore 64 – Programmer's Reference Guide** by Commodore (Prentice-Hall 1982). 450pp £16.95. This is the book that should have formed the instruction manual for the 64. If you want to know what's going on inside your machine then this book is a must.

**Learning to Use the Commodore 64 Computer** by William Turner (Gower Publishing 1983) 100pp £4.95. Another useful introductory book in the Learning to Use series.

**The PET Index** by Mike Ryan (Gower 1982) 192pp £10.95. A list of all the articles published about the PET in the UK and USA up to September 1981. Useful reference source.

**Beginner's assembly language for the PET 2, 3, 4 and 8000** by "Dr Watson" (Honeyfold 1983) £14.95. A very good introduction with the assembler on cassette.

**Beginner's assembly language for the VIC 20** by "Dr Watson" (Honeyfold 1983) £14.95 Ditto.

**Beginner's assembly language for the CBM 64** by "Dr Watson" (Honeyfold 1983) £14.95 Ditto.

**Mastering the VIC 20** by Jones, Coley and Cole (Ellis Horwood 1983) 178pp £5.95. An introduction to machine code programming using the VICMON assembler.

**Introduction to microcomputing with the PET** by Arotsky, Taylor and Glassbrook. (Edward Arnold 1983) 288pp £5.95. A rather simple approach to programming to the PET in BASIC.

## APPLE II

**Apple Machine Language** by Don & Kurt Inman (Reston 1981) 296pp £17.95HB £12.70PB. Goes from PEEK and POKE up to the use of the Apple Mini-Assembler.

**Apple II User's Guide** by Lon Poole et al (Osborne/McGraw Hill 1981) 385pp £12. Popular single volume takes you from switch-on, via BASIC and advanced programming to the machine language monitor.

**Apple BASIC** by Richard Haskell. (Prentice-Hall 1982) 184pp £11. A solid introduction to programming the Apple II computer in Apple Soft BASIC.

**Learning to use the Apple II/IIe** by William Turner (Gower publishing 1983) 100pp £4.95. Another good introductory text.

**Apple II assembly language** by Marvin de Jong (Prentice-Hall 1982) 336pp £13.55. An introduction to 6502 programming with the Apple.

**Accountant's BASIC programming for the Apple II** by Alan Parker and John Stewart (Prentice-Hall 1983) 302pp £12.20. Sample programs and many ideas for small business uses.

**The Apple personal computer for beginners** by Seamus Dunn and Valerie Morgan. (Prentice-Hall 1982) 300pp £9.95HB £6.95PB. The Apple followup to their successful PET book.

**Learning LOGO on the Apple II** by Anne McDougall and Tony and Pauline Adams (Prentice-Hall 1983) 262pp £11. Both MIT LOGO and Apple LOGO explained in relatively non technical terms.

**Using 6502 assembly language programming** by Randy Hide (Prentice-Hall 1983) 250pp £16.95. An update of a good book originally from Datamost (1981).

**The Visicalc book** by Donald Beil (Prentice-Hall 1982) 308pp £20.65HB £12.70PB. A straightforward guide to using Visicalc on the Apple.

### TANDY TRS-80 MODEL I/II/III/ Video Genie

**TRS-80 Basic: A Self-Teaching Guide** by Albrecht, Inman & Zaamora (Wiley 1980) 351pp £7. Introduces and reinforces each new concept for a good grounding in Level II BASIC.

**Microsoft BASIC Decoded and Other Mysteries** by James Farvour (IJG 1981) 310pp £18. Annotated dis-assembly of the major portions of the ROM with chapters on the detailed data structures and software methods. Tremendous value if you need it.

**Learning TRS-80 BASIC 1, II/16, III** by David Lien. (Compusoft 1982) 544pp £16.50. This book is basically a tutorial written with simple step-by-step instructions. The style is informal and the material is well organised.

**TRS-80 Assembly Language** by Hubert Howe Jr. (Prentice-Hall 1981) 184pp £14.35HB £8.45PB. An introduction to the TRS-80 monitor.

**The easy way to programming in BASIC using the Video Genie system** by John and Judy Deane. (Lowe Electronics 1980) 110pp £5.95. A good introduction to back up the rather thin Video Genie manual.

**TRS 80 Color Computer graphics** by Don Inman and Dymax (Prentice-Hall 1982) 308pp £12.70. A look round the Tandy Color Computer's 16K extended colour BASIC graphics.

**Assembly language graphics for the TRS 80 Color Computer** by Don and Kurt Inman and Dymax (Prentice-Hall 1983) 280pp £12.70. Using the 6809 assembly language for advanced graphics.

## SINCLAIR ZX81

**Learning Timex Sinclair BASIC** by David Lien (Compusoft 1983) 331pp £7.95. As usual with David Lien's books this one is a clear and concise introduction to ZX81 BASIC.

**Learning to Use the ZX81** by Robin Bradbeer (Gower Publishing 1983) 100pp £4.95. A useful introductory text by a well known author!

**Mastering Machine Code on your ZX81** by Tony Baker (Interface 1981) 188pp £17.50. A very comprehensive look at the inside of the computer. Not for the faint-hearted or inexperienced.

**Hints and Tip for the ZX81** by Andrew Hewson (Hewson Consultants 1981) 50pp £4.50. Contains many routines useful for programmers. Display explained in detail.

**Getting acquainted with your ZX81** by Tim Hartnell (Database Consultancy 1981). 128pp £5.95. Many programs with some useful information scattered through the text.

**Understanding your ZX81** by I Logan (Essential Software Company 1981) 200p £6.50. Illustrates all the attributes of the ZX81 monitor, how it works, and how to use it in writing useful programs.

**49 Explosive Games for the ZX81** by Tim Hartnell (Interface 1981) 138pp £5.95. Galactic Intruders, Breakout, Draughts, Star Trek etc. etc.

**Machine code and better BASIC** by Ian Stewart and Robin Jones (Shiva Publishing 1982) 188pp £7.50. Covers most of the features in Sinclair BASIC, and also contains 50 games.

**The Sinclair ZX81 – programming for real applications** by Randle Hurley (Macmillan 1981) 120pp £6.95. From word processing, through home banking to education... a book for those wanting to go beyond playing games.

**More real applications for the ZX81 and ZX Spectrum** by Randle Hurley (Macmillan 1982) 172pp £7.50. A follow up book for those inspired by the first volume.

## SINCLAIR SPECTRUM

**Learning to use the ZX Spectrum** by Robin Bradbeer (Gower Publishing 1983) 100pp £4.95. Yet another introductory text.

**The complete Spectrum ROM Disassembly** by Ian Logan and Frank O'Hara (Melborne House 1982). 185pp £9.95. Really for serious programmers who want to know what's going on.

**Spectrum Machine Language for Absolute Beginners** by Beam (edited by Tang). (Melbourne House 1982) 199pp £6.95. Really is for beginners with some programs.

**Over the Spectrum** by Fred Milgrom. (Melbourne House 1982) 180pp £6.95. Yet another book full of games listings (30).

**Advanced graphics with the ZX Spectrum** by Angell and Jones (Macmillan 1983) 256pp £10. Covers everything in quite good detail.

**Spectrum spectacular** by Roger Valentine (V & H Computer Services 1983) 138pp £4.95. No more than 50 games programs, some quite good.

## BBC COMPUTER

**Assembly Language Programming on the BBC Microcomputer** by Ian Birnbaum. (1982) 305pp £9.90. Teach yourself 6502 programming on the BBC Micro. Highly recommended by the User Group.

**Creative Graphics on BBC Microcomputer** by John Cownie. (Wiley 1982) 242pp £8.50. Includes 36 programs demonstrating the highest resolution graphics on the Model A and B.

**BASIC Programming on the BBC Microcomputer** by Neil and Pat Cryer. (Prentice-Hall 1982) 200pp £5.95. Probably the best introductory book for the BBC system. Clear, concise and comprehensive.

**BBC Micro An Expert Guide** by Mike James. (1983) 158pp £7.90. A guide to the functions of the BBC computer, especially the VDU interface.

**Learning to use the BBC microcomputer** by P. N. Dane (Gower Publishing 1983) 100pp £4.95. The BBC version of this best selling series.

**Easy programming for the BBC micro** by Eric Deeson (Shiva Publishing 1983) 136pp £5.95. Eric Deeson has made quite a name for himself in writing clear articles in the mags. This book is typical of his style.

**Assembly language programming on the BBC micro** by John Ferguson and Tony Shaw (Addison-Wesley 1983) 192pp £7.95. Based on a series of articles in Acorn User magazine.

**The BBC micro revealed** by Jeremy Ruston (Interface 1983) 144pp £7.95. A good poke around inside the BBC has revealed a whole host of tricks. Jeremy Ruston has well documented them in his book.

## RESEARCH MACHINES 380/480Z

**Microcomputing in BASIC with the 380Z/480Z** by W. R. McDonough (Edward Arnold 1983) 180pp £5.95. A first introductory book aimed at schools and colleges.

**Problem solving in BASIC – a guide for beginners** by Hugh Vincent (Addison-Wesley 1983) 150pp £4.95. Really does look at problem solving techniques.


## ATARI

**Paint** by Capital Children's Museum (Prentice-Hall 1983) 160pp £35.22 (includes program diskette). A novel program and book designed to use the good colour graphics of the Atari 800.

**Making the most of your Atari** by Paul Bunn (Interface 1982) 178pp £8.95. A lot of useful programming information with a few good games programs.

**The Atari assembler** by Don and Kurt Inman (Prentice-Hall 1981) 270 £12.70. Another book from the Inmans on the 6502 this time orientated to the Atari.

**Atari BASIC – a self teaching guide** by Bob Albrecht, Leroy Finkel and Jerald Brown (Wiley 1979) 332pp £6.95. A good introductory book looking at the Atari BASIC interpreter.

**Atari sound and graphics – a self teaching guide** by Herb Moore, Judy Lower and Bob Albrecht. (Wiley 1982) 234pp £4.95. The next steps on from the previous book.

**Your Atari computer: a guide to Atari 400/800 personal computers** by Lon Poole, Martin McNiff and Steven Cook (Osborne/McGraw Hill) 464pp £10.95. A well illustrated introductory text and reference book.

## ORIC 1

**Learning to use the Oric 1 computer** by Steven Blake (Gower Publishing 1983) 100pp £4.95. The Oric book in the Learning to Use series.

**Meteoric programming for the Oric 1** (Melborne House 1983) 120pp £5.95. Another collection of games and utility programs.

## DRAGON 32

**Learning to use the Dragon 32 Computer** by George Knight (Gower Publishing 1983) 100pp £4.95. A good introductory text.

**Enter the Dragon** by Colin Carter (Melbourne House 1983) 120pp £5.95. Really nothing more than a collection of 30 games programs.

**The working Dragon** by David Lawrence (Sunshine Books 1983) 158pp £5.95. A book designed to put the Dragon to "serious" use; not for the beginner.

**Dynamic games for the Dragon 32** by Robert Young, Roger Bush and Robert Shrimpton ed. by Tim Hartnell (Interface 1983) 180pp £4.95. Another compilation of games programs from Tim Hartnell's program generating team.

**Making the most of your Dragon 32** by Clive Gifford (Interface 1983) 200pp £5.95. A collection of 150 programs and tricks for the Dragon.

**Easy programming for the Dragon 32** by Ian Stewart and Robin Jones (Shiva Publishing 1983) 128pp £5.95. An introductory book.

**Inside the Dragon** by Duncan Sneed and Ian Sommerville (Addison-Wesley 1983) 192pp £3.95. An introduction to the 6809 processor as used in the Dragon.

## LYNX

**Learning to use the Lynx computer** by Felix Chapman (Gower Publishing 1983) 100pp £4.95. Another user friendly introductory text.

## TI 99/4

**Learning to use the TI 99/4 computer** by Kevin Townsend (Gower Publishing 1983) 100pp £4.95. The usual clear Learning to Use text.

**Programming BASIC with the TI home computer** by Herbert Peckham (McGraw-Hill 1979) 306pp £14.95. This book goes beyond the normal beginner's BASIC and looks at graphics and sound.

**Explorer's guide to the TI99/4** by Kaspar Boon (Addison-Wesley 1983) 272pp £7.95 book £8.95 cassette. A "gentle" introduction with the printed programs available on cassette.

**Computer art and animation: a user's guide to TI99/4 LOGO** by David Thornburg (Addison-Wesley 1983) 224pp £9.50. A good introduction to the LOGO language.

# APPENDIX G

**Glossary**

## A

*access time:* the time it takes to obtain information from a storage device.

*accounts payable/receivable:* American software/documentation uses the terms 'purchase ledger/sales ledger' respectively. As American accountancy procedures are different to ours, most US software has to be altered to European and UK practice.

*acoustic coupler:* converts pulses of sound from a telephone line into the digital signals computers understand, and vice versa. It is a form of modem (viz) that the telephone handset plugs into.

*A/D, analogue-digital converter:* used for converting analogue electrical signals to digital form. The opposite is called a digital/analogue converter (DAC).

*address:* a digital number stating a certain specific storage location in the computer memory.

*algorithm:* a prescribed set of well-defined rules or methods for the solution of a problem. The input of an algorithm into the computer takes the form of a sequence of instructions.

*alphanumeric:* a code containing the digits 0 to 9 and the letters of the alphabet.

*ALU, Arithmetic Logic Unit:* that part of the computer which performs basic mathematical operations such as addition, subtraction, multiplication and division of binary numbers.

*analogue:* means that a physical quantity can be represented analogously to a voltage, or other variable physical quantity. Example: a velocity can be presented in analogue fashion by the voltage across a meter.

*ASCII:* American Standard Code for Information Interchange. A standardized code used extremely frequently for data transmission. The code comprises 128 large and small letters, digits and some other special characters. Each of these is coded with its own unique 7-bit binary number.

*assembler:* a computer program that translates a program written in symbolic assembly language into machine language (binary code).

*assembly language:* a programming language built up with memory codes or mnemonic codes designed to facilitate programming ("mnemonic" means "assisting the memory"). Examples: ADD meaning "add", SUB meaning "subtract". Programs coded in assembly language are converted by a so-called assembler into machine code which the computer can understand. The process is called assembly.

*asynchronous:* asynchronous communication means that when an operation is finished it starts the following one. The opposite is *synchronous* procedure, which requires control by a clock signal.

# B

*backup:* a procedure, or facility, that allows users to retain information in the event of a failure.

*BASIC:* Beginner's All-purpose Symbolic Instruction Code, a procedure-orientated programming language built up of simple words and abbreviations. This language is very commonly used in the personal computer world and is best suited to systems with so-called interactive terminals, i.e. where the operator converses with the computer.

*baud:* a baud is the unit of signalling speed, which is approximately equal to one bit per second (a bit of a binary signal element).

*BCD:* Binary Coded Decimal. The binary equivalents to the digits 0 to 9 consist of groups of four bits each.

*benchmark:* a program to test and compare different computers for speed, programming simplicity, etc.

*binary:* a number system with only two digits, 0 and 1, i.e. the base is 2. Computers work fundamentally with binary numbers.

*bit:* an abbreviation for binary digit. The smallest unit of data in computer. Eight bits make one byte.

*bit parallel:* a method for simultaneous transmission of all the bits in a group by parallel conductors, one for each bit in the group.

*bit parallel:* a method for simultaneous transmission of all the bits in a group by parallel conductors, one for each bit in the group.

*bit serial:* refers to the sequential transmission of the bits in a group — i.e. one by one — via one single conductor.

*bootstrap:* a short program routine read into the computer at the time of starting up. The bootstrap instructions tell the computer where to look for data and what to do with it. Sometimes abbreviated to "boot".

*bubble memory:* a new type of memory which has a large storage capacity despite its small dimensions.

*bug:* a fault in the program or computer.

*bureau:* a company that runs other people's work on its computer. Of limited benefit to most small businesses.

*bus:* a number of conductors forming the communication path for data, addresses and control signals between different units (processor, memory, etc.) in a computer.

*byte:* a group of usually eight bits which is treated as a unit and stored at a storage location.

# C

*character set:* the collection of numbers, letters, graphics and symbols that are used by a computer.

*chip:* the piece of silicon that makes up a transistor or integrated circuit; also often used to apply to the whole integrated circuit (IC).

*clock:* an electric pulse-generator synchronizing all the signals in a computer.

*CMOS:* Complementary Metal Oxide Semiconductor, a family of digital integrated circuits characterized by extremely low power consumption and high complexity, but also by moderate working speed and sensitivity to static electricity.

*COBOL:* The Common Business Orientated Language — a high level programming language. Designed for commercial applications; CIS COBOL is one of the more common versions for microcomputers.

*compatible:* one item of equipment is said to be compatible with another if in certain respects it is constructed to the same standard. The term is also used for programs to express the possibility of running the program in a different model of equipment from that for which it was made.

*compiler:* a specialised program that translates a high level language program, in toto, into the machine language of the computer.

*computer:* a system which can receive data and, without human intervention, execute the usually complicated processing of the data, and also produce the results in the desired form. A computer consists of CPU, memory and input and output units.

*CP/M:* a disk operating system (viz) that has become a world wide de-facto standard, thus allowing software packages to be run on may different systems. Comes in two versions — one based on the 8080 — the other the 8086.

*CPU:* Central Processing Unit — the heart of any computer system.

*CRA:* Computer Retailers Association; a grouping of retail outlets whose code of conduct is a step towards establishing standards for selling and aftersales service.

*CRT:* Cathode Ray Tube; the glass tube in any video system, although it sometimes is used to describe a complete video display unit.

*cursor:* a square, dash, or other symbol, used on video display units to indicate where the next character is to be written.

## D

*D/A:* digital-to-analogue.

*daisywheel:* a form of printhead that has the characters embossed around the edge of a petal-like disk. A daisy-wheel printer is used for high quality printer output.

*data:* representation of facts or ideas in a formalised manner which can be processed or transferred by persons or machines.

*data base:* a file of data organised so that users can call on an up-to-date pool of information.

*database management system:* (DBMS) a software system for designing, setting up and managing a data base.

*debugging:* the detection and correction of faults in software and hardware.

*device:* often used synonymously with "Peripheral equipment".

*digital:* refers to a method of representing all the quantities in problem by the binary numbers 0 and 1; a digital circuit is an electronic circuit working in principle as a switch, i.e. with ON/OFF positions.

*digitizer:* an input device that converts the analogue information — whether pictorial or positional — into a digital form.

*DIP:* Dual Inline-Package, the name for the most commonly used chip form for integrated circuits.

*disk:* a rotating plastic medium for storing data. The plastic disk may be solid or flexible and is coated with a magnetic oxide. Flexible disks come in 5¼" or 8" diameters, hard disks in 5¼", 8" and 12" diameters.

*disk storage:* a method for rapid mass storage of problems and data. Data is written (stored) or read (fetched) via the read/write head which usually searches over the rotating disk for the right location.

*display:* a presentation unit of some kind like a CRT or other unit which can show characters.

*distributed processing:* the use of a number of small microcomputers, interlinked so that they share the same data bases, program memory or even larger mainframe computer.

*DMA:* Direct Memory Access, a method of transferring data quantities directly between a peripheral unit and the computer memory, without going via the CPU. This is a way of increasing the speed and thus the efficiency of the system.

*DOS:* Disk Operating System, a program enabling the disk storage to store and output data.

*dot matrix:* the technique used for building up characters from a matrix of dots, which make up a rectangular pattern. Used by video display units and matrix printers.

*dual processor:* a computer system based around two CPUs. Usually one handles the main processing involving data whilst the other handles input, output and, maybe, the disk access and video display.

*duplex:* a construction designed to allow transmission in both directions at once.

*dynamic memory:* a type of semiconductor memory where the presence or absence of an electric charge in a small capacitor represents the logic status in the binary memory cell. A dynamic memory must periodically be "refreshed".

# E

*edit:* to prepare data for a later operation.

*editor:* a program used for editing other programs, to revise, adapt and correct or supplement them for correct running and documentation.

*electronic office:* sometimes called "the office of the future", or "automated office"! Basically an office structure that uses computer-based systems to handle all the information processing in an integrated manner.

*EPROM:* an erasable, programmable ROM; this means that it is possible tfor the user to "zero" the program and then reprogram it.

*execute:* to carry out an operation in a program, to "run" a program in the computer.

*external store:* also called a mass memory. A memory with considerable greater capacity than a working memory, but often with considerable longer access time. Data is often transmitted in blocks between memories. Examples: floppy disk, magnetic tape.

# F

*FET:* Field Effect Transistor. A certain type of transistor (unipolar instead of bipolar) characterised by small dimensions, lower power requirements and low price.

*fetch:* the CPU fetches an instruction from the memory and decodes it.

*file:* a collection of data that can be considered in some way complete and is treated together.

*firmware:* a program (micro-instructions) stored in a permanent ROM.

*floppy disk:* also called diskette. A mass memory in the form of a soft plastic disk enclosed in a protective square envelope. The storage of data is magnetic. There are two sizes of floppy disk: standard — 200mm or 8" diameter and a smaller mini disk that is 5¼" diameter. See also disk storage.

*flowchart:* a graphic representation of a system or program, used as an aid to efficient programming or system design.

*format:* refers to the structure of data.

*FORTRAN:* FORMula TRANslator — a high level language developed for scientific use and the "father" of BASIC.

*function keys:* Keys that are un-allocated on a keyboard. The user can change the action, or meaning, of the key at will.

# G

*gate:* a logic element with two or more inputs and one output. The state of the output depends on the logic state of the input signals. The connection between incoming and outgoing signals is described in what is called the truth table of the circuit.

*graphics:* output that is not alphanumeric, usually symbols or pictorial characters.

# H

*handshaking:* control signals making it possible for two electronic circuits to synchronize their work.

*hard copy:* a printout of data on paper.

*hard sectored:* method used on some disk drives that positions the read/write head by a series of holes punched into the disk.

*hardware:* the actual apparatus of a computer system in contrast to software.

*hexadecimal:* the hexadecimal number system has 16 as its base and comprises the digits 0-9 and letters A, B, C, D, E and F.

*high-level language:* a programming language which is largely independent of the type of computer being used; the most used high-level language is BASIC.

# I

*IEEE-488:* a standard interface consisting of sixteen parallel lines as defined by the Institution of Electronic and Electrical Engineers (IEEE) in the United States.

*IEEE-696:* The officially accepted version of the S.100 bus (viz).

*Input/Output:* also known as I/O. General designation of peripheral equipment units making it possible for the computer to communicate with the outside world.

*instruction:* a set of characters defining a certain specific computer operation.

*instruction repertoire:* the different instructions with which a certain computer can work.

*integrated circuit:* also known as IC. A semiconductor circuit in micro form; on a small silicon chip a few millimetres square there are a large number of active and passive semiconductor elements dovetailed and connected in such a way that the circuit is given a specific electronic function.

*interface:* a connection between two units of apparatus with different functions.

*internal store:* a memory built into the computer; it is on-line i.e. directly controlled by the computer.

*interpreter:* a program controlling the execution of another program without the necessity for the latter to have been compiled or assembled first.

*interrupt:* this means that present program execution is interrupted in favour of a routine with higher priority; when this routine has been run, the computer returns to the original program at the point where the execution was interrupted.

# J

*jump:* a deviation from the normal sequence of orders followed by a computer to execute instructions.

# K

*K:* read as "kilo". It means 1024, e.g. a memory with storage space for 2K bits manages 2048 bits, Cf. k, which represents 1000, e.g. 1000 g = 1 kg.

*keyboard:* a set of keys similar to that on a typewriter, used for the input of data into the computer.

*key-to-disk:* a data entry technique whereby data goes directly from the keyboard to a disk file.

*keyword:* a word in a file that is used to retrieve its contents.

## L

*lcd:* Liquid crystal display. A form of display device that does not use cathode ray tubes, or any light emitting device. It works by varying the reflectivity of a crystal surface. Used for displays on portable, hand-held computers and televisions.

*line number:* used by some high level languages to indicate the start of a new instruction in a program.

*line printer:* a printer that prints a line at a time, as compared to a serial printer that prints a character at a time.

*loader:* a program controlling the operation of the peripheral equipment while other programs are being read in to the computer memory.

*logic:* the study of fundamental principles and applications of specific portions of symbolic logic, connection theory and other related methods used for instance for the designing of equipment for computers.

*logic circuit:* a coupling up of logic elements giving a certain specific function.

*LOGO:* a high level language designed for educational use.

*LSI:* Large Scale Integration, a highly complex integrated circuit which can execute complicated operations. On a chip only a few millimetres square there are several thousand transistors.

## M

*machine language:* the fundamental language with which a computer works; instructions are in groups of ones and zeros.

*matrix printer:* a printer that uses a single, or row, of needles to print characters using dot matrix techniques.

*Mega:* (M) means one million; as in 12M bytes i.e. 12 million bytes.

*memory:* a general term for any unit intended for the storage of binary data.

*memory map:* a graphic picture of the total storage in the computer and the disposition of this space: the map starts with the address 0000 (hex) at the bottom and goes up to the address FFFF for 8-bit processors.

*micro:* prefix signifying one millionth. Example: one microsecond: one millionth of a second.

*microcircuit:* another name for an integrated circuit.

*microcomputer:* a computer family characterised by being built up with only a few integrated circuits on a circuit board, with a word length usually not exceeding 16 bits, and with a low price.

*microprocessor:* an extremely complex integrated circuit giving the function of a central processing unit in a computer.

*Microsoft:* An American company that developed the first acceptable BASIC interpreter for microprocessor based systems. Now used as a standard by which other implementations are measured.

*mnemonic code:* data instructions written in concise, easily remembered symbolic or abbreviated forms, e.g. SUB which may symbolise "subtract".

*modem:* an item of equipment for signal conversion in data transmission: it is an abbreviation for modulator/demodulator.

*monitor (1):* a program — a typical part of a large operating system — which supervises or controls the operation of the computer system e.g. the input and output of data.

*monitor (2):* a special type of television set that does not receive off-air signals (uhf) but accepts video information in RGB or composite-video form.

*MOS:* Metal Oxide Semiconductor, a field effect transistor characterised by extremely high ingoing resistance.

*mother board:* a large circuit board to which one can plug in a number of smaller board modules.

*MP/M:* a multi-user version of CP/M (viz).

*MS-DOS:* a disc operating system (viz) developed by Microsoft for 16-bit, and pseudo-16-bit systems.

*multi-access:* a system that allows several users to access at the same time.

# N

*nano-:* prefix signifying one thousand millionth. Example: one nanosecond is one thousand millionth of a second (in common usage this is called one billionth).

*network:* a system of interconnected microcomputers.

*nibble:* a system of four binary digits — half a byte!

*nonvolatile:* when this term is used of computer memories it signifies that stored data is permanently retained even if the supply voltage should be turned off. Examples: nonvolatile memories include magnetic tape, disk storage and ROM.

*numeric-keypad:* a small keyboard, usually by the side of an alphanumeric keyboard, with numeric and/or cursor control keys only.

# O

*object program:* the binary form of a source program (the source program is what has been written by the programmer).

*octal:* a number system with 8 as its base, consisting of the digits 0-7.

*OEM:* Original Equipment Manufacturer. A company that takes individual parts of a system, plugs them together, and sells a complete unit.

*on-line:* refers to a control system whereby one unit is controlled by another without manual intervention, e.g. a data terminal is often on-line with regard to the computer.

*operating system:* software making it possible for the user to communicate with the computer in a convenient way.

*output:* what you get out of the computer!

# P

*package:* a package is a program developed for a particular application, hopefully with good operating manuals.

*paper tape:* a tape made of paper, usually 25mm wide, with punched holes in specific code positions, used as a data carrier.

*parallel I/O:* a method of transmitting all the bits in a bit group at the same time, for example a whole byte at once: this is done via parallel conductors, one for each bit.

*password:* a string of characters allowing restricted access to programs or files.

*peripheral equipment:* general designation of equipment used with a computer but not part of the CPU. Examples: printers, keyboards, video terminals, and floppy disk units.

*pixel:* a picture-element, or smallest piece of information e.g. a dot, that can be displayed on a television screen.

*plug-in:* any additional module, e.g. a memory board, that can be connected to the computer bus structure by means of the bus connector.

*port:* a communication channel through which data can pass into or out of the computer.

*Prestel:* British Telecomm's Viewdata (viz) network.

*printed circuit:* a fibreglass board with a circuit pattern of thin copper conductors, to which electronic components can be added; when it already contains these components it is called a circuit board.

*printer:* an item of electromechanical equipment which is fed with signals from the computer and prints out graphic characters on paper; the opposite is a plotter.

*printout:* printed output from the computer.

*program:* a complete sequence of computer instructions needed to solve a specific problem with the aid of the computer. (Can be spelt programme.)

*PROLOG:* a high-level language designed for educational use, but developed by the Japanese as the main language for their so-called fifth generation computers.

*PROM:* Programmable Read Only Memory, a permanent ROM which can be programmed by the user. Sometimes also called a "write once memory". See also ROM, EPROM.

*proprietary software:* a copyright program sold on a commercial basis.

# R

*RAM:* Random Access Memory, a memory where the access time depends on the location of the data in the memory.

*real time:* a way of running a system where the operations in the computer are carried out so fast in relation to a physical system that the result of the operations can be used by the physical system.

*record:* a group of related information or items of data.

*register:* a temporary storage place in a processor.

*reset:* to return a counter to the original position, usually the zero position.

*reset:* a key or button that re-initiates the computer system following a system "crash".

*ROM:* Read Only Memory, a memory where one can only read and not write.

*routine:* a sequence of data needed to effect a certain specific function.

*RS-232:* a standard specifying the electrical properties for input and output of data from peripheral units.

# S

*S-100:* a standard bus consisting of 100 parallel lines as defined by the IEEE in the United States.

*semiconductor store:* a memory consisting of active bistable semiconductor elements: the internal store of a mini- or micro-computer is a semiconductor store.

*serial I/O:* a method of transmitting data between the computer and a peripheral unit one bit at a time via a single conductor.

*simplex:* a connection designed to allow transmission in one direction at a time.

*soft-sectored:* a method of partitioning a disk using software, not physically on the media itself, as in hard-sectored.

*software:* a systematic collection of programs and associated documentation concerning the use of a data processing system. Examples are operating systems, monitors, compilers, editors, auxiliary programs and user programs.

*software documentation:* program listing and/or manuals telling you how to use the software.

*source language:* the language in which the programmer writes the program and from which translation is made.

*source program:* a program — either in the form of a list or stored in a memory unit — written in a language (source language) other than machine language and requiring translation by means of an assembler, compiler or interpreter program.

*static memory:* a semiconductor memory of the RAM type which does not require refresh pulses.

*statement:* in some programming languages, a designation of certain types if instructions.

*string:* an ordered sequence of signs or characters.

*subroutine:* a number of instructions which execute part of the work in a later program; a subroutine can, for example, be started by a command from the main program.

*synchronous:* used of a method of transmitting serial binary data between for instance the computer and the peripheral equipment; the transmission takes place at a fixed speed, and transmitter and receiver are synchronised with a clock.

*syntax:* rules determining how programming statements are constructed. Sometimes defined as the "grammar" of the language.

*syntax error:* message from the interpreter or compiler that a program has a "grammatical" error.

*system:* a collection of hardware and software that performs a particular, or general computing function.

*system software:* software that enables a programmer to develop and run applications programs.

*systems analysis:* the procedure for analysing the phases of all the activities of an organisation, and then developing detailed procedures for implementing a computer system.

## T

*tape:* usually refers to magnetic tape and sometimes to punched paper tape.

*teletext:* a computerised, and computer compatible, version of Telex.

*teletex:* a non-interactive method of receiving digitally encoded text and graphics via the broadcast television network.

*Teletype:* this is the everyday term of a teleprinter although it is actually a printer made by the Teletype Corp. in America. This machine is often used as I/O device in computer systems and an a keyboard and printer, and sometimes also a paper-tape reader and punch.

*terminal:* an I/O unit connected to a computer.

*time sharing:* a computer system where the CPU time and other system resources are shared by many users with many different tasks:some time sharing systems work so that the users contact the computer by telephone.

*transaction:* any event which requires a record to be generated in a computer system.

*turnkey:* a system started by the "turning of key". This usually "boots" the system and is thus immediately available for use.

## U

*UART:* Universal Asynchronous Receiver Transmitter, an often used LSI circuit for transmitting and receiving digital data.

*UCSD:* The University of California: San Diego — the inventors of a version of the high-level language Pascal. This has become a de facto standard for Pascal running on CP/M systems.

*UNIX:* A disk operating system (viz) that was developed by Bell Labs (USA). It is designed for 16-bit microprocessor systems.

*USART:* As UART but capable of synchronous transmission as well.

*utility program:* a program which is often part of the operating system and is used to facilitate running and testing of written programs.

## V

*validation:* checking input to ensure that it is correct.

*VDU:* video display unit.

*Viewdata:* An interactive method of receiving and transmitting text and graphics developed by British Telecom. Known in the UK as Prestel.

*video:* that part of a TV signal which transmits the information (intensity, colour and synchronization) required for the formation of an image on a TV screen. The standard video output has a magnitude of 1V peak to peak (1Vpp).

*volatile:* refers to a property of a computer memory whereby stored data disappears when the supply voltage is turned off. Example: a RAM is volatile.

## W

*Winchester:* a hard disk system developed by IBM. Usually refers to a hermetically sealed, non-removable disk unit.

*word:* a group of binary symbols treated by the computer as a single unit of information: the word length is determined by the design of the computer. A typical microcomputer has 8 bits to the word: In an 8 bit system the term byte has the same meaning as word.

*word processing:* the automatic processing of text. This is possible using a dedicated system — a word processor; or by using software on a general computer system.

## X

*Xenix:* Xerox Inc's version of UNIX (viz).

# APPENDIX H

**Some Hints on Kit-built Systems**

There has been a great deal of interest recently in kit-built peripherals. With the introduction of peripherals to machines like the Sinclair ZX81, kit building has shown itself to be very popular.

There are a number of reasons for building a computer or peripheral from a kit:

The price is lower — around 20%

It's interesting, and instructive; and there is a certain amount of pride when the thing actually works!

It is sometimes easier to repair a system that you have built yourself — especially if you learnt how it works in doing so.

Unfortunately there are a number of pitfalls to be avoided. It is not just a matter of going to the shop and buying the bits.

Most systems are sold by mail order — make sure that the manufacturer has stocks before you send any money. Also check that the system actually exists and is not just a figment of his (or his advertising manager's) imagination!

You must also check that it is a good design — and that it actually works. As this is difficult for the inexperienced, ask other people who have bought one. Don't be the first in your group to buy a new system. Let someone else have all the headaches first!

Another area of weakness in most kits is the instruction manual. It is usually written by somebody with years of experience who may have difficulty writing for a novice.

Are the components of reasonable quality? Some kit suppliers use "seconds" — chips which do not meet their specifications and are really rejects. Again, a reputable firm will not risk their reputation — it may cost you a bit more but in the long run it will be worth it.

What happens if the computer doesn't work? Is there a good backup — in information, trouble-shooting, and even repair facilities?

**Tools**

Some basic tools are required for building any kit. These are:

A light electric soldering iron (say 15-25 watts) with a fine bit.

Fine solder with a resin flux core: NOT acid type flux.

A sharp pair of side cutters.

A magnifying glass — very useful when looking for short circuits and inspecting solder joints.

Something to get solder off components that are in the wrong place or the wrong way round. Desoldering braid or a solder-sucker will be needed as double sided printed circuit boards with plated through holes are used.

If you have no experience of soldering, spend some money on buying cheap components and a pcb and get some practice. Don't use your computer as a way of learning to solder!

*Follow the instructions carefully.* This may be obvious, but the fact is that most people are careless. Read through everything from start to finish before you begin work. There are often important corrections to be noted and these are usually given on an errata sheet. During the work, follow the instructions, one after the other, and then you won't have to make unnecessary mistakes.

*Have a good place to work in.* You need good lighting, a good sitting position, and plenty of space so that you can keep all components and papers in order. Don't work when you are tired.

*Take your time.* Work quietly and methodically, spreading out the assembly over several evenings instead of doing a "quick job" that turns out wrong. Trouble-shooting can actually be very time-consuming and frustrating.

*Ask questions.* If the instructions are ambiguous on any point, don't guess. Take nothing for granted. Ask someone who knows!

*Watch out for solder shorts.* This is one of the most common mistakes. The circuit boards used for computers are usually highly complex and there's not much room between the conductors. Drops of solder flying around can very easily cause a short circuit. Keep the tip of the iron clean!

*Use IC sockets.* Integrated circuits (IC) with their many connector pins are troublesome to exchange. Invest in IC sockets if these happen not to be included in the kit. This makes life much easier when it comes to jobs such as trouble-shooting or repairs.

*Handle the components carefully.* Turn them the right way up — components such as transistors, integrated circuits, electrolytic condensers, diodes and others often tend to finish the wrong way up. **Double check!** Some integrated circuits are constructed with what is known as MOS technology and are sensitive to static electricity. Follow the instructions carefully.

*Get hold of reference literature.* The manuals do not always contain enough information about the components, for instance the socket connection of integrated circuits, colour-marking of resistors and so on. A good handbook is a valuable aid.

*Check your work carefully.* Before current is switched on you must carefully check that everything is connected according to the description. Look for unintentional soldering bridges with a magnifying glass. This is a small price to pay when you think of how disastrous a wrong connection can be.

If, after all this effort, the system doesn't work, what can you do? Well, don't put the system into its full casing until it does. It is very frustrating taking panels off, or unscrewing bits and pieces. It is also easier to check what's wrong if you can get at all the parts. If it is mains powered, however, be **very** careful when prodding about the power supply area.

Quite a bit can be done without having to resort to expensive equipment. Check the mains fuse — are the voltage regulators getting warm? That usually indicates something may be wrong. Check that the video display, or printer, is connected properly — and working. If things get **very** hot, then switch off and check for short circuits, or components the wrong way round. The microprocessor and memory chip tend to get warm — if they don't check back along the power rails.

If simple feeling, pushing, and looking achieves nothing, get onto your supplier. If you send it back then expect a charge for the service. Most suppliers will **not** repair half-made kits though — so don't give up halfway through!

# NOTES

# NOTES

# NOTES

# NOTES

# NOTES

# NOTES

# NOTES

# NOTES

# NOTES